America in Vietnam

America in Vietnam

The War That Couldn't Be Won

Herbert Y. Schandler

ROWMAN & LITTLEFIELD PUBLISHERS, INC.
Lanham • Boulder • New York • Toronto • Plymouth, UK

Published by Rowman & Littlefield Publishers, Inc.
A wholly owned subsidiary of The Rowman & Littlefield Publishing Group, Inc.
4501 Forbes Boulevard, Suite 200, Lanham, Maryland 20706
http://www.rowmanlittlefield.com

Estover Road, Plymouth PL6 7PY, United Kingdom

British Library Cataloguing in Publication Information Available

Library of Congress Cataloging-in-Publication Data
Schandler, Herbert Y., 1928–
    America in Vietnam : the war that couldn't be won / Herbert Y. Schandler.
        p.   cm.
    Includes bibliographical references.
    ISBN 978-0-7425-6697-2 (cloth : alk. paper) — ISBN 978-0-7425-6699-6 (electronic)
    1. Vietnam War, 1961–1975—United States. 2. Vietnam—History—20th century. 3. United States—History—1945– I. Title.
    DS558.S329 2009
    959.704'3373—dc22

                                                                          2009007189

⊗™ The paper used in this publication meets the minimum requirements of American National Standard for Information Sciences—Permanence of Paper for Printed Library Materials, ANSI/NISO Z39.48-1992.

Printed in the United States of America

We have won and you have failed. . . . If our generation cannot win, then our sons and nephews will continue. We will sacrifice everything but we will not again have slavery. This is our iron will. We have been fighting for 25 years, the French and you. . . . But you have read our history. We fought against the French for nine years. We were empty handed . . . yet we won victory.

—Le Duc Tho, 1970

They [the North Vietnamese] were more interested in the unification of Vietnam than they were in achieving peace.

—Herbert Y. Schandler, 2009

Contents

Vietnamese Participants

Luu Van Loi (Loo Van Loy). A retired journalist and Foreign Service officer, Luu Van Loi is Vietnam's foremost historian of Vietnam's negotiations with the United States. He was an army officer during the anti-French resistance. In 1954, he joined the mission of the Vietnam People's Army to the International Control Commission, where he became a deputy to Hanoi's principal delegate. In 1961, he was named deputy director of South Vietnam affairs in the Ministry of Foreign Affairs; in that capacity, he participated in the Geneva Conference on Laos from 1961 to 1962. Between February and April 1965, Luu Van Loi helped draft the Four Points, which remained Hanoi's basic negotiating stance from that point forward. Following the announcement of the Four Points on April 8, 1965, he monitored all the secret peace probes between Hanoi and Washington from the Foreign Ministry in Hanoi. From 1968 to 1973, he was in Paris and participated in all phases of the peace talks. He has written (along with Nguyen Anh Vu) on the secret diplomacy between the Hanoi government and Washington prior to the Paris Peace Conference and is co-author (along with Nguyen Anh Vu) of *Le Duc Tho–Kissinger Negotiations in Paris*, published in English in 1995.

Colonel Quach Hai Luong (Kwok Hy L'wong). Senior researcher, Institute of Strategic Studies, Ministry of Defense, Hanoi. During the war with the United States, he was an artillery officer, trained to operate Soviet surface-to-air missiles protecting the city of Hanoi. Since joining the Institute of International Relations, Colonel Quach Hai Luong has become one of Vietnam's leading specialists on U.S. strategy during the war.

Nguyen Khac Huynh (Nwinn Kok Hwinn). Senior researcher, Institute for International Relations, Ministry of Foreign Affairs, Hanoi. He joined the anti-French resistence while in high school and, after 1954, joined the Foreign Ministry as an analyst. Beginning in 1967, he was a principal coordinator of information relating to U.S. affairs, including the many peace initiatives occurring via third-country intermediaries. In 1968, he moved to Paris to participate in the peace talks, working closely with Nguyen Van Hieu, the National Liberation Front representative to the Paris talks. On his retirement, he was ambassador to Mozambique. On his retirement from the Foreign Service, he has become one of Vietnam's most active historians of the French and U.S. wars.

Luu Doan Huynh (Loo Zwann Hwinn). Senior researcher, Institute for International Relations, Ministry of Foreign Affairs, Hanoi. He joined the Vietnam People's Army in 1945 as a teenager. After joining Hanoi's Foreign Ministry, he served throughout South Asia and Southeast Asia (in Delhi, Bangkok, and Canberra). In part because of his fluency in English, he served in 1966 as an intelligence analyst in the Department of U.S. Affairs; later, he was a member of a five-person team that prepared the basic documents for entering negotiations with the United States. He is Vietnam's outstanding historian of the war currently publishing in English. He is the co-editor (along with Jayne S. Werner) of *The Vietnam War: Vietnamese and American Perspectives* (1993).

General Doan Chuong (Zwann Chong). Director, Institute of Strategic Studies, Ministry of Defense, Hanoi. A specialist in military strategy and tactics, he has written widely on military issues in both the French and the U.S. wars, both of which he participated in as a member of the People's Army of Vietnam.

General Dang Vu Hiep (Dahng Voo Heep). Deputy director general, General Political Department, Vietnamese Army, Hanoi. A historian of the war, having written several studies of various battles and campaigns occurring toward the end of the war, in 1965, he was a People's Army of Vietnam adviser to the People's Liberation Army Forces in the central highlands and, in this capacity, was closely involved with two events of pivotal significance in the escalation of the war: the attacks on Pleiku and Qui Nhon in 1965.

Nguyen Co Thach (Nwinn Co Tock). Retired foreign minister of Vietnam. He joined the anti-French resistance when he was fourteen. He became principal private secretary to General Vo Nguyen Giap. In 1954, he was named director general of the Ministry of Foreign Affairs. In October 1954, he became director of the Bureau of Foreign Affairs of the Military and Political

Commission, which took over from the French the administration of the city of Hanoi. He returned to the Foreign Ministry in 1956, serving as consul general in New Delhi. In 1960, he was named deputy foreign minister and participated in the 1961–1962 Geneva Conference on Laos. From 1962 until 1968, he had principal oversight of the Foreign Ministry for policy toward the United States and was the senior Foreign Ministry official involved in Hanoi's participation in the many peace initiatives at that time. From 1968 to 1973, he was the principal deputy in Paris to Le Duc Tho and Xuan Thuy during the peace talks. He was head of the Vietnamese delegation to the June 1997 conference with former secretary of defense McNamara and the American scholars who accompanied him. He died in April 1998.

Preface

This book had its genesis in the inquiries of former secretary of defense Robert McNamara and the technique of "critical oral history" developed by James Blight, a professor at the Thomas J. Watson Jr. Institute for International Studies at Brown University. McNamara, in writing his memoirs on his time as secretary of defense during the Vietnam War, stated that it was clear he was presenting only part of the story. He also recognized, as he felt most Americans did not, that the lessons of Vietnam, if properly drawn, would be applicable to the world of today—and will continue to be applicable to the world of tomorrow.[1]

Critical oral history postulates a conference (or a series of conferences) of former protagonists with opposing viewpoints responding directly to one another concerning the conflict they had recently had and with reference to a common factual baseline of knowledge would at least inform each side of the intelligence the other had relied on, the decision-making process of either side, the objectives being pursued, and the way each made decisions on the basis of the information available to them. Each side would be unable to speak exclusively to those who were like-minded and would agree with them. In fact, they began to listen to one another, some for the first time, in the "safe haven" of these critical oral history conferences. McNamara and Blight first utilized this method to examine the Cuban missile crisis. In a series of six conferences in Cuba and in Moscow, McNamara was shocked to learn how close the two nations had come to nuclear war, that Fidel Castro was quite willing to initiate nuclear warfare against the United States even if it meant the annihilation of Cuba.[2]

With the success of the Cuban–American–Soviet conferences, former secretary of defense McNamara quickly realized that this technique could be applied to the Vietnam War. Were there missed opportunities before and during that war when each side could have taken actions to achieve its objectives without the great loss of life suffered by both sides? Could these missed opportunities serve as lessons for decision makers in the future?

McNamara, through diplomatic channels, succeeded in convening an exploratory conference in Hanoi on June 20–23, 1997. His party consisted of former U.S. government officials, American scholars on Vietnam, and two generals who had commanded forces there. After frank but limited discussion, it was agreed to meet again in February 1998. However, the Vietnamese wanted the principals excluded so that the discussions would not be entirely limited. Former secretary McNamara and the American delegation agreed to this condition.

This is where I became involved in this process. I knew the two generals involved in the first meeting and wrote them volunteering to participate in the next conference. I had served twice in Vietnam as a combat commander and had served in MACV-J3. In the Pentagon in between Vietnam tours, I had served on the army staff and the secretary of defense's staff on Vietnam strategy. I felt that I was qualified. Both generals and, finally, former secretary McNamara agreed that I would replace the generals so that the military point of view would not be excluded.

Therefore, I attended the meetings in Hanoi in February 1998 and 1999. In addition to the regular sessions, I had several one-on-one discussions (along with our interpreters) with a Vietnamese colonel, Quach Hai Luong, Vietnamese Institute of Strategic Studies, who had been an air defense commander during the war and was now a military historian and strategist.

In the book that was expected to follow these conferences, I was assigned the task of writing a chapter concerning the possibility of military victory in Vietnam. The book was titled *Argument without End: In Search of Answers to the Vietnam Tragedy* by McNamara and others, published in 1999. The chapter I wrote was titled "U.S. Military Victory in Vietnam: A Dangerous Illusion?" The book was favorably received and favorably reviewed. My chapter, in particular, however, was criticized for not going beyond the Tet offensive of 1968. The Tet offensive was certainly discussed in Hanoi insofar as its effect on future combat and future negotiations was concerned. But certainly there was the opportunity to revise and expand the history beyond 1968, and that became one of the rationales of this book.

Following President Johnson's speech on March 31, 1968, subsequent to the Tet offensive, Vietnamese and Americans established negotiations concerning the cessation of the bombing of North Vietnam. These negotiations, once completed, could then lead to negotiations to end the war. I have written about the negotiations that followed in the remaining ten months of the

Johnson administration concerning the cessation of the bombing of North Vietnam. This piece was presented at a conference held by the LBJ Library and was published by the Texas A&M University Press under the title *The Search for Peace in Vietnam, 1964–1968* (2004), a collection of essays. The chapter referred to is titled "The Pentagon and Peace Negotiations after March 31, 1968."[3]

I resolved to write the history of the Vietnam War from the point of view of what I had observed and learned while serving in Vietnam and in the Pentagon as well as what I had gleaned in discussions with the Vietnamese in Hanoi. Most of the incidents described are by now well known to scholars and the public as well. Therefore, these detailed secondary sources that were developed by copious and extended research by others are now used throughout. The discussion in almost every paragraph of my work probably has been examined in an entire book based on detailed original sources and copious research. But the revelations by the Vietnamese leadership during the Hanoi conferences are not available elsewhere except in the notes of those conferences taken from recorder tapes. They can be taken as original sources and are used throughout this text. They are identified in the text with the names of the Vietnamese who made the accompanying remarks.

Most of the high-level American participants in the decision-making process concerning the Vietnam War believed that they were fighting a "massive communist international conspiracy," of which the North Vietnamese leadership were willing and eager participants. Ho Chi Minh, the leader of North Vietnam, was a recognized communist, an organizer of the original French and Vietnamese communist parties. But Ho seems to have been something more. He was also a dedicated Vietnamese who was determined to rule a complete Vietnam free of colonial rule. He often stated that he was a nationalist first and only secondarily a communist.

After discussion with the Vietnamese, it is the thesis of this book that nationalism was Ho's and his followers' primary objective. Therefore, the American fear of a "massive communist international conspiracy" was misguided as far as Vietnam was concerned. No leader in South Vietnam could compete with Ho Chi Minh in his drive for a complete and independent Vietnam. Because of the irrational fear of North Vietnam's participation in a "massive communist international conspiracy," American presidents were misinformed by their secretaries of state, John Foster Dulles in the administration of President Eisenhower and Dean Rusk in the case of presidents Kennedy and Johnson. Each accepted Eisenhower's "domino principal" completely and uncritically and felt that South Vietnam could be defended as a non-communist entity against the North. But as Luu Doan Huynh stated in Hanoi, "The main [North] Vietnamese objective has always been independence, freedom, and unification. That was the common hope of the Vietnamese people."[4]

I am indebted to former secretary of defense Robert S. McNamara and to Professor James Blight of the Thomas J. Watson Institute for International Studies, Brown University, for allowing me to accompany the group of scholars who visited Hanoi in 1998 and 1999. We interviewed and held discussions with Vietnamese officials who had been associated with decisions made during the years of the war with the United States and before. The Vietnamese leaders, unlike those of the United States, stayed in power for long periods of time and could discuss the whole post–World War II period. I also offer my thanks to Professor Thomas Biersteker, director of the Thomas J. Watson Institute for International Studies, Brown University, for allowing me to use specific quotes that were made at those conferences with Vietnamese leaders. janet Lang of Brown University set up the conferences at the Vietnamese Institute for International Relations and arranged for my interviews with Colonel Luong. Kathy Le, a graduate of Brown University and a Vietnamese American, served as translator in my discussions with Colonel Luong. I would have been lost without her.

Major General John S. Cowings and Brigadier General (Ret.) Gerald E. Galloway, respectively, commandant and dean of the Industrial College of the Armed Forces (ICAF), National Defense University, where I was employed during this period, allowed me to take time off from my duties in order to travel to Hanoi and to take part in those discussions. Drs. Alan Gropman and Benjamin F. Cooling, succesive chairmen of the Department of Grand Strategy at ICAF, each excused me from a semester of teaching in order to devote that time to finishing this manuscript. I am grateful to all of them. I am also grateful to my distinguished colleagues who filled in for me during those absences.

The opinions provided and the events stated or alluded to are from my own research and are my own interpretation. Any discrepancies, omissions, or errors are mine alone.

Indochina

Chapter One

The Illusion of Military Victory

Could the United States have won militarily in Vietnam at a reasonable cost in terms of human life, both Vietnamese and American, and without an unacceptable risk of extending the war to China and Russia? The persistent, burning question of the American failure in Vietnam has haunted and fascinated American political scientists, politicians, historians, journalists, military officers, and military doctrine before and since the last U.S. helicopter left the roof of the American embassy in Saigon in July 1975 as triumphant North Vietnamese forces entered the city and unified the nation.[1]

The Vietnam War had a profound influence on a generation of Americans, military as well as civilian. It also has influenced U.S. domestic and foreign policy for decades. Literally thousands of books have been written, many recounting the experiences of individuals and of military units in Vietnam, others seeking to place the blame for America's first failure in wartime. In recent times, some authors, under a dangerous illusion, have argued that we actually won the war or were on the edge of winning but perhaps withdrew too soon—after 58,000 American dead and a million Vietnamese dead—to exploit our victory.

The arguments regarding the breakdown of American strategy in Vietnam have several facets. Many senior military leaders point to the political constraints on military power, denouncing the government policy of limited and gradual application of military power, both in the air and on the ground, in both North and South Vietnam, as being one of the critical causes of our unprecedended military failure. Most military leaders saw the war as a conventional aggression by the communist-controlled Democratic Republic of Vietnam (North Vietnam) against our noncomunist and newly created ally, the Republic of Vietnam (South Vietnam). Clearly, the United States had to

1

intervene to stop the march of communism and to protect other small Asian countries from having this ideology imposed on them, as President Eisenhower's "domino principle" prophesied. Military leaders frequently have charged that the military tools and strategy were available to repel that aggression and to "defeat" North Vietnam and thus preserve the independence and legitimacy of South Vietnam. However, it is stated, constraints on the use of force imposed by political leaders tied the hands of the military and was one of the major causes of our unprecedented military failure to defeat the enemy and achieve "victory." They argue that had the military been free to employ its military power quickly, decisively, and without limit, the war against a third-rate military power could have been won, this so-called North Vietnamese aggression could have been defeated, and the independence of South Vietnam could have been maintained. Other opinion leaders have charged that other political limitations prevented an American victory. "Reasonably plausible theories of victory," it has been stated by them, were to convince the North Vietnamese that their theory of unity was implausible; to have denied Vietnam the ability to conduct the war in the South by cutting off North Vietnamese access to South Vietnam through massive bombing of the North or of the rail lines leading to China and the Soviet Union or even the invasion and threatened U.S. occupation of North Vietnam; or to cut North Vietnamese supply lines in Laos and Cambodia. These are efforts that President Johnson refused to approve. They are options that President Nixon later adopted but that did not lead to the achievement of U.S. objectives. These options are examined in detail.

Others indicate that the war was lost by an unsympathetic press or by dissenters within the nation who refused to support the war and indeed actually demonstrated their opposition to it and attempted to influence the will of the nation. The media, of course, were initially sympathetic to the war but increasingly followed the American public as disillusionment with the lack of success in the war grew.[2] As the war progressed, there was a great deal of public dissent within the United States in the media as well as on college campuses both before and after the commitment of American troop units. There is evidence to indicate that these press reports were generally accurate even though they did not reflect official positions. There is also evidence that demonstrations against the war initially were often ineffective, even leading to greater support for the war in the heartland of America.[3]

Other Americans have stated that the war in Vietnam was a civil war, that North Vietnam expressed and represented Vietnam nationalism, and that initially the people of South Vietnam rose up against their corrupt and ineffective leaders and attempted to unseat them. They indicate that North Vietnam assisted this "southern resistance" and sent military help to fight the new colonial power initially represented by American advisers and subsequently represented by the armed forces of the United States. American military leaders, it has been charged by civilian critics, were both unimaginative and inflexible in meeting the new challenge of people's war, insurgency, and nation building that they confronted in South Vietnam. Faced with a new challenge, these critics maintain, the military responded in a conventional manner, attempting to follow doctrine and strategy that had been developed on the basis of World War II and Korean experience. Military leaders sought to fight a conventional war based on old doctrine designed for a far different foe and a far different circumstance where the objective had been the more traditional one of destruction of the enemy largely free of political and resource constraints.

It is true that the building and strengthening of a civil democratic government in South Vietnam was not a military responsibility. Whose responsibility was it? No agency of the U.S. government even to the present day has such a responsibilty. Nation building at that time was anathema to U.S. military forces. Thus, it is not surprising that most American programs in South Vietnam were not designed to strengthen that government. Few large programs or great resources were devoted to making the South Vietnamese government more effective in delivering social programs and security to its population to gain their loyalty and support.

This did not go unnoticed. The U.S. military evidenced little or no confidence in the government or the army of our ally and ignored both of them in taking over the war to fight it American style. In addition, American military leaders neither clearly understood nor accepted this nation's limited political objectives in Vietnam. Their illusion of a military victory divorced from political considerations ignored or overlooked the causes of the war, failed to consider the weaknesses and interests of the ally on whose behalf we were fighting, neither feared nor cared about overt Chinese or Soviet participation in the war, and did not appreciate or clearly understand the history, motives, objectives, or will of the enemy. It seems to have never occurred to the Joint Chiefs of Staff that in order to win they had to adopt a strategy that would meet the president's political goals, that defeating North Vietnam was really not the American objective, and that the U.S. field commander had adopted a military strategy that could probably not succeed in accomplishing that objective. As General Bruce Palmer Jr. stated in his analysis of the war, *The 25-Year War: America's Military Role in Vietnam*, "Not once during the war did the Joint Chiefs of Staff advise the commander-in-chief or the secretary of defense that the strategy being pursued most probably would fail and that the United States would be unable to achieve its objectives."[4]

Several of the principal senior leaders in Vietnam have written memoirs that state their views. Both journalists and scholars, some unfamiliar with either the national decision-making process or the uses of military force, have analyzed both of those flawed processes in great detail. In this one-sided process of description and analysis, few have given any knowledgeable consideration to the views, objectives, and strategies of the North Vietnamese leadership during this period of struggle or to the history of Vietnam prior to this war.

The questions—or the answers—that exist in the minds of the North Vietnamese, what the opposing side has to say about the war, and what it can teach us in our quest to better understand this pivotal moment in our nation's history have been largely ignored. Both the United States and North Vietnam had completely different mind-sets, and understanding those differences may help us avoid such catastrophes in the future. A new perspective on the U.S. intervention in Vietnam can, I believe, reveal mistakes made by both sides in their efforts to protect or defeat South Vietnam. Indeed, instead of asking why the United States failed in Vietnam, it might be equally fruitful to ask why North Vietnam achieved victory.

I have been fortunate in recent years to have had extensive direct contact with some knowledgeable members of the North Vietnamese leadership who served their nation during the period of the American phase of their war as well as before that phase and subsequent to it. My in-depth interviews and conversations with them provide for the first time some insight into their mind-sets as well as their thinking, their motivation, their objectives, and their understanding of and response to American actions, both diplomatic and military. It is my hope that with this new knowledge we can now develop a definitive narrative and analysis of the American failure in Vietnam and learn lessons from the perspectives of our victorious enemy.

THE OBJECTIVE

In an article in *Parameters* magazine in 1983, Harry Summers reminds us of a Jules Feiffer cartoon in which one of the characters, having made what he believes to be the telling point of a long and involved argument, is devastated by the riposte, "Now let us define your terms."[5] To avoid such a fate, it is best to define our terms in advance. For this particular discussion, the main term to be defined is "to win militarily." For in a limited war with limited objectives, winning may have a far different, far more limited definition than the traditional military concept of defeating the enemy's military forces.

Although it is—or should be—the common understanding that the United States "lost" the war in Vietnam, that is, that it failed to achieve its objectives, it is also clear that our military forces "won" every major military engagement and were never defeated, although they lost small-scale ambushes and lost men in them. Clearly, in these cases, there was something more to "winning" than simply defeating the enemy's military forces. As Harry Summers has indicated in *On Strategy*, his flawed analysis of American military actions in Vietnam, a North Vietnamese officer admitted to him that the United States had won every battle but also pointed out that this fact was irrelevant to the outcome of the war.[6]

In his seminal book, *The War Managers*, Dr. Douglas Kinnard found through responses to his questionnaires that 70 percent of U.S. Army generals who managed the war in Vietnam were uncertain of the nation's objectives in that war. As Kinnard points out, this represented a deep-seated strategic failure, the inability—or unwillingness—of policymakers to frame tangible obtainable political goals to be achieved through the use of military power.[7]

This failure—or unwillingness—to translate understandable and limited political objectives into military goals remains with us today. Many military leaders have attacked the political leaders of the time for their gradual escalation of the war, for geographic limitations on operations, for manpower limitations by failure to utilize major reserve forces, and for significant restrictions on the bombing campaign against North Vietnam. Clearly, many of these senior leaders had and continue to have little appreciation for the limited and political nature of the war and little understanding for some of the limitations that political objectives and civilian control necessarily may place on military operations. Winning, to the minds of these leaders, remained defined, as it had been in previous wars, as defeating the enemy's military forces by overwhelming combat power exerted against both his military forces and his civil economy.

I examine these views in more detail later when I trace the political and military decisions that eventually involved this nation in an air and ground war in Southeast Asia without a clear understanding on the part of many senior leaders as to the national objectives that were being pursued. As a recent book on leadership states, "It's difficult to get there if you don't know where you are going." In a limited war conducted for political purposes, I define winning militarily as "accomplishing the nation's political purposes through the use of military force." Military operation must always have a political purpose. They do not stand alone. Leaving it to the military to "fight the way it wants to" is almost always, in a limited war, an incorrect policy devoid of civilian control and not directed toward achieving the nation's political purposes. The military is only one instrument of a nation's policy, perhaps the last to be used when the other instruments of diplomacy—economics, psychology, or information—fail to achieve the political end desired. Thus, in order to determine whether the United States could have "won militarily" in

Vietnam, we must be clear on our political objective(s) there as well as our enemy's objective there.

American objectives in Indochina were initially spelled out in a basic National Security Council document in December 1949 during the Eisenhower administration and remained remarkably consistent even as the U.S. commitment to Indochina grew. That document, which was modified in 1950, set forth what later became known as the domino principal. The operative paragraphs are as follows:

> It is important to United States security interests that all practicable measures be taken to prevent further communist expansion in Southeast Asia. Indo-China is a key area of Southeast Asia and is under immediate threat. The neighboring countries of Thailand and Burma could be expected to fall under Communist domination if a Communist-dominated government controlled Indo-China. The balance of Southeast Asia would then be in grave hazard.[8]

Thus, "preventing further communist expansion in Southeast Asia" became the keynote of American policy throughout this nation's efforts in Vietnam. That became the political objective, and this nation committed large resources, to include military forces, in attempting to achieve that objective. President Lyndon B. Johnson restated the same objective in National Security Action Memorandum (NSAM) 288 approved in March 1964. This document reiterated the American objective as "an independent non-Communist South Vietnam" and reaffirmed the domino principle. NSAM 288 even saw increased threats to India, Australia, Korea, and Japan if South Vietnam were to fall to communism.[9] Just a few days later, on April 7, 1964, in a speech at Johns Hopkins University, President Johnson reiterated the objective of "an independent South Vietnam" but with an important caveat. He stated, "We will do everything necessary to achieve that objective, and we will do only what is absolutely necessary."[10]

Clearly, this objective was a political objective and, some charge, did not provide specific guidance to military commanders. It did not involve defeating anyone or winning anything. It was a rather vague, rather defensive objective—that of doing what was necessary and only what was necessary—to stop a communist power from defeating the government of South Vietnam. This objective seemed to put limitations on military power and other national resources and was a requirement foreign to the military. Military doctrine taught that winning meant defeating the enemy by the violent, quick, decisive application of superior and overwhelming military combat power. But in Vietnam, the stated objective was different. How does a military leader commit "only what is necessary" in order not necessarily to defeat the enemy but simply "not to lose" South Vietnam to communism? This was a dilemma that the American military attempted to solve in its own manner throughout the course of America's involvement in the war in Vietnam.

A concomitant requirement, it seemed, was to provide significant assistance in developing a competent, independent, and representative government in South Vietnam where none had existed before. That government should be capable of winning the loyalty of its people and of providing needed services and security to them. This to a large extent was not a military responsibility. But without positive achievement in this field, military progress by an outside power could be an endless task. Helping to build an indigenous government where one had never existed before would not be an easy task for the United States. Political science offers no clear prescription for the development of a viable democratic political system in a traditional society recently freed from colonial rule, with limited physical, administrative, and leadership resources and in the midst of a civil war. As has been indicated, there is no American government agency charged with supervising such a task. Therefore, there must be some doubt as to what could have been accomplished by an outside power in an alien society even if a clear realization of the true objective had been present. So it is not surprising that the American response in large part was a conventional military one as it had been in previous wars. The military defeat of the enemy seemed an achievable goal, and the United States escalated and reescalated in order to progress toward that goal. But in a people's war, that could not be sufficient. How long could American arms hold off an enemy on behalf of a government that could not hold off the enemy itself— and on behalf of a government that finally was seen to be incapable of providing services and protection to its own people without major American assistance? For whom could that war be won?

Chapter Two

The Enemy

When the United States entered the Vietnam War, very little was understood about Vietnam, its history, its government, and its people. The Kennedy and later the Johnson administrations and their military leaders were confident that the United States could overpower the North Vietnamese, break the will of its people, and quickly bring them to the bargaining table. In this, they were mistaken. What the United States faced in Vietnam were determined, nationalistic, fanatical warriors, hardened by a history of warfare and fighting for a government with an ideology, an objective, and a will that would not be broken.

Few nations have as long a history as Vietnam, and few nations are as conscious of their history. Through the veneration of ancient national heroes and heroines in shrines and cults, through historical dramas, through the recital of legends, national and ethnic history has always been an intimate part of Vietnamese life. The main feature of Vietnamese history is its unity and continuity. For more than 2,000 years, the Vietnamese people have occupied and fought for their land. Their survival and their way of life has been ascribed by scholars to a vitality that was lacking in the peoples whom they defeated, displaced, or absorbed. Although a part of the Chinese Empire for almost 1,000 years, the Vietnamese never lost their character as a non-Chinese people. After years of struggle, they asserted their right to a separate national existence against the Chinese, defeated all attempts at reconquest by their skillful and tenacious resistance, and have stood as a barrier to Chinese advance into Southeast Asia to this very day. After defeating first their Chinese masters and later other inhabitants of the peninsula, Vietnam became independent in the middle of the tenth century (A.D. 939). This inaugurated a process of territorial defense and expansion that lasted more than 900 years. It was carried on gradually by a form of peasant soldiering for which this people seemed to have developed an aptitude at a very early time and spread the Vietnamese people from the Red River valley all the way down the east coast of Indochina to the Gulf of Siam. This was the famous "march to the south," which has the same mythology in Vietnamese history that "manifest destiny" has in our own. Through this process, Vietnam grew to its present size and took on its present shape. The Vietnamese also developed a stable and efficient political regime built around a hereditary monarch. Although the succession of hereditary monarchs was fought over from time to time, in general this national independence was defended and has endured for some 900 years. The intervention of the French put an end to Vietnamese territorial expansion in the Mekong Delta region and Cambodia. In 1883, the French completed their twenty-five-year struggle for the domination of the country. In order to maintain order and make their rule easier, they decided to destroy the unity of Vietnam and divided it into three parts to be administered separately: Tonkin, Annam, and Cochinchina. The French knew how to run a colony. In order to make it pay, they worked the peasants and exported rubber and rice in quantities that often caused starvation among the Vietnamese. Their harsh colonial administration accentuated the growth of an intense awareness of national identity among Vietnamese intellectuals, producing a variety of nationalist resistance groups. The French replied with sharp punitive measures, executing and imprisoning thousands of Vietnamese. But the nationalist movement continued. Every time the French educated a Vietnamese to take a subordinate position in the colonial bureaucracy, they also created a nationalist opposed to French rule. The nationalist movement in this case was led by the Vietnamese educated middle class and intellectuals.

Nguyen Ai Quoc (Nguyen the Patriot) was one of these nationalist leaders. Prior to World War I, he toured the world as a cabin boy before settling in Paris as a student and nationalist agitator. He petitioned the allies at Paris in 1919 asking for democratic freedoms for Vietnam. At that time, Vietnam was so obscure that the petition was not answered.[1] After his rejection in Paris, he soon decided that only the communists had the potential and interest to spark the anticolonial fire that would free Vietnam. Nguyen became a charter member of the French Communist Party. As he explained years later, "It was patriotism and not communism that . . . inspired me." By the early 1920s, the French police were tracking him, and in 1924 he moved to Moscow. There he changed his name to Ho Chi Minh—a name we now recognize more prominently—and became a party organizer. In 1929, he organized the Indochinese Communist Party in reaction to continued economic and political turmoil in his native Vietnam.

At the beginning of World War II, Ho returned to Vietnam after a twenty-year absence. He aligned himself with the allies, expecting them to defeat

Japan, oust the discredited French from Vietnam, and reward his country with independence. Ho's sole concern was focused on Vietnam. He organized a broad front of all nationalist groups in Vietnam to fight both the Japanese—who occupied Vietnam in 1941—and the French, who were cooperating with them. This organization was called the Viet Nam Doc Lap Dong Minh (the Vietnamese Independence League), soon to be known simply as the Vietminh. His organization was helpful to the allies during the war by rescuing downed airman, in harassing the Japanese, and in collecting intelligence. A U.S. Office of Strategic Services (OSS) team was parachuted in and provided rudimentary military training.

After the allied victory, the Vietminh were able to seize control of most of Vietnam. They were strongest in the North. On September 2, 1945, in Hanoi, quoting from the American Declaration of Independence and with a U.S. OSS adviser at his side, Ho Chi Minh declared the independence of the Democratic Republic of Vietnam (DRV). Emperor Bao Dai, the Vietnamese puppet whom the French had set up to rule Vietnam under their authority, immediately abdicated and handed over "sovereign power" to the Vietminh.

Ho hoped to win American support. He wrote letters to President Truman through the American consul in Hanoi requesting such support. None were answered, probably having never reached the U.S. president. At this time, the United States and its wartime partners were inexorably if not deliberately proceeding to restore French rule in Indochina. At Potsdam in July, the allies decided—it was a minor item on their agenda—that the British would take the surrender of Japanese forces in Indochina south of the sixteenth parallel, and Chinese nationalists would effect this surrender in the North. In the South, the British released the French legionnaires from captivity and rearmed them. The legionnaires went on a rampage, attacked Vietminh forces, and ousted Vietminh administrators. The Vietnamese called an effective general strike that paralyzed Saigon. The first Vietnam War (subsequent to World War II) had begun in the South.

In the North, 200,000 Chinese nationalist occupiers descended like locusts and attempted to install their own government. Ho, feeling trapped and desperate to get rid of the Chinese, decided he had to make an accommodation with the French under which they would replace the Chinese—on condition that they recognize Vietnamese independence and stay for no more than five years. He is said to have commented, "The last time the Chinese came, they stayed a thousand years. The French . . . are weak. Colonialism is dying. I prefer to sniff French shit for five years than to eat Chinese shit for a thousand years."[2]

In March 1946, France agreed to recognize an independent Vietnam within the French Union and to station 25,000 troops in Annam and Tonkin. But the fate of Cochinchina—South Vietnam—was not resolved. In the North, as the French army moved back in, there were clashes over who controlled what. In November 1946, in a customs dispute, the French decided to reassert their control and attacked Haiphong with infantry and armored units supported by naval gunfire. The Vietnamese claimed 20,000 were killed; the French say they only killed 6,000. France's desperate effort to cling to its reluctant and defiant Asian possession escalated quickly into war—and the American commitment took shape. The United States initially was indifferent to Southeast Asia and to the French colonial war, but Vietnam soon was linked to activities taking place in other parts of the world.

The American indifference to France's colonial war in Vietnam ended on June 25, 1950. On that date, North Korean military forces surged across the thirty-eighth parallel and quickly captured Seoul. Six months earlier, Chinese communist forces reached the borders of Vietnam after conquering all of mainland China. Both the Soviet Union and China, despite growing differences, recognized the DRV, the first two nations to do so. It seemed clear to American leaders that communism was on the march throughout Asia and that the government of North Vietnam was its agent in Southeast Asia.

American foreign policy after World War II generally followed two tracks: those of anticolonialism and anticommunism. When the nationalist leader of a former colonial nation identified himself as a communist, a choice had to be made. To the United States, the choice was not difficult. The national anticolonial leader became a part of the massive communist conspiracy that threatened the West. He was seen as a puppet of the Soviet Union and the People's Republic of China and was a communist enemy of the West. Acting on the principle of containing the spread of communism throughout the world, the American military commitment in Indochina took shape. With the U.S. intervention in Korea, President Truman had added a new dimension to American foreign policy; NSC-68 cast the containment of communism in military terms and extended its focus worldwide. The United States saw the Soviet Union as perfectly willing to use proxies to achieve its ends. Almost overnight, the United States amended its approach to France's war in Indochina. The secretary of state announced that "the resources of the United States" would henceforth "be deployed to reserve Indochina and Southeast Asia from further communist encroachment."

But the United States saw as the more important effort the stopping of the spread of communism in Western Europe. The two efforts soon became linked. The French attempt to defeat Ho Chi Minh's manifestation of Vietnamese nationalism quickly became an important part of American efforts to gain French support for a European military organization and for American anticommunist efforts in other parts of the world. But while the French repeated that theme, they were fighting in Indochina primarily to preserve a colonial possession, and their goal was relatively narrow. The United States, playing for global stakes, therefore became more determined than France to persevere in Vietnam. Thus, America's view of Ho Chi Minh's Indochina as a part of a unified international communist conspiracy gave the French enormous "leverage." Now they were fighting the good fight against communism in Southeast Asia. The French threatened to undermine American military efforts in Western Europe unless the United States fulfilled its requests for aid in Indochina. The United States was even persuaded to recognize the emperor Bao Dai, whom the French had resurrected as the emperor of Vietnam.

The unity of the communist threat remained an axiom of American foreign policy. American officials repeated the warning that the war in Vietnam against the French was a part of that conspiracy and was controlled by Moscow and Peking. If Indochina fell to the communists, the other countries of Southeast Asia would quickly follow, American leadership proclaimed. While the French picked up and repeated that theme, they actually were fighting to preserve their colonial possession, and their objectives remained relatively narrow. They resisted American efforts directed toward political reform in Vietnam and threatened to undermine American military efforts in Western Europe unless the United States fulfilled its requests for aid and assistance in Indochina. By 1954, American aid accounted for 80 percent of French expenditures in the conflict. But this aid and support for the French in time adversely affected containment in Europe. The French became too bogged down in Indochina to meet their military obligations in Western Europe.[3]

The efforts of the United States to assist the French in their colonial war were noticed carefully in the DRV. Hopeful of U.S. support for their freedom and independence after World War II, the Vietnamese were upset, disappointed, disillusioned, and bitter that President Truman had not responded to Ho Chi Minh's advances to him. They were further alienated with this U.S. support for their former colonial overlords. "Blood," said North Vietnamese diplomat Luu Doan Huynh, "speaks with a terrible voice. . . . Our slogan by the end of 1950 was to 'fight and defeat the French colonialists and the American interventionists.'" And, as Nguyen Khac Huynh, another veteran North Vietnamese diplomat, pointed out,

> Without U.S. aid, we believe we could have defeated the French in 1950, or 1951 at the latest. If we had—if the United States had not rescued the French in 1950, just imagine: it is possible that there would have been no partition, no U.S.-backed Diem regime, and no U.S.-Vietnam War.[4]

Finding themselves in desperate straits in their ill-conceived defense of Dien Bien Phu, the French finally called on the United States for direct military support, to include air strikes and troops, in order to prevent their defeat. President Eisenhower refused to intervene without other allied support. He could find no allies willing to join in bailing out France, and although the Chairman of the Joint Chiefs of Staff, Admiral Arthur Radford, was said to have "encouraged the French," the other members of the Joint Chiefs strongly recommended against beginning an American version of the Vietnam war in 1954.[5]

The first Indochina War ended with the Geneva Conference of 1954. That conference met just as Dien Bien Phu fell. It produced what actually turned out to be a military truce, confirming the independence of Laos and Cambodia and the withdrawal of the French from all of Indochina. But under intense Chinese pressure, Ho Chi Minh was forced to agree to a temporary partition of Vietnam pending nationwide elections two years hence in 1956 to unify the country. The agreement stated that the border between the two "countries" was not to be considered an international border and that Vietnam would be unified after the promised election. But only the DRV (North Vietnam) and France, the two nations at war, actually agreed to and signed the document.

The North Vietnamese viewed the Geneva Convention of 1954 as the beginning of the end of their long struggle for Vietnamese unity and independence. Pressured in 1954 by their Chinese and Soviet mentors to agree to a temporary partition of the country at the seventeenth parallel, they were cheered by the defeat and departure of the hated French colonial army and the prospect of Vietnamese reunification through elections in two years. They had no doubt that those elections would ratify the reunification of the country under the revered Vietnamese nationalist leader, "Uncle" Ho Chi Minh, who had for so long led the fight for Vietnamese freedom from colonial rule. While grateful for the help of their Soviet and Chinese mentors, the Vietnamese leadership had no intention of becoming subservient to the policies of those two countries. Communism had been an effective way to gain support against Western colonialism and imperialism, but, as Ho Chi Minh often pointed out, Vietnamese nationalism had always been the overriding goal.[6]

In this case, the Vietnamese were to be disappointed. As Nguyen Khac Huynh, Luu Doan Huynh, Luu Van Loi, and others carefully explained, the North Vietnamese, after ten years of fighting in the jungles, considered themselves to be "not well versed" in international diplomacy. Their friends and allies, the Soviets and the Chinese, urged the North Vietnamese to agree to a division of Vietnam at the seventeenth parallel, with elections to be held in two years to unify the country. This was done, according to the Vietnamese, to avoid what the major communist powers felt to be imminent American military intervention in Indochina.[7]

The United States saw the Geneva Convention of 1954 as a disaster for the United States and the free world, bringing down the Iron Curtain in Asia and surrendering another country to the worldwide communist threat. The experience of communist triumphs in China and in Czechoslovakia, the necessity for the Berlin Airlift, and the invasion of Korea had convinced the Eisenhower administration that there was a massive integrated worldwide communist conspiracy against the United States and its allies. The "domino principle" was promulgated by the Eisenhower administration as the plan of action for communist domination of all of Asia. American representatives attended the conference at Geneva reluctantly; refused to meet or even to shake hands with the Chinese foreign minister, Chou En Lai; and would not sign the document that "gave away" part of a country to communism.[8]

There is no evidence that the Americans ever spoke to any of the Vietnamese delegates. President Eisenhower stated that although the United States had not signed the Geneva agreements, this nation would "not use force to disturb this settlement."[9] But he and his secretary of state, John Foster Dulles, were convinced that the nationwide elections promised by the Geneva Accords would ratify the communist triumph in Indochina, thus defeating American objectives there. Communists were not going to take power in South Vietnam, according to Dulles, even if that is what the people there wanted as demonstrated by a national election.[10]

Thus, from the very beginning, the Americans and the North Vietnamese started from outlooks or mind-sets so different that it became difficult for each of them to understand the other. These different outlooks would lead inevitably to misunderstanding and conflict. Although disappointed with the results of Geneva, the North Vietnamese began to consolidate their government in the North to prepare for the elections to follow, which, they felt, would unify their country as called for by the Geneva treaty. That agreement clearly stated that the demarcation line would not be viewed as an international boundary and that the country would be unified by the elections that would follow in two years' time.

Chapter Three

The American Commitment

To the Americans, the Geneva agreements at best provided a means for saving the southern portion of Vietnam from communist rule. In South Vietnam, a nation had to be created where none had existed before. That nation, an invention of the Geneva agreement, was supposed to disappear after elections in two years. From the American point of view, this weak and artificial nation was to be the new anticommunist bulwark in Southeast Asia against the menace of communist expansion and the loss of all of Southeast Asia to communism under the "domino principle," accepted uncritically by the American political leadership.

In a speech at Gettysburg on April 4, 1959, President Dwight D. Eisenhower reiterated the American commitment: "We reach the inescapable conclusion that our own national interest demands some help from us in sustaining in Viet-Nam the morale, the economic progress, and the military strength necessary to its continued existence in freedom."[1] Thus, from the beginning, U.S. planning focused not on elections but on providing necessary military and other assistance to the new noncommunist entity of South Vietnam—everything it needed to defend itself against the communist threat from the North. This, as noted, would be the fundamental objective of U.S. policy in the region from 1954 until the middle 1970s: the South Vietnamese "domino" must not be allowed to "fall" to communism and thus ostensibly present a threat to the rest of Southeast Asia. The North Vietnamese, on the other hand, expected that the country would be unified in two years as promised by the Geneva Treaty. They went about consolidating their rule in the North in preparation for the eventual and inevitable unification of their nation by the forthcoming election. It is little wonder, then, that the agreements made in Geneva quickly began to unravel. Clearly, the United States had no intention of allowing this Southeast Asian country, the newly created government of South Vietnam, to accede voluntarily to communism through elections in 1956.

In South Vietnam, reputable Vietnamese nationalists who were outside the ranks of the coalition formed by Ho Chi Minh or who had not served the French were hard to find. Ngo Dinh Diem, a French-trained Catholic who was in the United States at the time, had courted American legislators, academics, and religious leaders for a position in the new government. He had a reputation as being both anticommunist and anticolonial. He was promoted as president by Archbishop (later Cardinal) Spellman and finally by the United States because, as John Foster Dulles, the American secretary of state put it, "There is no one . . . to serve U.S. interests better."[2] Diem had several disadvantages, however. He was a Catholic, and Catholicism was a religion that had been favored by the French in a largely Buddhist country. Diem, furthermore, had little recognition or backing among the people of South Vietnam. The United States committed its resources to Diem's support and went about building up South Vietnam as a bulwark against the threat of communist expansion led by a militant North Vietnam under Soviet and Chinese influence and direction.

Another step in developing a defense for Southeast Asia by the United States was the creation of the Southeast Asia Treaty Organization (SEATO). This treaty, entered into by the United States, Great Britain, France, Australia, New Zealand, Pakistan, Thailand, and the Philippines, was less clear in pledging an "automatic response" to aggression than had earlier treaties signed by the United States (the Rio and NATO treaties) because of the insistence of the U.S. Congress that this country abide by its constitutional provision to consult Congress prior to entering a war. But Secretary of State John Foster Dulles attempted to put teeth into the agreement by making the three Indochina states, Laos, Cambodia, and South Vietnam, "protocol states" to the treaty and insisting that the treaty cover only "communist" aggression.[3] Some analysts in hindsight have stated that the weakness of this agreement did not commit the United States to go to the defense of South Vietnam, and therefore this nation had no obligation to do so.[4] But this analysis overlooks the fact that President Eisenhower was determined to defend South Vietnam by force if necessary. As he saw it, the SEATO Treaty was all that was needed. He stated, "The dilemma of finding a moral, legal, and practical basis for helping our friends of the region need not face us again."[5]

American strategic military planning for the use of ground forces in the defense of Indochina began in the days following the signing of the Geneva Accords and the establishment of SEATO. The United States had inherited from France a poorly trained, ill-equipped South Vietnamese army of 250,000 with low morale, poor leadership, and limited national spirit. A Military Assistance Advisory Group (MAAG) was established by the Americans in 1956 with responsibility for training this Army of the Republic of Vietnam (ARVN). With roughly $85 million per year, the United States provided the ARVN with uniforms and small arms as well as a small quantity of tanks and helicopters. It underwrote the entire cost of the training program, including officer's salaries. In the second year, the United States undertook a massive reorganization campaign, scaling the ARVN back to 150,000 troops and creating an officer training program. Many junior officers were sent to military schools in the United States for further instruction.

The American strategy seemed to reflect U.S. combat experience in Korea, to include the U.S. view of the Chinese threat to Southeast Asia. It also reflected the new-look military doctrine of the Eisenhower administration with its emphasis on U.S. air, naval, and particularly nuclear supremacy. It had very little to do with insurgency.[6] American contingency plans for the defense of South Vietnam provided for countering a conventional enemy offensive by North Vietnamese or combined North Vietnamese–Chinese forces. South Vietnamese troops would occupy blocking positions while American forces, generally those already based in the Pacific Command, would secure major air and sea facilities in South Vietnam and would then deploy to occupy these blocking positions north and west of Saigon. After the invasion had been contained, a counter-offensive would be undertaken, featuring joint airborne, amphibious, and ground attack into North Vietnam. To support these plans, provisions were made for selecting potential targets for nuclear strikes, for occupying key cities, and for interdicting the enemy's critical lines of communication. These plans anticipated and were based on a mobilization of U.S. reserve units.[7]

Contingency plans did not change markedly during the 1955–1965 time period even though the political and military situation on the ground changed significantly. The escalating threat posed by the resistance to the Diem regime in South Vietnam and a growing interest in "counterinsurgency" in the American military appear to have been only superficial distractions to the military planners. In general, they had difficulty translating counterinsurgency doctrine and strategy into plans and tactics for use of American combat forces in Southeast Asia. As they were unsure how to deal militarily with an insurgency, the Americans tentatively proposed to train indigenous forces for this mission. Under this scheme, American units would continue to occupy blocking positions to stop the invading North Vietnamese forces while South Vietnamese internal security forces would take on the indigenous guerrilla forces.[8]

American military leaders quickly realized that they could not effectively train the ARVN for two diverse and, in retrospect, impossible missions: internal security and defending South Vietnam from a cross-border attack from the North.

To solve this dilemma, responsibility for training and equipping paramilitary and internal security forces was vested not in the military at all initially but rather in other U.S. agencies that differed in their views of the proper mission, composition, coordination, and employment of those forces.[9] The U.S. military training mission in Vietnam during the period 1954–1960, therefore, tended to concentrate on building a South Vietnamese army more or less in the image of the American army and geared to resist attack from the North. This was a logical application of American doctrine to a rather unique situation. American efforts to create an effective South Vietnamese military force during this period were critically affected by perceptions of the threat, by exaggerated estimates of the value of recent American military experience in responding to similar threats, by implementing military standards and doctrines designed for a major conflict against the Soviet Union in Europe, and by fragmentation in determining and administering the overall program of assistance to Vietnam.

The general belief in U.S. Army doctrine, based on experiences in Greece and Korea, was that revolution could not be instigated or successful without the support of an external sponsoring power. Experience in Korea taught that guerrillas were the "early warning of cross-border conventional attack, a much greater danger." The focus of the army's doctrine of guerrilla warfare, therefore, was on the defeat and destruction of a cross-border invasion through mobility, firepower, and conventional combat. Experience seemed to teach that conventional forces could meet a guerrilla threat by interdicting supply lines, communications, and command between the guerrilla and the external power and by sealing the border with the external power. And so the American military, in training the ARVN and in developing contingency plans for the region, concentrated on the assumption that any conflict in the region would be a repetition of the Korean model and would be a mixture of guerrilla and conventional war, with an invasion of the South by the North the most likely scenario.[10]

Although it might be an exaggeration to claim that the United States created a "mirror image" of its own forces in the South Vietnamese defense forces, the emphasis was on conventional forces (as opposed to paramilitary forces) based on the concept of superior weaponry and technology against a guerrilla force that was potentially the spearhead of a more massive cross-border thrust out of North Vietnam. Considerations of the mission, organization, equipment, and training of the ARVN, according to American doctrine, dictated that it have a capability similar to that of American forces.

Bad doctrine and incorrectly applied experience combined to ensure that the very nature of the war in Vietnam would not be recognized initially by American military planners. Ultimately, U.S. strategy and training forced the South Vietnamese forces to the road, making them dependent on a motorized or helicopter-borne offensive force that was hard to supply and totally inappropriate for the people's war in the countryside. Furthermore, the South Vietnamese were ill prepared to fight the political war. Few of the top South Vietnamese military leaders had strategic training of any kind and were incapable of conceiving, planning, and directing a complex political and military struggle in a hostile or indifferent countryside. Thus, in attempting to put down insurgent groups, the ARVN took heavy casualties in an often futile attempt to spread government control throughout South Vietnam. Furthermore, ignoring the advice of American advisers, Ngo Dinh Diem tended to promote officers on the basis of their loyalty to him and their casualty avoidance rather than their combat success.[11]

The elections of 1956 promised by the Geneva Accords never occurred, of course. Although President Diem had a great deal of success initially in meeting the challenge of building a new nation in South Vietnam, he soon began to encounter a great deal of resistance to some of his policies. Many of these policies, arbitrarily promulgated and inefficiently implemented, were unpopular with many disparate elements of the population of South Vietnam. Soon dissident forces, communist and noncommunist, were arrayed against him, and his forces, with or without their American advisers, were hard put to deal with the increasing insurgency that threatened his regime. As Diem became more threatened, he also became more arbitrary and more isolated and less amenable to American advice and counsel. Aware of his weakness, he had no intention of implementing the elections of 1956 promised by the Geneva Convention. In this, American political leadership backed him. The Eisenhower administration was not prepared to have a country vote freely to be under communist control.

As far as the North Vietnamese side was concerned, the elections to unify the country had been canceled, American puppets had replaced the French, and their "brothers" in the South were being eliminated by Diem. As Luu Doan Huynh stated,

> But at the end of 1954 and early '55, things changed. The French are leaving. Now it is *you*, the Americans, who are in South Vietnam supporting Diem, who has refused to hold elections, who is persecuting our people. So you then become the bulwark of Diem, who is the enemy—who opposes—our goal of reunification.[12]

By 1956, the North Vietnamese regime, denied the unification it had been promised, saw the Americans as the colonial successors to the French in Vietnam and the Saigon regime as the illegitimate sucessor of that colonial power. Vietnamese diplomat Luu Van Loi stated,

> Our assessment by 1955 [was] that the United States had now replaced the French as our principle enemy. . . . Our calculations and judgements were based

[on] this fact, which we saw every day in our country: the U.S. was intervening in Vietnam, replacing the French imperialists, providing critical support to Ngo Dinh Diem, and had thus become, by these means, the enemy of the Vietnamese people.[13]

The United States and its president, Dwight D. Eisenhower, from the outset focused not on elections but on providing military assistance to South Vietnam, a newly created "country." Ngo Dinh Diem was installed to establish a government in the South as a separate entity. That government would supply a "free and democratic" legitimate alternative to the communist regime in North Vietnam. He was financially underwritten by the United States and moved quickly to consolidate his control of the South. With money pouring in from Washington, with the South Vietnamese security forces being advised by the U.S. MAAG in Saigon, and with a tough determination to prevail, Diem at first seemed to be the great foreign policy success Washington had been looking for. He was hailed as an "Asian liberator" who had succeeded in stopping the spread of communism in Indochina.[14]

Conflict appeared to be inevitable. Ho Chi Minh and the North Vietnamese would not long be denied the victory they had won on the battlefield and had been promised in the peace negotiations, the goal that their nation had sought for so long—the unification and independence of Vietnam. Initially, however, Democratic Republic of Vietnam representatives insisted that they focus on internal consolidation. The North Vietnamese, in recent conversations, indicate that following the Geneva agreements, they applied the line of "peaceful unification" to all their dealings with Diem. Their main objective was to have his cooperation in holding the promised elections. To that end, they state, they were willing to give Diem and some of his colleagues important posts in the all-Vietnam government that would follow.[15]

But while the North Vietnamese may have played an ill-defined part, one that they still deny, it is clear that a structured rebellion against the government of Ngo Dinh Diem began in the South in 1957 and 1958. Most of those who took up arms or otherwise resisted initially may have been indigenous South Vietnamese, and the causes for which they fought were by no means contrived in the North. Indeed, there is proof that the North Vietnamese tried to stop their followers in the South from participating in the insurgency that was endemic in South Vietnam. Diem's policies and government organization often engendered animosity toward the government of South Vietnam. The Diem regime alienated itself from one after another of those elements within South Vietnam that might have offered it political support. The numerous manifestations of religious preference was one element in developing a volatile climate of resentment in South Vietnam. So the insurgent movement in South Vietnam initially seems to have been indigenous, neither started by nor controlled by Hanoi. Although there is little evidence that Vietminh militants were directed to structure an insurgency, the Vietminh "stay behinds" in the South were exposed to Diem's retribution, and they resisted.

The American perspective on the matter was quite clear, however. To the Americans, the guerrilla movement quite simply was not only instigated by the North but also controlled by the Democratic Republic of Vietnam as a preparation for a cross-border invasion. The organization of the National Liberation Front (NLF) by the "southern resistance" in 1960 was taken as another indication not simply of northern involvement but also of the pending invasion. The manifesto of the NLF was issued on December 20, 1960. From its inception, the NLF was designed to encompass all anti-GVN activists, communist and noncommunist, and to provide an alternative government in South Vietnam to the Diem regime. Diem's publicists gave it a pejorative label, the Vietnamese communists, or Vietcong, and the name stuck.

And although the North Vietnamese government now insisted that there was no difference between the members of the DRV and the southern resistance, that they were all Vietnamese striving for the freedom and unity of Vietnam, there were serious divergences between the northern communists and the southern resistance. These differences manifested themselves throughout the struggle. For one thing, the northerners state that they were convinced that they needed to consolidate their victory in the North before addressing the unification of the country. The southerners, subject to Diem's retaliation, were unwilling to wait.

Chapter Four

The Road to War

It is little wonder that the agreement made in Geneva quickly began to unravel. Clearly, the United States had no intention of allowing this Southeast Asian nation, the newly created government of South Vietnam, to accede voluntarily to communism through elections in 1956. After the Geneva Accords of 1954, the Democratic Republic of (North) Vietnam never seemed to waver in its belief that the nation would finally be unified under Ho Chi Minh's and Hanoi's leadership in two years as provided by the Soviet Union, China, and France. Ho Chi Minh indicated that the burden of the Geneva Accords would fall hardest on his southern compatriots. He called on them nevertheless to "place national interest above local interests and permanent interests above temporary interests" over the next two years until the nationwide elections leading to unification could be held. The North Vietnamese leadership went about consolidating its rule in the North in preparation for eventual unification of their nation or for whatever followed if that did not occur.[1]

The elections of 1956 promised by the Geneva Accords never occurred, of course. They were desired neither by the South Vietnamese nor by the U.S. leadership and were never planned for by either. Aware of his weakness, the South Vietnamese president had no intention of implementing these elections. In this, American political leadership backed him. The Eisenhower administration was not prepared to have a country vote freely to be under communist control.

Insofar as the North Vietnamese side was concerned, the elections to unify the country in 1956 had seemed to have been canceled. American puppets had replaced the French and were standing by while their "brothers" in the South were being eliminated by South Vietnamese forces. By 1956, the North Vietnamese regime, denied the unification that it had been promised, saw the

Americans as the colonial successors to the French in Vietnam and the Saigon regime as illegitimate puppets of that colonial power. As veteran (North) Vietnamese diplomat Luu Van Loi stated,

> Our assessment by 1955 [was] that the United States had now replaced the French as our principle enemy. . . . Our calculations and judgments were based [on] this fact, which we saw every day in our country: the United States was intervening in Vietnam, replacing the French imperialists . . . and had thus become, by these means, the enemy of the Vietnamese people.[2]

Conflict appeared inevitable. Ho Chi Minh and the North Vietnamese would not long be denied the victory they had won on the battlefield with France and had been promised in the peace negotiations. The goal that their nation had sought for so long—the unification and independence of Vietnam—was being taken from their grasp. Their main objective was to have the promised elections after eliminating Diem. The situation in South Vietnam had become so desperate that Hanoi felt forced to abandon its strategy of pure political struggle and agreed to direct support of an armed revolution south of the seventeenth parallel. Ho could not avoid addressing his deep concern that the United States increasingly was "becoming our main enemy." Leaders in Hanoi had fears of their own about the course of events in the South. They never wavered in their commitment to reunify Vietnam under Hanoi's communist leadership, even after it became clear that the U.S. government would back Ngo Dinh Diem's government to a degree they had not anticipated. The northern leadership felt that events in the South seemed to be moving too quickly, too chaotically. Their fear was that an uprising or revolt against Diem might occur prematurely, before Diem's political apparatus and military capability had been sufficiently weakened.

So timing and careful political calculations were now very important and were the key to success for Hanoi. Le Duan was the Hanoi leader most responsible for coordinating events in the South in such a way as to maintain this delicate balance. On the one hand, as a southerner who had traveled clandestinely throughout the South in the 1950s, he saw firsthand the brutal effects of Diem's campaign to eradicate the "southern resistance." It was important that the southerners understood that they had not been forgotten by Hanoi and that they receive tangible support for resisting Diem. On the other hand, seeing the strong commitment Washington had made to Diem, Le Duan had to worry about inadvertently moving too fast and inviting American intervention. Le Duan and John Kennedy, the successor to President Eisenhower, had this in common, and each leader groped for a way to support his ally in South Vietnam without encouraging the other to intervene.[3]

The North Vietnam concept of "people's war" had evolved over a millennium of invasion and occupation by foreign powers. The objective of this strategy placed the emphasis on political consolidation—on building a core of revolutionaries who were committed to a long-term struggle. The goal was to create a revolutionary movement first before engaging the enemy in the field. Although the pace of the southern war was to be constrained by revolutionary doctrine and Hanoi's wariness about Washington's response, it nevertheless was propelled inexorably forward. Hanoi attempted to increase pressure on the Diem government consistent with the doctrine of people's war. But the southern resistance could not be so patient. The violence in South Vietnam increased. The reaction to these developments in Hanoi and Saigon were diametrically opposed. Diem and his circle saw signs of ominous escalation by the North and attributed all violence to "northern mercenaries" and communists. But Hanoi often had great difficulty in getting its ostensible southern allies to wait and to topple the enemy at an appropriate time. Instead, the southern resistance, aggrieved members of various groups who had run afoul of Diem and his followers, were forced to take a stand. As Luu Doan Huynh, a Vietnamese diplomat, saw the situation after Geneva, "The French are leaving. Now it is you, the Americans, who are in South Vietnam supporting Diem, who has refused to hold elections, who is persecuting our people. So you are then the bulwark of Diem, who is the enemy—who opposes our goal of reunification."[4]

Thus, there was an implied assumption that, in defeating and overthrowing Diem, Hanoi and the southern resistance would have to reckon with the United States as well. By 1961, the United States had become every bit as much an enemy as Diem, yet few Vietnamese outside of Saigon had ever seen an American. Why was the United States in such a position? Part of the answer is that Hanoi and the southern rebels did not only believe that the Americans had helped the French with money and equipment that had killed Vietnamese. Now they were replacing the French in the South, and they were just like the French, interested only in subjugating and exploiting the Vietnamese people. It appeared obvious to Hanoi in 1961 that Ngo Dinh Diem had been put in place by the United States to do its bidding. As Luu Doan Huynh put it, "[Diem] was your guy, and he was killing our people. You see, blood . . . speaks loudly when you are the one who is bleeding."[5]

Because of the outcome at Geneva, Hanoi's military and diplomatic flexibility would be severely constrained in its appraisal and interactions with the United States. At Geneva, they listened to their big friends, the Soviets and Chinese. In the future, they would not. At Geneva, they compromised in order to secure a promise of reunification, which was broken. In the future, their willingness to compromise would seem virtually nonexistent to the United States. At Geneva, they tried to play the game of diplomacy with the big powers and lost.

In the future, diplomacy with the United States would be conducted only between Hanoi and Washington—or not at all. And, most important, at Geneva they felt that they had, in effect, betrayed their compatriots south of the seventeenth parallel, who had already suffered greatly in the war with France.[6]

There is no doubt that the North Vietnamese as well as the southern resistance saw Ngo Dinh Diem as closely linked to the United States. This caused a direct military confrontation between Hanoi and Washington to draw even closer. The brutality and arbitrariness of the Diem regime had, by the time of President Kennedy's election, begun to pull the United States more directly into the civil conflict in the South.

At the same time, it seems that Hanoi was having its hand forced by its desperate southern colleagues. Hanoi saw the writing on the wall and took the necessary steps, to the extent possible, to establish command over the resistance in the South. Hanoi was radicalized by its southern allies and had to respond to their desperation and commitment. A fight to the end apparently was the only option left to Hanoi. As veteran Vietnamese diplomat and journalist Luu Van Loi stated, "The U.S. was intervening in Vietnam, replacing the French imperialists, providing critical support to Ngo Dinh Diem, and had thus become, by these means, the enemy of the Vietnamese people."[7]

For the United States, all members of the resistance to Ngo Dinh Diem's regime were considered to be "communists." Hanoi's view was that the repressive measures of Diem were conceived, directed, and certainly financed by the United States as part of a plan whose ultimate end was to crush the Democratic Republic of (North) Vietnam itself. So, the North Vietnamese claim, they were forced to take up arms by the actions of Diem and the United States. After 1956, they realized that a peaceful reunification of Vietnam as called for by the Geneva Accords would not be possible. As Nguyen Khac Huynh explained it,

> We had to give up a strategy of political struggle, which could not succeed due to Ngo Dinh Diem's brutal tactics against our people . . . we were forced to take up arms in the south because the United States and Diem's regime forced us to. We wanted a peaceful solution, but it was not possible to have reunification without arms.[8]

To the United States, however, the Geneva Accords were seen as the best way of "saving" the southern portion of Vietnam for the free world. On October 26, 1955, with U.S. backing, Ngo Dinh Diem proclaimed the Republic of (South) Vietnam, evidently in violation of article 6 of the Geneva treaty, which declared that "the military demarcation line [the seventeenth parallel] is provisional and should not in any way be interpreted as constituting a political or territorial boundary." The action was justified by the United States, as was the cancellation of elections on the grounds that prior communist aggression from North Vietnam proved that it had already violated the Geneva Accords, necessitating the action taken by Diem with the encouragement of the United States.[9]

From the moment the United States brought Ngo Dinh Diem to Saigon as its designated architect for South Vietnam's anticommunist nation building, the main objective of the Hanoi government was to dislodge Diem and reunify the nation. But there was one overriding caveat: do not provoke the United States into a U.S.–Vietnamese war. One of the ironies of the history of the escalation to such a war is that the major objective of both Hanoi and Washington initially was to avoid escalation to the level in which North Vietnamese and U.S. combat forces would be fighting each other directly. An additional irony is that Hanoi's strategy of achieving its twin objectives—replacing Diem with a neutral government able to reunify the nation and avoiding an American war—was in many respects the mirror image of Washington's strategy.

In the lexicon of war planners in Hanoi, the "special war," the war between Vietnamese and Vietnamese, using South Vietnamese forces and American equipment and advisers, was now under way. The emphasis was on political consolidation to get Washington to accept a political settlement and the formation of a coalition government in the South. The objective of Hanoi and Washington was to break the will of the other at the lowest rung of the ladder of escalation and to do so not by gaining an outright victory but by preventing the other from winning.

In January 1959, the party plenum in Hanoi passed what came to be known as Resolution 15. Declaring that the "basic path of development of the revolution in the South is to use violence," Resolution 15 essentially gave permission to southerners to protect themselves and fight back when necessary. The fates of the Hanoi government and the southern resistance were officially joined on December 20, 1960, at a secret location in South Vietnam, where the National Liberation Front (NLF) was founded. It was intended to be an alternative southern government. Its formation, however, did not indicate that Hanoi had given the go-ahead for an all-out offensive against Diem. In fact, it was quite the reverse. It meant that Hanoi's alternative government structure was taking shape and that the time had come to unite "partial and spontaneous uprisings" with a systematic strategy to take over the South, beginning with the rural areas, and, when they were secured, to move on to the cities and the Diem government. Hanoi was taking charge of the southern resistance.[10] As Nguyen Khac Huynh explained,

But by 1956, we realized that peaceful reunification was not possible. Therefore our leaders in both regions had to reassess the situation led by Le Duan in the south and Ho Chi Minh in the north. The combined efforts of Le Duan and Ho

Chi Minh resulted in the passage of Resolution 15 in January of 1959. As you know, this signaled that we had given up a strategy of purely political struggle which could not succeed due to Ngo Dinh Diem's brutal tactics against our people. . . . We were forced to take up arms in the south because the United States and Diem's regime forced us to. We wanted a peaceful solution, but it was not possible to have reunification without arms.[11]

The United States and its ally, Ngo Dinh Diem, in South Vietnam, was the big enemy. The brutality and arbitrariness of the Diem regime had, by the time of President Kennedy's election, begun to pull the United States more directly into the conflict in the South. Likewise, it is unclear if, when, and under what conditions Hanoi would have agreed to Resolution 15 and the formation of the NLF if it hadn't been forced—as it clearly was—by desperate southern colleagues. Hanoi saw the writing on the wall, took the necessary steps, and thus established control over the resistance in the South. The purpose was to organize the countryside and to defeat Ngo Dinh Diem before the United States was able to mobilize and intervene successfully.[12]

The Kennedy administration took office with the realization that the situation in South Vietnam was deteriorating steadily and would continue to do so without some major changes in the policies and efforts of the government of South Vietnam (GVN) and improvement in the proficiency of the Army of the Republic of Vietnam (ARVN). The new president was inclined to support Diem. As a member of Congress, he had often voiced support not only for the French war in Indochina but subsequently also for supporting our new South Vietnamese allies. He also felt that he could deal with the situation in Southeast Asia without great expenditure or difficulty.

What advice did the president receive concerning the growing problem in Vietnam? Initially, President Kennedy considered the merits of a new counterinsurgency proposal by Brigadier General Edward Lansdale and forwarded to him before the end of the Eisenhower administration. The report, dated January 17, 1961, urged that Vietnam be treated "as a combat area of the cold war, as an area requiring emergency treatment." The report also suggested that the United States send its "best people" to Indochina, people who were "experienced in dealing with this type of emergency." One of Lansdale's specific proposals was to increase South Vietnam's armed forces from 150,000 to 170,000 men, primarily for action against the NLF. The additional 20,000 troops, Lansdale reported, should "meet the immediate and serious guerrilla threat." The plan also called for Diem to institute political reforms, to include having opposition leaders in the cabinet.[13]

At a January 28 meeting, Kennedy asked his top advisers if the new counterinsurgency plan under debate would "really permit a shift from the defense to the offense" or whether the deteriorating situation in Saigon was not "basically one of politics and morale." Most concluded that there was indeed a problem with Diem; however, the administration seemed eager to show positive progress in Vietnam, so Kennedy approved Lansdale's counterinsurgency plan on January 30, 1961, in what was seen by most as quite a routine action. Lansdale's biographer reports that Kennedy offered Lansdale the ambassadorship to Vietnam, but this was unacceptable to both the State Department and the Defense Department because of his service in the Central Intelligence Agency (CIA) and was finally dropped by the president.[14]

The Joint Chiefs of Staff were not enthusiastic about Lansdale's recommendation to create special units for counterinsurgency efforts. They were especially concerned at that time and in the future about the availability of American conventional forces for a conflict in Europe, the theater considered to be of major threat at that time. Many thought that wars of national liberation in the developing world were a sideshow to distract the United States from the communists' main targets in the industrialized West. The Joint Chiefs at that time rejected counterinsurgency as a special need and trained all infantry units in those tactics as an added mission. Army Chief of Staff General George Decker is reported to have told Kennedy that "any good soldier can handle guerrillas." The marines felt the same way. But Kennedy is reported to have answered that counterinsurgency fighting was a "special art."

Kennedy hoped to stop the insurgency through local and limited war. The goal was to find a means of containing the deterioration of Diem's government in the South while minimizing the risk of doing anything to provoke war with North Vietnam's ostensible allies, China and the Soviet Union. The president sought to limit the amount of force used by the United States to what was absolutely necessary to achieve America's political aims in Vietnam. The goal was not to crush North Vietnam but rather to persuade the communists to cease their support of the southern insurgency. General Maxwell Taylor, former U.S. Army Chief of Staff who had been called from retirement to be Kennedy's independent military adviser, supported Kennedy's limited-war concept. Taylor had retired in 1959 largely in protest over Eisenhower's new-look strategy. The general did not think that heavy reliance on nuclear arms was a viable strategy in the Cold War. President Kennedy adopted a more "flexible response," one that would allow the United States to oppose in its own way the communist threat to the newly emerging former colonial nations.[15]

Initially, Kennedy sent his vice president, Lyndon Johnson, to meet with Diem. Johnson praised Diem as "the Churchill of Asia" and promised him American support. The outcome of Johnson's visit was a new program for South Vietnam announced in May 1961. Additional resources were added to the American aid program designed to strengthen the Diem government and improve its popular support. But another result of the vice president's visit was that Diem, assured of continued American support, could safely spurn American demands for reform. In order to pressure him into making reforms in his government, the United States would have had to threaten Diem with a credible withdrawal of American support. But U.S. officials repeatedly stated that America was determined to help South Vietnam preserve its independence and would not allow the country to be taken over by communism. Since the United States continued to proclaim the vital importance of maintaining an anticommunist South Vietnam and continued to assure the Diem government that it was committed to the defense of Southeast Asia from communism, a threat to cut off American support was not credible and was, in fact, never made by the United States. Consequently, Diem had complete confidence that the United States needed him as the anticommunist buffer in the region and would continue to support him. The United States, it seemed, had little leverage over his actions.

As the military situation continued to deteriorate, Diem demanded additional increases in the South Vietnamese forces—which would also require increases in the number of American advisers as well as more U.S. equipment and financial aid. In October 1961, President Kennedy dispatched his special military representative, General Maxwell Taylor, and his deputy national security assistant, Walt W. Rostow, to Saigon again to assess the situation. After a two-week tour of Vietnam, they recommended a substantial expansion of American aid to stem the tide. An increase in American advisers, they stated, could force a "much better, aggressive, more confident performance from the Vietnamese military and civilian establishment." They also recommended deploying three squadrons of helicopters, manned by American pilots, to provide mobility to the South Vietnamese forces. Their report also proposed an initial commitment of 8,000 American combat troops to be disguised as logistical forces dealing with floods in the Mekong Delta.[16]

In this report, there was no discussion whatsoever of the serious political problems in South Vietnam, nor did there seem to be any appreciation of the capabilities and intentions of the North Vietnamese forces. The report seemed to indicate that air power against the North could handle the situation if things were to get out of hand in the South. In concentrating on the military situation, the report showed a complete lack of understanding of the situation in South Vietnam. While Taylor did recognize that the communist strategy appeared "to aim at an essentially political denouement rather than the total military capture of the country," his recommendations were to support the Diem regime militarily while entering into a new relationship with the South Vietnamese president, moving from "advice" to "limited partnership."[17]

The secretary of defense and the secretary of state sent the president a memorandum in early November 1961 urging him not to send in American troops as Taylor and Rostow had recommended. Both believed that although additional U.S. forces might be necessary someday, the ARVN would have to bear the burden of the fighting at this stage. "If there is a strong South Vietnamese effort," Secretaries McNamara and Rusk suggested, "U.S. combat forces may not be needed. If there is not such an effort, U.S. forces could not accomplish their mission in the midst of an apathetic or hostile population." Thus, the two secretaries recognized the true situation in Vietnam. Indeed, at the core of American strategy at that time was the realization that South Vietnam eventually had to be capable of defending itself and standing on its own and that American arms were no substitute for this.[18]

President Kennedy shared this view and stressed to others that the effort in Vietnam could be only as good as the Saigon regime. He warned that "to introduce U.S. forces in large numbers there today, while it might have an initial favorable military aspect would almost certainly lead to adverse political and, in the long run, adverse military consequences. . . . The troops will march in; the bands will play; the crowds will cheer," Kennedy told White House Special Assistant Arthur M. Schlesinger Jr., "and in four days everyone will have forgotten. Then we will have to send in more troops. It's like taking a drink. The effect wears off and you have to take another." Thus, Kennedy balked at the commitment of American combat forces to shore up the Diem regime. He approved increases in the size of the ARVN and increased the number of American advisers. By May 1963, there were 12,000 American advisers in South Vietnam.[19]

Having been told by Diem in late 1961 that South Vietnam would not accept American troop units, Kennedy turned his attention to counterinsurgency efforts in that nation. One plan implemented by the Saigon regime with U.S. approval and financing had as its major purpose to win that loyalty and support in the countryside. The strategic hamlet program, as it came to be called, represented the unifying concept for a strategy designed to develop support among the rural population for the Saigon government. The program initially was much broader than the construction of strategic hamlets per se. It initially was seen as a comprehensive sequential plan beginning with clearing the insurgents from an area and protecting the rural population, progressing through the establishment of a government infrastructure and ultimately to the provision of services that would lead the peasants to identify with the government. It would help peasants defend themselves, improve their living conditions, and develop support among the rural population for the Saigon government.

The program, first proposed to Diem by Sir Robert Thompson, a British civil servant who had been permanent secretary of defense in Malaya, was a comprehensive proposal for an overall strategic effort to translate the newly articulated theory of counterinsurgency into reality for the country as a whole. Similar guerrilla-led insurgencies in Malaysia and the Philippines had been put down in the past in part by the successful implementation of this strategic hamlet concept. In Malaysia, large-scale resettlement was used to isolate sympathetic ethnic Chinese from the guerrillas, thus depriving those guerrillas of their essential source of food and protection among the people. At the core of the government's success in Malaysia was its ability to extend its administrative control over the entire population of the country. Government officials there understood that "winning the hearts and minds" of the peasants was the key to success. Guerrillas needed the local population for food, shelter, and recruitment, and thus they hoped to turn passive resistance into active support. The American Joint Chiefs condemned this concept, however. They warned that "the insurgency in Vietnam has developed far beyond the capacity of police controls."

But Kennedy was seeking cheap and effective answers without the use of American troop units. Officials in Saigon supported this program of "defended villages" in Vietnam. The United States, in the Taylor–Rostow report, had proposed that the United States enter a "limited partnership" with Diem to implement this program. Diem, on the other hand, not interested in a limited partnership where he shared power, saw this program as a vehicle to get the United States committed to South Vietnam with money and equipment while avoiding American recommended reform in his government organization and without giving up his independence. Diem's brother, Ngo Dinh Nhu, was put in charge of the program, and construction of these hamlets began in early 1961.

The strategic hamlet program demonstrated starkly the inflexibility of Diem and his unwillingness to give up some of his sovereignty to American advice. The objective was political, though the means to its realization were to be a mixture of military, social, psychological, economic, and political measures. Diem was determined to run the program in his own way. As it was implemented by Diem's brother, the program put achieving security before winning loyalty. Despite American material support, the program was characterized by poor planning, corruption, and alienation of the peasants, whose loyalty was the object of the exercise. Criticisms mentioned corvée labor, the failure of the GVN to reimburse the farmers for losses due to resettlement, the dishonesty of many officials, infiltration of hamlets by the NLF or the Vietcong, unwillingness of the peasants to resettle, and Diem's stress on exhortations rather than on the provision of social services.

The whole program demonstrated a lack of understanding of Vietnamese culture and tradition on the part of the Americans and the lack of concern for the rural population on the part of their own government leaders. Ancient patterns were wantonly disrupted in many areas. The populace, tied for centuries to its land, its hamlets, and even the graves of its ancestors, was reluctant to move into these stockades. Perhaps most damaging to the success of the strategic hamlet program was the inability of the Saigon regime to convince rural Vietnamese that the GVN was little more than a distant nuisance. That government did little to reform the land tenure system that left peasants paying high taxes and exorbitant rents on lands they had previously farmed without charge. Often these lands had been redistributed by the NLF from absentee landlords to local tillers of the soil.

Villagers often viewed these "strategic hamlets" as havens for corrupt government officials, and as a result they often conspired with NLF cadres. Since few leaders of the government in Saigon ventured much into the countryside, these corrupt officials, along with isolated security forces, became the only contact of rural Vietnamese with their government. The NLF often targeted Diem's appointees for assassination, adding to the proof that the Saigon regime could not provide security to the countryside. It was perhaps not taken into account by the government and by the Americans, nor, perhaps, was it even contemplated that attempts to separate the peasants from the guerrillas in this fashion were futile. Often, the peasants were the guerrillas. The Vietnamese government was unwilling to understand that establishing strategic hamlets would accomplish nothing unless other necessary measures were taken to achieve the three objectives of protection, of uniting and involving the people, and of development. The inept and corrupt strategic hamlet program died with its sponsors.[20]

The NLF's plan to defeat the GVN was directed toward the peasants: win the hearts and minds of the peasants throughout the South and foment urban unrest to topple Diem before the Americans would intervene directly with its forces. This strategy was helped by all the circumstances discussed previously. To accomplish this task, the NLF created associations at the village level organized around gender, age, occupation, and religion. These associations were the key to the political struggle during the early years of the war, as they helped organize the peasants at the "rice roots." The Saigon government had no similar organization in the villages. The NLF's people's war was not a small-scale war but rather a coordinated political struggle with guns, called a "people's war." It was directed toward the people of South Vietnam, highlighted the government's crimes, and promised security in the countryside.

People's war, therefore, as conceived by the NLF, was the combination of various interests and actions, all designed to make the Saigon regime appear reactive and arbitrary. The party exploited the government's often oppressive policies by helping to organize the rural population in legitimate forms of protest. Simultaneously, NLF cadres sought to alleviate hardships by providing food, restoring land use rights through redistribution, and tightening security in the countryside. People's war was a multilayered art form requiring careful planning and timing. According to *Needs of the Revolution*, the most important communist document on the subject, every action and reaction was crucial:

> Timing is most important . . . choose the right moment to launch it such as when the enemy is committing a mistake . . . or when the people's rights have been endangered . . . by corruption, high taxation, forced money donations, land robbing building strategic hamlets, forced membership in reactionary organizations, terror or killing, military draft. . . . Struggle movements can also be launched in favor of freedom and trade, freedom to move to a new part of the country.[21]

As one NLF official explained, "Every military clash, every demonstration, every propaganda appeal was seen as part of an integrated whole; each had consequences far beyond its immediate apparent results."[22]

By the end of 1962, President Kennedy understood that the strategic hamlet program was not enough to achieve American objectives in Vietnam, as he had been warned by his Joint Chiefs. As the Saigon regime and its army continued to suffer defeat after defeat in the hamlets but continued to resist the deployment of American troop units, Kennedy approved requests by the Military Aid and Advisory Group for more advisers and weapons. American military aid to Vietnam more than doubled between 1961 and 1962, and it included more than 300 military aircraft. In addition, Kennedy reorganized the American command system in Vietnam, replacing the old U.S. advisory group with a subordinate joint command, the Military Assistance Command, Vietnam (MACV). The president also endorsed initial plans to transfer all CIA paramilitary operations to the MACV.

MACV urged ARVN units to use their increased firepower and control to launch sweeps in the countryside. Buoyed by early successes, Kennedy announced plans to withdraw some American advisers by the end of 1963. General Paul Harkins, the detached but always optimistic MACV commander, is reported to have told the president that the war would probably be over by Christmas 1963. Others were not so optimistic. The CIA's National Intelligence Estimate warned that the situation was far more precarious and unstable than reports from Saigon indicated. In one report, the CIA analyst warned, "the Viet Cong by and large retain de facto control of much of the countryside and have steadily increased the overall intensity of their effort." By mid-1963, according to one official U.S. source, "the rate of Communist-initiated incidents and attacks increased by one-third over the first half of 1963 and exceeded the average level of such activity sustained during 1962."

As late as October 1963, Secretary McNamara and General Taylor, returning from Vietnam, again stated that the United States supported "the military effort" to suppress the insurgency and predicted that the task would be completed by the end of 1965. Once again, having sent military leaders to assess the situation, the president received a military recommendation. Once again, the political situation and its requirements were largely ignored. Thus, most of the advice that President Kennedy received concerned the use of increased military power to solve what was clearly a political problem—the inability of the Diem regime to establish a stable and effective government that could win the loyalty and support of the population of South Vietnam.[23]

This left President Kennedy in a quandary. Beginning in late 1961, some of the more outspoken of the American advisers, as well as many of the young newsmen in Vietnam, began to point out the deficiencies of the GVN and military leadership. The reports of the press in the early days of the American advisory effort in Vietnam were pessimistic and emphasized the lack of morale and competence of the ARVN and many of its leaders. These views, while not widely disseminated, contradicted the optimistic reports of the senior American military leaders in Vietnam and often were not welcomed or accepted in Washington.[24] But the ARVN remained largely ineffective, and the political leadership of Ngo Dinh Diem became more arbitrary, corrupt, and remote from the population of South Vietnam.

From the North Vietnamese point of view, they were participating in the "special war," where American "special" troops—the advisers—encouraged Vietnamese to fight other Vietnamese. Former North Vietnamese officials, in recent conversations, stated that they could see that Diem, while relying heavily on the United States and opposing communism in an uncompromising way, essentially represented a narrow and extremist nationalism coupled with autocracy and nepotism. As a result, the North Vietnamese found that the longer Diem stayed in power, the better it was for their struggle for "liberation" in South Vietnam. This was not only because his autocratic and brutal rule "increased the ranks of the revolution" but also because he rejected direct U.S. military intervention. This was very helpful to the North Vietnamese and their southern allies because their goal was to seize a decisive victory at the right moment and preempt U.S. direct military intervention. The idea, these North Vietnamese planners indicated, was to play on the contradictions in the enemy ranks—between Diem and the Americans—and thereby strengthen Diem's opposition to the commitment of U.S. combat forces to the war. This, they believed, would help their southern allies win a decisive victory before it was possible for the United States to undertake all-out, direct military intervention.

This decisive victory won in South Vietnam, they felt, would bring about the collapse and disintegration of the South Vietnamese main forces, paving the way for the formation of a national coalition government that would negotiate the exit of any U.S. military presence in South Vietnam. They felt that Diem's inclusion in a new government at that point would give a face-saving solution to the United States and thus make the United States more amenable to a neutral solution in South Vietnam. In that way, they saw that Diem could make a valuable contribution toward a gradual victory of the revolution without a big war with the United States.[25]

To help achieve what they saw as this historical inevitability, the North Vietnamese made decisions at the Third National Congress of the Lao Dong Party in September 1960 to increase the flow of aid from North to South and called for a unified front to lead the struggle. They felt, in any case, that the troubles of the "puppet" Diem regime were of his own making. They foresaw that this artificial regime imposed on the South Vietnamese people by a foreign power in violation of the Geneva Convention could not survive the enmity and opposition of its own people, the southern resistance. The North had only to sit back and cheer Diem's collapse at the hands of his own people. The organization of the NLF of South Vietnam in 1960, according to these North Vietnamese officials, was designed to unite the disparate groups opposing the Diem regime and to provide an alternative government structure to the discredited and failed regime imposed and supported by the Americans. The evidence supports the conclusion that whether or not the rebellion against Diem proceeded independently through 1958, Hanoi moved thereafter to capture the revolution. Thus, President Diem was confronted with a committed and organized indigenous foe supported with material, personnel, and political action by Hanoi.[26]

Diem had proved to be something of a disappointment for Washington. The brutality of his regime increased over time. Family had always been of great importance in Vietnamese culture, and the brutality was led by Diem's younger brother, Ngo Dinh Nhu, who directed internal security. Predictably, such brutality backfired, and by the late 1950s a guerrilla movement was already in control of some parts of South Vietnamese countryside. Moreover, Diem seemed to be remarkably uncooperative in resisting advice and counsel when it came from Washington. A mandarin, he believed that he ruled with the "mandate of heaven," an attitude that infuriated his American underwriters and estranged many of his fellow Vietnamese.

And so a vicious cycle was created in South Vietnam. Diem used even more brutal and arbitrary means to eliminate suspected communists and opponents, in turn leading to increased guerrilla activity. In response to the increased guerrilla threat, more American advisers were sent to South Vietnam, only to be rebuffed and ignored by an increasingly isolated brutal and unresponsive Diem and his brother. He refused to allow American combat forces into his nation. Nevertheless, throughout the early 1960s, Washington ignored Diem's arbitrariness and brutality for the most part because it was believed that he—and he alone—could transform South Vietnam into a bulwark against the spread of communism from the North. The Diem regime would turn out to be more efficient than expected in dealing with the southern resistance.

THE GOVERNMENT OF SOUTH VIETNAM

The insensitive military handling of Buddhist demonstrations in Huė by Diem's brother, Ngo Dinh Nhu, focused attention on the increasing arbitrariness of the Diem regime and of the increasing opposition of many of the people with the excesses of that regime. That feeling of disenchantment with Diem was expressed publicly by President Kennedy in a television interview in September 1963. But in the same week, in another television interview, the president indicated his opposition to reducing aid to the GVN. By November 1963, the U.S. troop level in South Vietnam was 16,500 advisers and pilots, and it still seemed to make little difference. The ARVN, led by its cautious political generals, remained largely ineffective, and the political leadership of Ngo Dinh Diem was becoming more arbitrary, corrupt, remote from the population, and unable to win the loyalty and support of the South Vietnamese people.[27]

In August 1963, President Diem's brother, Ngo Dinh Nhu, who had become an important but unpopular figure in his brother's administration, again cracked down on dissident Buddhists in Saigon. These Buddhists had been leading the civilian population in protest against Diem's harsh policies. At long last, the United States began to reassess its support of Diem. American officials decided to take a firm policy toward Diem's actions and particularly against the increasingly nefarious influence of his brother. Dissident generals approached the new American ambassador, Henry Cabot Lodge, seeking American support for a coup to oust Diem and his brother. Lodge, newly arrived as the American ambassador in Saigon, reported to Washington that he felt it unlikely that Diem would oust his brother and recommended that the generals be supported in ousting Diem. In a controversial cable from Washington on August 24, 1963, Lodge was instructed to

urgently examine all possible alternative leadership and make detailed plans as to how we might bring about Diem's replacement if this should become necessary

. . . you will understand we cannot from Washington give you detailed instructions
as to how this operation should proceed, but you will also know we will back you
to the hilt on actions you take to achieve our objectives.

In his response, Lodge agreed that "we go straight to the generals with our demands, without informing Diem." This decision, of course, set into motion a
military coup that quickly spiraled out of control and resulted in the deaths of
Diem and his brother.[28] Diem's death would have been unlikely without
American complicity. President Kennedy, shocked by the assassination of the
two Vietnamese leaders, would himself be assassinated three weeks later. But
Diem's death marked a new phase in the Vietnam conflict. America's responsibility for Diem's death haunted U.S. leaders during the years ahead, leading
them to acknowledge that the United States now had a larger responsibility in
Vietnam. In addition, the questionable legitimacy of the GVN, both internally
and internationally, was now largely questioned and undermined. From this
time forward, even more so than in the past, the claims of the North Vietnamese government and its southern supporters that the ineffective GVN was
a puppet supported only by American aid seemed to reflect the truth and
found a more ready audience among the rural population of South Vietnam.

Could Diem have succeeded with an expanded program of American military and civil support and assistance directed toward the rural population of
South Vietnam? Unfortunately for the United States, the problem was in the
South Vietnamese leadership and not in American support. Diem grew to realize that the United States was sufficiently committed to South Vietnam that
he could afford on occasion to resist and even to ignore American advice and
pressure. Diem knew, as the United States came to realize, that he himself
represented the only alternative to a coalition government that, the United
States felt, eventually would lead to a communist Vietnam. As long as that solution was anathema to the United States, America had no other choice than,
as a popular slogan stated, to "sink or swim with Ngo Dinh Diem."

This perceived American dependency reinforced Diem's political inflexibility. Almost as soon as the United States decided to increase its commitment, Diem began to renege on promised reforms. He was similarly handi-
capped in his attempts to build a nation based on his political concepts. Diem
remained as he had been raised, a mandarin of imperial Vietnam, steeped in
filial devotion to Vietnam's past history, modern only to the extent of an aes-
thetic, intense, conservative Catholicism. The political apparatus he created
to extend his power and implement his programs reflected this background,
personality, and experience: a rigidly organized, overly centralized familial
oligarchy. To the frustration of American officials, in no sense did Diem or
his brothers attempt to acquire a popular base for his government. His per-

sonality and his political methods practically ensured that he would remain, distant, and even isolated from the peasantry, his major constituency. Diem's political history and background practically ensured that over the long run, he would alienate one after another of the key groups within South Vietnamese society. By late 1960, his regime rested only on the narrow and disintegrating base of its own bureaucracy and army and on the Catholic refugees, many of whom had fled from the North with U.S. assistance.

The question arises, Was President Kennedy correct in believing that, in the end, the government and people of South Vietnam must carry the war themselves, that it could not be done for them? Clearly, that was the case. The military problem that the Americans intended to solve, the "defeat" of the insurgency by military force, did not address the real problem—the attitude of the rural population of South Vietnam toward their government and its leaders. The failure of Diem was not preordained, although the leaders of North Vietnam feel that it truly was. Diem's downfall and death was no surprise to the North Vietnamese. As Dinh Nho Liem explained, the northerners saw Diem as

> absolutely incapable of surviving long in South Vietnam. Since Diem and his family could not turn back the "historical wheel," [t]he overthrow of Diem's regime was inevitable. . . . If Diem's generals had not done away with him, then the people would have done so. Diem's days were numbered, no matter how you look at it.[29]

The strident outlook of North Vietnam notwithstanding, for the people of South Vietnam, the reunification of a partitioned Vietnam was not a burning political issue. There was, in fact, a certain historic distrust between North and South. A more sensitive and adroit leader might have captured and held a significant rural following if he had demonstrated a willingness to address the questions important to the populace—peace, security, improving standards of living, and land reform. The initial GVN "pacification" efforts combined promises of land reform with improvements in public health, education, and local government. Unfortunately, these programs never received the resources from the central government to allow them to be successful.

Diem's almost paranoid preoccupation with security meant that the bulk of the American aid he received was lavished on the ARVN. Little attention was paid to police and intelligence organization in the countryside, and security in the villages was relegated to the Self-Defense Forces, most often poorly trained and equipped and miserably led. In large part, the ARVN was withdrawn from the rural countryside. Diem had identified loyalty in his top army commanders as a sine qua non for his own survival. He took a personal interest in the positioning and promoting of officers and with the equipping of

his military forces. He—and his favorite officers—showed a distinct procliv-
ity toward heavy military forces of the conventional type. American advisers
were glad to accommodate him.

In light of Diem's policies, it is quite clear in retrospect that a focused and
overall government policy was required to win the loyalty and support of the
rural population of South Vietnam. Here, indeed, was a "missed opportunity"
for America. The answer to South Vietnam's internal political problems in
1963 was not an increase in American military forces, nor did it have much
to do with the bombing of North Vietnam. The situation called for an effort
directed toward the security and prosperity of the rural population of South
Vietnam. That effort was never undertaken.[30]

Another missed opportunity to avoid war occurred after the death of Diem.
The Hanoi leadership respected Diem's credentials as a nationalist and understood that he was unlikely to ask for or accept large numbers of American troops
in the South. Therefore, the party leadership did not desire to wrest control of the
south from Diem prematurely. The party felt that he was a strong enough nationalist to resist the Americans right up to the point where the party would remove him by force and liberate Vietnam. In the South, the NLF also wanted ultimately to remove Diem from power. But until they did, his intransigence and
his policies both filled NLF ranks and kept the Americans at bay. From the North
Vietnamese point of view, the death of Diem created an opportunity for both
sides. The NLF called on all parties to establish a coalition government on the
model of the Laos settlement of 1962. They state that they were eager to form
such a government, that there was an opportunity, but that the United States
missed that opportunity. They stated that this could have been an ideal time for
the United States to terminate its commitment to South Vietnam. They point out,
"In late 1964–early 1965, U.S. ground troops had not yet arrived. The full scale
bombing of the North had not begun. In short, the U.S. was not really—not
totally—committed to 'winning' some kind of ground war in Vietnam."[31]

But, as Secretary of Defense McNamara and North Vietnamese officials
have pointed out, the possibility of negotiations for a coalition government at
that time was really not considered seriously by either side. The North Vietnamese plan was to establish such a government by defeating South Vietnam
before the United States could deploy large numbers of troops. Although no
one could foresee the immensity of the struggle to come, the North Vietnamese point out, one truth was possible to see:

> The Saigon regime was bankrupt, morally bankrupt—absolutely worthless, es-
> pecially when compared to the high ideals for which . . . Americans believe they
> stand. So if, at that time, the U.S. had allowed the stinking Saigon regime to
> rot—to collapse—then the U.S. could certainly have avoided the costly war
> which U.S. public opinion eventually rejected.[32]

A group of South Vietnamese generals, led by Doung Van Minh, took control of the southern government after Diem's assassination. The new junta, including General Minh, seemed inclined from the moment they took power to be probing for a possible neutral arrangement. In the unexpected and chaotic situation in the South at that time following the coup, Hanoi put feelers out to the junta of General Minh to determine its interest in a neutral solution. But the new American president, Lyndon Johnson, was disquieted by these speculations. He tried to cut them short with a New Year's greeting to General Minh that stated, "We shall maintain in Vietnam American personnel and material as needed to assist you in achieving victory. . . . Neutralization of South Vietnam is unacceptable [and] would only be another name for a communist take-over." The ruling junta spurned the feelers after thus being encouraged by the United States.[33]

Faced with this American intransigence, the North Vietnamese, at the Ninth Party Plenum in late 1963, undertook several measures with the intent of increasing their military support for the southern insurgency and accelerating the struggle in the South to take advantage of the government crisis there. Throwing caution to the winds, these actions were as follows: (1) to strengthen the local armed forces, (2) to expand the secret forces in the cities (these forces would play an important role later in the Tet offensive), (3) to dispatch northern troops to the South (this is the first admission given by North Vietnam that they had dispatched troop units to the South), and (4) to step up the political struggle. But the North Vietnamese insist that they did not undertake any major changes in their grand strategy at this time. The shared objective of North Vietnam and the NLF, they state, was still to overthrow the puppet regime in Saigon, to liberate the South, and to establish a coalition government there that had good relations with Hanoi. These were goals, they state, before and after the assassinations of November 1963. If the United States had forced the South Vietnamese generals who succeeded Diem to come to the negotiating table, a coalition government could have been formed at that time, they indicate.[34]

The resolution paid lip service to what was seen to become a cataclysmic reality for North Vietnam—so-called limited war, meaning an American war with North Vietnam. In short, the document said that Hanoi would look for a quick victory in the South, where the situation was suddenly and unexpectedly advantageous, and would win before Washington knows what hit their allies in Saigon. The resolution stated,

That is the principal goal: to preempt a protracted war involving the United States. Second, it is possible that this won't happen, but we in Hanoi, with our sound doctrine, will win any protracted war and we will win it within the parameters of "special war," that is before the Americans can escalate to a Washington-Hanoi war.[35]

But Hanoi would not win a preemptive "special war" against the Saigon government at that time, although it came close. Moreover, it would not win quickly a protracted war, the "limited" American war begun scarcely a year later. Hanoi would win that war, but it would pay an enormous price for fighting that mutual war of attrition. In fact, the entire preemptive strategy adopted by the southern hawks in Hanoi in 1963 was based on a fundamental misunderstanding of Washington's view of escalation.

From the time of Diem's assassination forward, as the United States was to perceive in the months ahead, there was never an effective and stable independent noncommunist GVN, the objective of American policy. From this point forward, a stable, independent noncommunist South Vietnam was a chimera, a dangerous illusion. The government remained continuously weak, divided, and ineffective. As Gertrude Stein once wrote, "There was no there there." From this point forward, the survival of the GVN would depend directly on American arms and direct military support. The inevitable result of the withdrawal of that aid and military support should have been as easily and clearly foreseen in 1964 as it was in 1974. As General Westmoreland, the U.S. commander in Vietnam, has pointed out,

> If any generalization can be made about the war in South Vietnam it is that the U.S. effort, both military and political, prospered to the extent that the government of Vietnam was strong, coherent, and active. The corollary, of course, is that none of our efforts had any chance of success in the periods during which the government was weak, divided, and thus ineffective.[36]

Unfortunately, the government remained weak, divided, and ineffective throughout the American involvement in South Vietnam.

The North Vietnamese nearly succeeded in winning their "decisive victory" in the South. But Diem's overthrow and death in the November 1963 coup greatly increased the probability of direct U.S. military intervention. By conspiring in the death of Diem, the United States may have eliminated the possibility of a neutralist solution in South Vietnam, even if such a solution had been acceptable to the American leaders. From this point forward, it seems, a war between the United States and North Vietnam, considering American objectives, became more likely.

This was the situation that faced the new American president, Lyndon B. Johnson, as he took office after the assassination of John F. Kennedy. When made aware of Hanoi's December 1963 decisions, the decisions of the president and his adviser's reaction were reactive, as were Hanoi's. They felt an urgent requirement to respond, and they did so. Such were the fruits of Hanoi's purpose and Washington's actions. The ill-conceived removal of Ngo Dinh Diem in November 1963 by the Americans and the equally ill-advised decisions taken at Hanoi's party plenum in 1963 set these two nations on the road to a long war that would kill millions. Ngo Dinh Diem's brutal campaign brought the North into the conflict earlier than it had planned in order to protect the southern resistance, and the United States, having removed Diem and having lost President Kennedy, felt that it had a commitment to defend the Republic of Vietnam. Although Ngo Dinh Diem was no longer present, his actions had put both the United States and Hanoi on the road to war.

Inefficient as the Diem administration had been, his successors were worse. There were seven military coups in the year following Diem's assassination. There was no stability in the countryside, as resistance to the policies of the GVN continued and made significant gains. These gains were not—could not be—challenged either militarily or politically by the GVN and the army. South Vietnam was on the verge of collapse. By February and March 1964, it became increasingly clear to the American leadership, as perhaps it had not been clear before, that the situation in Vietnam was deteriorating so badly that the kind of American effort invested thus far could not reverse the trend. It also became clear during this period that previous optimistic reports of progress in the war had been overstated and that, despite significant American aid, the South Vietnamese had not been able to achieve political stability. Concern in Washington grew over American inability to arrest the imminent collapse of the GVN.

As the realization became clear that an ally on whose behalf the United States had steadily increased its commitment was in a state of political and military collapse, President Johnson undertook a determined policy reassessment of the future American role in the war. On March 8, 1964, he dispatched Secretary of Defense Robert S. McNamara and Chairman of the Joint Chiefs of Staff General Maxwell D. Taylor once again to Vietnam for a firsthand assessment of the situation there. Their report was presented to the president on March 16, 1964, and it was approved the following day. The report, by U.S. civilian and uniformed military leaders, predictably focused on military issues. The program contained in this document, subsequently labeled National Security Action Memorandum (NSAM) 288, reasserted the American objective in Vietnam as an "independent non-Communist South Vietnam." NSAM 288 called for enlarging the U.S. commitment of military aid to South Vietnam considerably. Although the report indicated that the political situation in South Vietnam had "unquestionably worsened," the major emphases of the program were on strengthening the South Vietnamese armed forces by providing them with increased quantities of new equipment so that they could add 50,000 men and by providing American budgetary and political support to the inept GVN. NSAM 288 publicly affirmed Washington's support for the government of General Nguyen Khan, Diem's latest successor, and warned that the Johnson administration was opposed to "any further coups." It also called for a national mobilization plan in Vietnam, lifting overall troop levels and placing Saigon on a war footing.

The McNamara–Taylor report of March 1964, however, specifically rejected the following options: (1) accepting a neutralized South Vietnam by withholding additional support, (2) placing military pressure on North Vietnam, (3) furnishing American troops to secure Saigon, and (4) fully taking over the South Vietnamese military command. McNamara did, however, recommend that plans be developed to allow the initiation of graduated U.S. military pressure against North Vietnam should this prove necessary in the future.

Johnson at this time replaced General Paul D. Harkins, the overly optimistic and ineffective American field commander in Vietnam, with General William Westmoreland, a highly regarded veteran of World War II and Korea. In response to the McNamara–Taylor suggestions, the president also assured Ambassador Henry Cabot Lodge in Saigon that he would have "whatever you need to help the Vietnamese do the job." At a National Security Conference meeting on March 17, the president's closest advisers expressed support and confidence that the increased military and economic aid would change the course of the war in Vietnam.

But the McNamara–Taylor report had failed to address the major issue in South Vietnam: the weakness of and lack of political support for the government. So from the beginning, it seemed evident that this limited program would not be enough. Almost uninterrupted political upheaval in Saigon was reflected in progressive military demoralization in the countryside. Throughout the late spring and into July, as the U.S. program was put into effect, the Buddhist–Catholic quarrel intensified. The civil administration in South Vietnam continued in a state of disarray and ineffectiveness. Military forces were becoming more and more defensive and demoralized. Desertions increased and combat operations ground to a near standstill.

At the same time, it appeared that the North Vietnamese were visibly strengthening their support base in Laos and stepping up their infiltration of supplies into South Vietnam. Party strategists had concluded that NLF forces should use their stronghold in the central highlands to launch additional attacks against the South Vietnamese in the lowlands to "tighten the noose around the neck of the Saigon regime." CIA sources detected this change in communist strength and concluded that "the situation in South Vietnam is very serious and prospects remain uncertain." Lyman D. Kirkpatrick, a high-ranking CIA official, and Peer de Silva, the new CIA station chief in Saigon, worried that the tide had turned quickly against the unstable Saigon regime. "Even with U.S. assistance," they concluded, "unless there is a marked improvement in the effectiveness of the South Vietnamese government armed forces, South Vietnam has, at best, an even chance of withstanding the insurgency." Outside the urban population centers and areas of traditional local religious power, the country once again was slipping, to a great extent by default, to the NLF. The president continued to search for a policy that did not involve escalation or the use of American ground forces.

If the United States must go to war in Vietnam, Lyndon Johnson wanted a limited war with limited resources in a limited geographic area for limited diplomatic objectives. The objective, as stated, was itself unobjectionable but perhaps hard to accomplish: an independent, noncommunist South Vietnam. It was the president's caveat that was to frustrate some. "We will do everything necessary," the president said, "to achieve that objective, and we will do only what is absolutely necessary."[37] It was the "only" that would cause concern because it would later seem to some U.S. military leaders to indicate a less-than-all-out approach to winning the war militarily, an approach they rejected. To the president, however, this policy meant that the allocation of American manpower, resources, and material would not be allowed to reach the point where the war would unduly affect the American civilian economy or interfere with the burgeoning programs of the Great Society. American manpower devoted to the coming war would be limited. Operations must be restricted geographically so as not to spread the war to neighboring states or to incite a direct confrontation with the Soviet Union or China. The entire effort was seen to be flexible, with a controlled sequence of events in response to and justified by the level of enemy activity in South Vietnam. The U.S. object was not to "win" or even to "defeat" an enemy but rather to influence the course of the struggle in the South while having a minimum impact on the American domestic scene. Victory, then, was defined as "not losing" South Vietnam to communism.

The objective—the war termination objective—was to demonstrate American resolve to the North Vietnamese and convince them over time that they could not win, that the cost of continuing the war in the South was prohibitive to them, and that they could not succeed in their war to unify Vietnam—that a diplomatic settlement involving two Vietnams would be all that they could hope for. There was, however, no clear conception in the United States as to when or if this elusive psychological goal would be achieved in the mind of Ho Chi Minh.

This rather naive U.S. strategy saw the current conflict in South Vietnam in NSC-68 terms—simply as a communist aggression on the Cold War model, a challenge to a free nation by expansionist international communism. The questionable legitimacy and demonstrated inefficiency of the fledgling GVN and the history and nationalist credentials of North Vietnam were overlooked. The enemy was much too simply described, and the Saigon government had ascribed to it, by Washington, capabilities and qualities that it would never possess. The war was seen by the United States as a traditional aggression by one sovereign power against another rather than as a civil war to settle long-standing and historic political issues.

The Joint Chiefs of Staff—the president's principal military advisers—saw the White House's limited political objective as essentially negative and ineffective. The thing they feared most was a partial war and a partial commitment. If the United States were to go to war, the Joint Chiefs felt that a more ambitious objective was necessary, that of defeating the enemy both in North and South Vietnam. They advocated the classic doctrine that victory depended on the rapid application of overwhelming military power through offensive action to defeat the enemy's main forces. American military leaders had been forced to fight a "limited" war in Korea for limited objectives and had no intention of again engaging in that sort of frustrating experience.

Thus, in any air war against the North, the military chiefs advocated a forceful, massive, and concentrated bombing campaign designed to break the enemy's will and to destroy his industry. In the South, the military chiefs advocated a campaign of taking the war to the enemy wherever he might appear, attacking his main force elements in South Vietnam and his sanctuaries and support installations in Laos and Cambodia. A strategy of attrition would kill more of the enemy than could be replaced and force North Vietnam to discontinue the war. This American strategy, of course, would require a virtually open-ended U.S. military commitment to the war in Vietnam.

But with the limits imposed by political authority, this campaign plan would give the enemy the strategic initiative. The pace and level of fighting could be dictated by Hanoi and not by the United States. The Vietcong and regular North Vietnamese units would not be vulnerable to U.S. ground forces until they crossed the borders into South Vietnam. Likewise, enemy units in South Vietnam could escape pursuit by crossing over the borders into Cambodia or Laos or beyond the Demilitarized Zone. Thus, the enemy could enter that battle when he wished and could withdraw from the battlefield when he chose.

Success in this kind of war did not depend on the American field commander's ability to defeat the enemy in South Vietnam; it depended instead on how long the North Vietnamese were willing to feed the pipeline with men and material. If they were willing to pay the price, the enemy could keep large American forces tied up indefinitely. The war could become a protracted war of attrition. As it turned out, Hanoi was able and willing to pay a very high price. But a war of attrition was something the American public over time could not tolerate. As indicated, the decisive "victory" over North Vietnam sought by the military actually was not the national political objective. Neither the military strategy nor the operational plan supported the political objective. As it turned out, the level of U.S. effort was, in fact, to be determined largely by North Vietnam. Its willingness to match American deployments to South Vietnam would result in a gradual but inexorable military escalation by both sides. The North Vietnamese, of course, were prepared to continue the fighting as long as necessary. First, they sought to defeat the GVN of Ngo Dinh Diem and to force the establishment of a coalition government before the Americans could intervene. Failing this, they would see each American escalation as an admission of defeat for the previous policy. As the "special war," the war of Vietnamese against Vietnamese, with American advisers, failed, they saw an American air war and, later, American ground force deployment each as a change in strategy as the previous strategy failed.

And there was a vital missing element from the so-called American strategy, that of a viable independent noncommunist government of South Vietnam capable of providing services and security to its citizens. Clearly, the operational plan adopted by the Joint Chiefs—a massive bombing campaign against all targets in the North and the reinforcement trails (the Ho Chi Minh trail) in Laos, accompanied by ground incursions into Laos and Cambodia to deny the enemy sanctuary—was one for which their civilian superiors in Washington, for domestic and worldwide political reasons, would never provide the necessary operational leeway or, finally, the necessary level of forces that the military leaders required as essential to a favorable outcome.

A debate within the administration concerning the limited strategy advocated by the president and his civilian advisers and the more forceful strategy advocated by the military chiefs continued throughout Lyndon Johnson's presidency. General Westmoreland had adopted a strategy that could perhaps win only if the president would lift his political restrictions. The Joint Chiefs continued to echo their field commanders' requests for additional American troops for South Vietnam, increased bombing of North Vietnam, and expanded authority to attack on the ground and in the air in Laos and Cambodia. Further, they advocated calling up reserves forces to respond to military contingencies elsewhere. Military strategy states that if your strategy is bad, you may win every battle and still lose the war. The United States had no agreed-on strategy during its fight in Vietnam. The definition of "victory" was different for the president and for his military leaders. Thus, not only was the strategy bad, but it was virtually nonexistent as well.

President Johnson made every effort to ensure that the costs of the war would not become unacceptable to the American people. If the United States were to pursue the war according to the president's strategy—at a low level over an extended period of time—it was essential that the American public maintain the will to pursue that strategy. It has often been stated that Americans dislike long, indecisive wars and that our political system is incapable of fighting such wars. President Johnson realized this. He saw American public opinion as a major objective—the essential domino—in his ability to pursue his strategy in Vietnam while emphasizing the programs of the Great Society at home. Domestic politics, therefore, demanded that America intervene to stop communism in Southeast Asia. But domestic politics also demanded the minimum disruption of American life.

In his search for the elusive point at which the costs of the effort in Vietnam might become unacceptable to the American people, the president settled on mobilization—the point at which reservists would have their lives disrupted by being called up to support the war. This domestic constraint, with all its political and social implications, not any argument concerning long-range military strategy, appears to have had a major impact on the level of American effort in South Vietnam. The president's top priority continued to be the passage by Congress of the programs of the Great Society. He would not be a wartime president seeing an America with its resources mobilized to fight an extended ground war in Southeast Asia. Nor would he be a president who lost Southeast Asia to communism. As late as 1966, President Johnson declared to the Congress, "I believe we can continue the great society while we fight in Vietnam."

Chapter Five

America Enters the War

At 3:40 A.M. local time on Sunday, August 2, 1963, the U.S. destroyer *Maddox* was attacked by North Vietnamese patrol boats in the Gulf of Tonkin off the North Vietnamese coast. *Maddox*, joined by aircraft from the U.S. aircraft carrier *Ticonderoga*, damaged two of the attacking boats and disabled another. President Johnson chose not to retaliate, though he issued a protest and warning to the Hanoi government. Two days later, on the morning of Tuesday, August 4, *Maddox* again reported the presence of hostile boats and that an attack might be imminent. The question was whether an attack had actually occurred on *Maddox* and another U.S. destroyer, the *Turner Joy*.[1] Having decided that the second attack was "probable but not certain," President Johnson decided that this time the "probable" attack would not go unanswered. Just before midnight on August 4, the president announced on radio and television that a retaliatory strike was then under way on North Vietnamese port and oil facilities that were associated with the activities of the torpedo boats that had attacked U.S. ships.[2]

Hanoi Defense Minister Vo Nguyen Giap, in a conversation with Robert McNamara on November 9, 1995, as well as other Vietnamese sources, recently revealed that Washington erred in interpreting these actions. According to General Giap, the August 2 attack was ordered by a local commander and not by Hanoi, as Washington had assumed from analysis of intercept data from North Vietnamese communications.[3]

On Friday, August 7, Congress overwhelmingly approved the Southeast Asia Resolution, better known as the Tonkin Gulf Resolution. This resolution allowed the president to use armed force if necessary and was to act as a de facto go-ahead from Congress to allow the president to get the United States deeply involved in a war in Vietnam.[4] The swift reprisal and the nearly unanimous congressional support demonstrated in dramatic fashion the U.S. commitment to South Vietnam, a commitment that was undertaken with little domestic criticism or questioning. In addition to the congressional support, these air strikes were accomplished with virtually no domestic criticism, indeed, with an evident increase in public support for the administration. Johnson's popularity in the ratings increased dramatically in the wake of the reprisal attacks, from 42 to 72 percent.[5] The precedent for U.S. military action against North Vietnam had been established. These air raids represented the crossing of an important threshold in the war. They were intended as a clear communication to Hanoi of American firmness and resolve and of what it could expect if it continued to support its current course of action. Encouraged by this reprisal and dismayed by the continued political turmoil in the government of South Vietnam (GVN) and the apparent ineffectiveness of other U.S. programs, consensus grew within the administration that some form of continued additional military action against the North at an increasingly faster tempo would have to be conducted in order to have any lasting effect in arresting the deteriorating situation.

The president and the secretary of state, however, continued to feel that such moves were not worth the risk of Chinese or Soviet retaliation and that they could not be effective without a degree of government stability in the South. On August 6, South Vietnamese President General Khanh declared martial law and imposed severe restrictions on civil liberties in South Vietnam. He enacted such measures to try to save his government from the growing urban unrest, but, predictably, these moves sparked even more protest. During this period, American concern was focused on how the United States could retrieve the situation in South Vietnam. However, the usual palliatives—more aid, more advice, more pressure on the GVN to reform, and more verbal threats to Hanoi—were seen as having little or no effect. Continuing pressures for further U.S. action against the North culminated in a series of strategy meetings of administration officials in Washington on September 7, 1964. The president again rejected proposals by the air force and navy chiefs for an immediate bombing campaign against the North. He did approve, however, preparations for retaliatory action against North Vietnam on a tit-for-tat basis in the event of any further attacks on U.S. forces or installations. The consensus seemed to be that emphasis at this time should be placed on further strengthening the structure of the GVN. These demands for increased government stability in South Vietnam, however, were not matched by any American programs designed to enhance that stability. The American government apparently continued to look on government instability in South Vietnam as a military rather than as a political problem.[6] There was a growing conviction among close advisers to the president, both political and military, that sometime in the near future, hopefully after the political stability of the GVN improved, it would be necessary to subject North Vietnam to overt U.S. military pressure through aerial bombardment. Without such direct pressure, it was generally felt, it would not be possible to stop what was seen as North Vietnamese sponsorship of the insurgency or to reverse the deteriorating situation in the South. In short, the United States had exhausted its alternatives in South Vietnam, and government leaders saw no option other than to exert military pressure against the North. The GVN was not reforming, the Army of the Republic of (South) Vietnam (ARVN) was being hit hard and was ineffective, further U.S. aid and advice did not seem to help, and something was needed to keep the GVN afloat until the president was ready to decide on stronger actions at a later date. Bombing the North seemed to fill that bill, as this, it was felt, would demonstrate to North Vietnam American support for the government in the South. This anticipation of the eventual need to resort to the use of American force against North Vietnam was reinforced during the remainder of 1964 by the continued deterioration of the political structure in South Vietnam, by evidence of increased levels of North Vietnamese troop infiltration into South Vietnam, and by the actions of North Vietnamese and National Liberation Front (NLF) forces in the South.

On August 13, McGeorge Bundy, President Johnson's holdover national security adviser, writing on behalf of himself and the secretary of defense, sent the president a memorandum that was to drive discussion of Vietnam within the administration for the next several months. Although acknowledging that General Kanh's staying power was questionable, it also contended that trying to negotiate a solution under these circumstances would be equivalent to surrender in the South. Bundy also laid out plans of action:

> The larger question of action is whether a number of contingency plans for limited escalation are in preparation. They involve three kinds—there is any course of action that can improve the chances in this weakening situation of activities— naval harassment, air interdiction in the Laos panhandle, and possible U.S. fleet movements resuming a presence on the high seas in the Gulf of Tonkin. The objective of any of these would be more to heighten morale and to show our strength of purpose than to accomplish anything very specific in a military sense—unless and until we move toward a naval quarantine.[7]

But the Joint Chiefs of Staff were not interested in "heightening morale." They felt that the Johnson administration should indeed prepare for U.S. air strikes against the North and the Ho Chi Minh Trail in North Vietnam and Laos, which the North Vietnamese used to supply forces in the South. The objective would be to convince Hanoi that it could not win the fight and should desist in its attempts to take over South Vietnam. On August 28, the Joint

Chiefs submitted a proposal for "strong military actions" in both the North and the South. This proposal was an effort to identify those sites in North Vietnam that must be knocked out in order to crush its industrial capacity. Several members of the Joint Chiefs believed that U.S. airpower could knock out these essential targets in a matter of weeks, forcing Hanoi to quit the war. President Johnson rejected this thinking, however, concerned that such a massive air strike against a small nation was impractical and dangerous. He reasoned that the Soviets and the Chinese would not sit back idly while the United States launched such a massive campaign near Vietnam's northern border. He also doubted that Hanoi's war economy was as concentrated and industrialized as the Joint Chiefs seemed to suggest with their list.

In any event, the president called a meeting at the White House on September 9 to discuss the various proposals. In preparation for the meeting, William Bundy and Michael Forrestal drafted a working paper, "Courses of Action for South Vietnam," in which they summarized the emerging consensus of the president's top national security advisers. The paper called for the following military actions: (1) U.S. naval patrols in the Gulf of Tonkin, (2) covert operations in the South against the North, (3) limited South Vietnamese ground and air operations in the corridor areas of Laos, and (4) a tit-for-tat response against the North in the event of any attack on U.S. units or any special communist attack against the South—but no continuing attacks on the North.[8] These, of course, were all direct U.S. military options. There were no proposals or programs for strengthening the GVN or the ARVN. There was no suggestion of a coordinated U.S. strategy for South Vietnam.

President Johnson asked his advisers one by one to respond to the report. General Maxwell Taylor, now U.S. ambassador to South Vietnam, commented that the situation in Saigon was as grave as ever. He therefore supported most of the proposals, agreeing that there should be no major military operations against the North. Secretary McNamara agreed with General Taylor, adding that more could be done later if necessary. Secretary Rusk told the president that the decision to launch direct attacks against the North Vietnamese could be taken at any time but that now was not appropriate. The Joint Chiefs split on the issue of direct action. Generals Wheeler (chairman) and Johnson (army) were joined by Admiral David McDonald (navy) in support of delaying any direct attacks, whereas Generals McConnell (air force) and Greene (marines) believed that "time is against us and military action against the DRV should be taken now."[9]

As the president considered his options, events in Vietnam were forcing the administration's hand. On November 1, the NLF attacked the U.S. air base at Bien Hoa, killing four Americans and destroying several aircraft. This singling out of the major air base in South Vietnam as the target for a damaging attack was seen as the most spectacular and deliberate anti-American incident in the conflict to date. The Joint Chiefs, along with Ambassador Maxwell Taylor, felt that this attack warranted the immediate retaliation against North Vietnam that had been contemplated at the September conference, and they so recommended. But this attack was an unwelcome reality on the eve of the American presidential election, and the recommendations were rejected by the president.

Convinced now more than ever that the South was on the ropes and that the United States must soon respond to this open aggression against Americans, the president ordered his advisers to formulate a strategic plan for bombing the North. Johnson believed that "bombing was less risky than deploying ground forces" at that point of the war. Simultaneously, he instructed Ambassador Taylor in Saigon to do all he could to stabilize the GVN. The president correctly understood that American bombing raids against communist supply lines would prompt an immediate response from Hanoi, and he wanted to make certain that South Vietnam could withstand such an attack. President Johnson at the September policy review had asked whether any of his advisers doubted that "Vietnam was worth all this effort." All had agreed that the loss of South Vietnam would be followed, in time, by the loss of all of Southeast Asia.[10]

In the election campaign, Johnson was presenting himself as the candidate of reason and restraint as opposed to the warlike, unpredictable, and irresponsible Barry Goldwater. Throughout the campaign, Johnson had made plain his disinclination to lead the United States into a wider war on the Asian continent. Speaking in Manchester, New Hampshire, in late September, he had reiterated,

> I have not thought that we were ready for American boys to do the fighting for Asian boys. What I have been trying to do was to get the boys in Vietnam to do their own fighting—we are not going north and drop bombs at this stage of the game.[11]

The war in Vietnam would not be allowed to intrude on the campaign. Thus, the administration refrained from direct military action for the time being. Similarly, the bombing of the Brinks Hotel, an American billet in Saigon, on Christmas Eve evoked the same recommendation and the same response from the president. Even though the idea of increasing military pressure against North Vietnam had been generally agreed to in September, the president was still reluctant to order the war to be extended in this manner without some greater degree of political stability in South Vietnam. In addition, President Johnson, as was his custom, was not going to make this difficult decision until all available alternatives could be carefully and thoroughly re-examined.[12] Therefore, on November 2, subsequent to the Bien Hoa bombing but before the election, the president appointed a working group to conduct another thorough review of U.S. Vietnam policy and to present him with viable future courses of action and alternatives open to the United States in Southeast Asia.

The representatives of the Central Intelligence Agency in the working group deliberations pointed out that "the basic elements of Communist strength in South Vietnam remain indigenous." They also predicted that although the U.S. ability to halt DRV support of these insurgents depended on eroding Hanoi's will, it was quite likely that the DRV was willing to suffer significant damage "in the course of a test of wills with the United States over the course of events in South Vietnam." In any case, the intelligence analysts pointed out, "lasting success would depend upon a substantial improvement in the energy and effectiveness of RVN [Republic of South Vietnam] government."

The representative of the Joint Chiefs challenged this view as too "negative" (even though it was amazingly accurate and even prescient), and the working group's report to the senior advisers was rather noncommittal on this subject. The alternative of withdrawing American support from a Saigon government demonstrably incapable of pulling itself together and organizing a stable government in its own defense was briefly considered but was rejected quickly as being in conflict with the stated American objective listed in NSAM 288—that of an independent noncommunist South Vietnam. But there was no indication that that government could survive without massive American intervention.

Short of that extreme, however, two other alternatives were considered. One would have placed an immediate low ceiling on American personnel in South Vietnam while taking vigorous efforts to build on a stronger base in Southeast Asia, probably Thailand. The second alternative would have been to undertake a highly visible action to support South Vietnam, such as bombing raids against the North, to be accompanied by a public relations campaign about the inability to win the war given the ineptness of the Saigon government.

However, these strategic issues and options considered by the working group were not presented to the president. There was no fundamental reassessment of the American commitment to the fatally flawed government in South Vietnam. There were to be no "doves" in this group. The alternative of cutting American losses and abandoning a weak and virtually hopeless GVN, which was demonstrably incapable of organizing its own defense, was briefly considered and quickly rejected. Clearly, here was another "missed opportunity" to reassess the American commitment to a failing GVN incapable of winning the loyalty and support of its people or of mounting a successful military effort to provide them with adequate security. All the options presented to the president by this policy review consisted simply of greater military pressure against North Vietnam. After almost a full month of deliberation, the president's advisers failed to come up with any promising new strategic alternatives and, at a December 1 meeting with the president, could only repeat old military options, now divided into two phases. Phase I would merely comprise a continuation of current actions, tit-for-tat reprisals against North Vietnam for attacks on U.S. forces in the South, and increased efforts to reform and strengthen the South Vietnamese government. When this had been accomplished or was well under way, Phase II, a sustained and gradually increasing air campaign against North Vietnam, would be undertaken to dissuade it from further support of the war in the South.

These were not fundamentally new proposals, and no prospect was held out for speedy results. The president again emphasized the need to strengthen the Saigon government before beginning any military action against the North. He approved Phase I and gave assent, at least in principle, to Phase II. President Johnson, however, did not at this time make a commitment to expand the war either on the ground or in the air. Although the president's advisers had reached the consensus by the end of 1964 that increased military pressure against North Vietnam would be necessary, this consensus reflected neither a precisely defined strategy as to the subsequent course of American military action in Vietnam nor any commonly held expectation as to the result to be gained by military pressure. In any case, there seemed to be no dearth of reasons, once the U.S. commitment to South Vietnam was affirmed, for striking North Vietnam.

The decision to use military power against the North, in the end, seems to have resulted as much from a lack of alternative proposals as from any compelling logic advanced in its favor. Getting North Vietnam to remove its support and direction of the insurgency in the South was the basic objective, but there was no general agreement as to the likelihood of that result or of a strategy to attain it. And the president's reluctance to approve these actions was based on a rather unrealistic and rather weak hope that the GVN would be able to become more effective and thus preclude the need for additional American military action.

But the hoped-for improvement in South Vietnamese governmental stability failed to materialize. The continuing struggle for political power in Saigon clearly was impeding military operations, as large elements of the best units of the South Vietnamese army were maintained on constant "coup alert" in or near Saigon. A highly visible setback occurred during the period from

December 26, 1964, to January 2, 1965, when the NLF virtually destroyed two South Vietnamese battalions at Binh Gia. This was the first time that enemy forces had chosen to remain on the battlefield and meet government forces in sustained combat.[13]

From that low point, the remainder of 1965 saw major and historic decisions concerning the level of both North Vietnamese and U.S. efforts in South Vietnam that transformed the character of the war and the United States role in it. These decisions foreshadowed a dramatic increase in the U.S. commitment and led eventually to a virtual American takeover of the war. From 1965 on, U.S. involvement grew in slow stages, with each step preceded by an agonizing policy review by a reluctant president involving the highest levels of government. Throughout the course of this involvement, however, none of the policymakers involved in these reviews and decisions seemed capable of looking ahead to the long term, of developing an overall, coherent, long-range strategy for the achievement of specific U.S. objectives. And none showed an understanding of the historic North Vietnamese commitment to the unification of Vietnam.

THE AMERICAN COMMITMENT GROWS

As 1965 began, the Johnson administration continued to be beset by frustration and considerable anguish over the imminent collapse of the GVN. The debate in Washington continued to focus on developing the means for generating more intensive military pressure against North Vietnam. Discussion turned inevitably to the desirability and likely effectiveness of Phase II reprisal strikes on the North. But enthusiasm for these operations, although increasing, was far from boundless. The intelligence community continued to express little confidence that these military pressures would have much impact on reducing Hanoi's support for its southern allies to any significant degree. The proposed program of graduated military pressure against North Vietnam that emerged from this reassessment in late 1964 had three major objectives: (1) it would signal to North Vietnam the firmness of the U.S. commitment to its South Vietnamese ally; (2) in the South, it would boost the sagging morale of the GVN; and (3) the increased human and material costs and strains imposed on North Vietnam would ultimately affect its will as well as its ability to continue to support the NLF. Underlying the rationale of the program was the hope that it might restore some equilibrium to the balance of forces, hopefully increase U.S.–GVN bargaining leverage, and interfere with North Vietnam's ability to continue the war in the South.[14] This estimation by the U.S. military of the potential impact of a U.S. air war against the North, an estimation not shared by the intelligence community, would turn out to be wrong.

The long months of planning, hesitation, and agonized study and debate within the American government reached a sudden climax at 2:00 A.M. local time on February 7, 1965, when the NLF conducted well-coordinated and highly destructive raids on U.S. advisers' barracks and an American helicopter base near Pleiku in South Vietnam. Eight American soldiers died in the two attacks, and losses of equipment were characterized as severe. This was the heaviest and most destructive attack up to that time against American military installations in South Vietnam, and the attack had come at the very beginning of a visit to Hanoi by Soviet Premier Kosygin, a visit that the administration felt presaged increased Soviet aid to Hanoi. President Johnson's national security adviser, McGeorge Bundy, was also in South Vietnam at this time. Telephoning from General Westmoreland's command post in Saigon, he recommended to the president that, in addition to immediate retaliatory strikes against the North, the United States should initiate Phase II of the previously planned military measures against North Vietnam.

This time the president showed the same decisiveness he had displayed six months earlier during the Gulf of Tonkin incident. The decision to retaliate against North Vietnam was reached in a seventy-five-minute meeting in the Cabinet Room of the White House on the evening of February 6, with Senate Majority Leader Mike Mansfield and House Speaker John McCormick present. Summarizing their views, George Ball, the senior State Department representative present (Dean Rusk was traveling), told the president that everyone believed that action must be taken. In fact, retaliatory air strikes were conducted by U.S. naval aircraft against North Vietnamese barracks and staging areas at Dong Hoi, just north of the Demilitarized Zone (the seventeenth parallel), within fourteen hours of the president's directive.[15]

This dramatic action, long on the U.S. planners' drawing boards, precipitated a rapidly moving sequence of events that transformed the nature of the Vietnam War and the U.S. role in it. It also became the opening move in what soon developed into an entirely new phase of that war: the sustained U.S. bombing effort against North Vietnam. Thus, these attacks in reprisal for the NLF attack on Pleiku became the first U.S. move in the events of 1965 that, by December, would transform the war into a U.S. war against North Vietnam and its southern allies. As Ambassador Taylor expressed it, "The inhibitions which had restrained the use of our air power against the enemy homeland were broken, and a new phase of the war had begun."[15]

From the North Vietnamese point of view, retaliatory air raids had been anticipated for a long period of time, and preparations had been made. Many civilians had been evacuated from the major cities. The North Vietnamese leaders were somewhat surprised, they state, by the Pleiku attacks being the trigger for the beginning of raids against the North. Those attacks, the North Vietnamese have stated, were planned and directed by local regional commanders and in no way were related to the visits of either Kosygin or Bundy. They were merely in accord with the regional plan and were a "normal battlefield activity." The North Vietnamese cited the attacks on the Officer's Club at Tan Son Nhut on August 11, 1964, and the attack on the Brinks Hotel in Saigon on December 24, 1964, as being larger and more significant than the Pleiku attack and had caused more American casualties. But they indicated that at those times they felt that the United States was not ready to escalate. "By the time of Pleiku, you were."

The beginning of this air campaign also indicated to the North Vietnamese that the previous American strategy of building up the ARVN and GVN had been a failure. The North Vietnamese saw the beginning of the American air effort against the North as an admission of that strategic failure on the part of the United States. Bombing the North, they stated, was "a desperate attempt to somehow save the Saigon regime from collapse. That is the real reason for the bombing. You wanted to take the pressure off the Saigon government and the whole situation in the South, which was getting bad—very bad."[17]

The fact that the raids had come so swiftly after the Pleiku attack also indicated to the North that they had long been preplanned by the Americans, that the attack on Pleiku had been an "excuse not the main reason, the 'trigger' for the U.S. expansion of the war into the North." From the North Vietnamese point of view, "We can affirm that in the history of our resistance war against U.S. aggression, 7 February 1965 was the day which led to the direct involvement of North Vietnam in the people's war against the U.S." Prior to that, they claim, the war had been conducted largely by southerners, by the NLF and its People's Liberation Army against the Diem regime and its American advisers. No North Vietnamese organized units had been in the South, they claim, although there were North Vietnamese advisers and logistical personnel.

Events began to move more swiftly in Washington. On his return from Vietnam on February 8, McGeorge Bundy presented to the president the conclusions his group had reached concerning the situation in South Vietnam. The report stated, "The situation in Vietnam is deteriorating, and without new U.S. action, defeat appears inevitable—probably not in a matter of weeks or perhaps even months, but within the next year or so." (This conclusion, incidentally, had been also reached by North Vietnam.) Bundy saw no way of "unloading the burden on the Vietnamese" or "negotiating ourselves out of Vietnam." He therefore indicated that the development and execution of a policy of sustained reprisal against North Vietnam was the most promising course of action open to the United States. "That judgment," he added, "is shared by all who accompanied me from Washington and I think by all members of the Country Team."[18]

Although there was near unanimous support among the president's advisers by early 1965 that increased military pressure against North Vietnam was necessary, this consensus reflected neither a precisely defined strategy nor any commonly held expectations as to the results to be gained by such military measures. Indeed, those advisers differed significantly as to the intensity of the bombing effort that would be desirable or required and as to its likely effectiveness in influencing Hanoi's will and determination to continue its aggression in the South.

Generally, the military leaders consistently continued to argue that a most dramatic, forceful, and quick application of military force would be the only feasible means to exert significant pressure on North Vietnam. They firmly reiterated that such application would achieve satisfactory results and could and would affect the enemy's will. In general, they were also indifferent to Chinese or Soviet reaction to unlimited and forceful air strikes against all of North Vietnam. Most civilian officials, on the other hand, continued to see the program as a flexible one, with a more controlled sequence of actions, "progressively mounting in scope and intensity" in response to and justified by the level of Vietcong violence and terror in the South. The military pressure against the North could be decreased if Vietcong terror visibly decreased in the South. The objective would not be to "win" an air war against Hanoi or to break the will of North Vietnam but to influence the course of the struggle in the South. The prospect of greater pressure to come was at least as important as any damage actually inflicted. But these civilian officials for the most part also tended to have much less confidence that such pressures would have much impact on Hanoi's actions. They also felt that this limited campaign, if carefully controlled, would not provoke Chinese or Soviet reaction.

This difference of opinion as to how the air war should be conducted continued throughout the war and, indeed, afterward. In spite of these differences and the rather hesitant judgments that not much would be achieved by this bombing campaign, the graduated approach was adopted for the time being. The decision to use military power against the North in the end seems to have resulted as much from a lack of alternative proposals as from any compelling logic advanced in its favor or any expectation of its success. Detailed preparations were made to carry out bombing strikes against limited targets in North Vietnam.

Chapter Six

The Air War: The Futile Effort to Break Hanoi's Will

The air strikes subsequent to the Pleiku attacks were not characterized by the United States as a one-time reprisal for the immediate incident as they had been after the Gulf of Tonkin strikes of August 1964. These new strikes were characterized as a more generalized response to a long series of "continued acts of aggression" that had long been considered normal features of the war in the South. This change in terminology, from "reprisal" to "response to continued aggression," was clearly deliberate and reflected the president's conscious though unannounced decision to broaden the reprisal concept as his advisers were urging and to do so as gradually and as imperceptibly as possible. Thus, although the February air strikes set the stage for the sustained and continuing bombing program that was now to be launched, this change in policy was instituted with a minimum of drama so as to make it appear as almost a logical sequence of unavoidable steps in response to enemy provocations.[1] On February 13, 1965, President Johnson formally approved a program for American action in Vietnam that included "measured and limited" air action against selected military targets in North Vietnam. Details of these air actions, which were to be conducted jointly with the South Vietnamese, were deliberately left vague, indicating that the president still wished to preserve as much flexibility as possible concerning the scope and character of this activity. Although the first air strike under the new program, dubbed "Rolling Thunder," was scheduled for February 20, 1965, continued political turbulence in South Vietnam prevented obtaining clearance from the South Vietnamese government, and the strikes had to be continuously postponed. The first Rolling Thunder air strikes were executed against North Vietnam on March 2, 1965. The next strike occurred eleven days later, and the program became a series of limited, measured, and spaced air attacks against the North occurring about once a week. The pattern adopted was designed to preserve the president's options to proceed or not and to increase the tempo or not, depending on North Vietnam's reaction. The carrot of stopping the bombing was deemed as important as the stick of continuing it. All-out bombing, the president apparently continued to feel, would pose far greater risks of widening the war, would transmit signals to Hanoi and the rest of the world out of all proportion to the limited objectives and intentions of the United States in Southeast Asia, might carry unacceptable internal political penalties, might foreclose the possibility of achieving U.S. goals at a relatively low level of violence, might induce Chinese or Soviet reaction, and would not be more likely to get North Vietnam to decrease or call off its support of the insurgency in the South.[2]

Almost immediately after the initiation of the Rolling Thunder air strikes, however, efforts began within the administration to make the program more forceful, continuous, and effective. Secretary of Defense McNamara expressed his dissatisfaction with the military damage caused by the raids, and Ambassador Taylor voiced his annoyance over what he considered to be unnecessarily timid approaches to these air operations, the long delays between strikes, and their marginal effectiveness. He recommended that they be increased in intensity and in tempo. The Army Chief of Staff, General Harold K. Johnson, returning on March 14 from a presidential survey mission to see what more could be done in South Vietnam, also recommended increasing the scope and tempo of the air strikes and removing self-imposed restrictions that had limited their effectiveness. "To date," General Johnson reported, "the tempo of punitive air strikes has been inadequate to convey a clear sense of U.S. purpose to the DRV [Democratic Republic of North Vietnam]." The president accepted most of General Johnson's suggestions, and on March 15, 1965, the Rolling Thunder program against the North was transformed from a sporadic, halting effort into a regular, continuing, and militarily significant effort.[3]

In the initial Rolling Thunder attacks, target selection had been dominated by political and psychological considerations. With this gradual acceptance of a militarily more significant, sustained bombing program, serious attention began to be paid to the development of a target system or systems that would have a more tangible and coherent military rationale. The first and most obvious target system for Rolling Thunder was that of interdicting the flow of men and supplies from the North into South Vietnam by striking lines of supply and communications (LOCs). The objective, of course, would be to reduce the capability of North Vietnam to supply forces operating in the South—which U.S. leaders, both military and civilian, regarded as the most visible manifestation of Hanoi's aggression.

Predictions as to the effect of the interdiction of aid from North Vietnam varied widely. Admiral U. S. Grant Sharp, commander in chief of the Pacific Command (USCINCPAC), bore ultimate military responsibility for air action over North Vietnam. Admiral Sharp, a zealous proponent of airpower, predicted in a January 12, 1966, message to the Joint Chiefs of Staff that a properly executed bombing program "will bring the enemy to the conference table or cause the insurgency to wither from lack of support." A more moderate but still optimistic view was taken in a Special National Intelligence Estimate (SNIE) of July 23, 1965. The SNIE estimated that a bombing program that included destruction of the petroleum facilities and military targets in the Hanoi–Haiphong area, together with sustained interdiction of the lines of communication from China, could significantly reduce communist capabilities in the South. It reasoned that

> if additional PAVN [North Vietnamese Army] forces were employed in South Vietnam on a scale sufficient to counter increased U.S. troop strength [which the SNIE said was "almost certain" to happen] this would substantially increase the amount of supplies needed in the South. The Viet Cong also depend on supplies from the North to maintain their present level of large-scale operations. The accumulated strains of a prolonged curtailment of supplies received from North Vietnam would obviously have an impact on the Communist effort in the South. They would certainly inhibit and might even prevent an increase in large-scale Viet Cong military activity, though they would probably not force any significant reduction in Viet Cong terrorist tactics of harassment and sabotage.[4]

Following a meeting called by Secretary McNamara in Honolulu on April 20, the decision was made to "plateau the air strikes more or less at the prevailing level" rather than to pursue the relentless dynamic course ardently advocated by Ambassador Taylor and Admiral Sharp in February and March or the massive destruction of the North Vietnamese target complex consistently pressed by the Joint Chiefs. At the Honolulu conference, it was also decided that "interdiction" would now be the major objective of the bombing, and Secretary McNamara devoted a special Pentagon briefing for the press corps to that objective.

Nonetheless, the president and the secretary of defense continued to keep this air effort under strict and careful control. The attacks were carried out only by fighter-bombers utilizing low-altitude, precision-bombing tactics. Final target determinations were made in Washington, and population centers were scrupulously avoided. The secretary of defense set a ceiling on the number of missions, prescribed the areas within which they could be flown, and defined the types of targets to be hit. Areas near the Chinese border and in

Hanoi and Haiphong were off limits to attack. The use of B-52 bombers in the North was considered but not accepted.[5]

Bombing proposals from the Joint Chiefs were approved only in weekly target packages. Extended bombing programs, which would permit greater latitude in the field, were not approved. Each target package, moreover, had to pass through a chain of approvals in the Department of Defense, the Department of State, and the White House; this chain often included the president and the two secretaries. Clearly, a major unannounced consideration of the air strikes was that they would not be allowed to become so threatening as to call forth Soviet or Chinese reaction. The Rolling Thunder campaign always had goals that were explicitly political in nature. Thus, close control by the administration was entirely appropriate and clearly necessary.[6]

Within this framework of political control, the Rolling Thunder program was allowed to grow in intensity, in geographic coverage, and in assortment of targets. By mid-1965, the number of strikes had increased from one or two per week to ten or twelve per week and the number of sorties to about 900 per week, four or five times what they had been at the outset. During the closing days of February and throughout March, the administration undertook publicly and privately to defend its rationale for air strikes against North Vietnam. Official and public reaction to the strikes was fairly predictable. Much of the American press initially regarded the air strikes as necessary and justifiable, but many admitted either to confusion or to serious doubt as to just what U.S. policy in Vietnam was and where this policy was heading. The president spent much time with members of Congress, talking to many of them in his office, reiterating the continuity of his policy with that of his predecessors, and emphasizing the restraint and patience he was showing. But despite the full use of his powers of persuasion, the president could not stop a rising tide of criticism. Condemnation of the bombing spread to the campuses and to a widening circle of congressmen.

In addition, despite official hopes of some that the Rolling Thunder bombing campaign would rapidly convince Hanoi that it should agree to negotiate a settlement to the war in the South or that it should cease to support the insurgency in the South in exchange for a halt in the bombing, these hopes were not realized. After a month of continued and regular bombing with no response from the North Vietnamese, official optimism began to wane. Although enemy military activity in the South had been reduced, the North Vietnamese showed signs of adjusting to the limited bombing campaign and preparing for a long siege while they continued to support the National Liberation Front (NLF) in South Vietnam. A weeklong pause in the bombing from May 12 to 18 was initiated by the United States to determine if the North Vietnamese would respond to suggestions for negotiations. No response was received.[7]

The Joint Chiefs from the very beginning were opposed to this gradual and limited bombing campaign. They continually advocated a more decisive, more forceful, more continuous air campaign designed to force North Vietnam to its knees, making it incapable of or unwilling to continue to support the insurgency in the South. To accomplish this, the air chiefs on the Joint Staff in particular continued to advocate a forceful, massive, and concentrated strategic bombing campaign. They sought from the president and the secretary of defense a freedom to pick targets in North Vietnam, the elimination of restrictive zones around Hanoi and Haiphong and the Chinese border, and expanded authority to strike in Laos and Cambodia. This military criticism stemmed from a basic disagreement with an air campaign centered on tactical interdiction rather than a punitive rationale more in keeping with strategic uses of airpower, a campaign in which the apparent target was the infiltration system rather than the economy as a whole.

The bombing was criticized, therefore, for failing to focus on the kinds of targets that strategic bombing had been concentrated in World War II—power plants, oil depots, factories, and transportation and harbor systems. Many air planners felt that the doctrine for the use of strategic airpower developed after World War II, that it be directed at the nation itself and its war-making capability rather than against its deployed armed forces, was violated by these political restrictions. Many senior air planners believed, in effect, that U.S. airpower was being dissipated and was not being utilized in the way that best suited U.S. capability and strategy. Secretary McNamara was pressed hard on these points when he appeared before congressional committees in August 1965 with a major supplemental budget request for the war. In defending the policy of not attacking strategic targets concentrated in the Hanoi–Haiphong area, the secretary stressed the risks of widening the war through Chinese intervention as well as the irrelevance of those targets to the limited interdiction purposes of the bombing. The secretary's arguments had difficult sledding at this time, however. As 1965 ended, these bombing restrictions were still under attack. As U.S. ground forces began to be heavily involved in the war in the South, a limited bombing campaign against the enemy in the North did not make much sense to those who were determined to win that war. There was mounting pressure among the supporters of the Joint Staff to put more thunder and lightning into the air war.[8]

A bombing pause was initiated by the United States on December 24, 1965, and extended to January 31, 1966, in order to see if North Vietnam would respond with deescalatory measures of its own. It was taken for granted, of course, that bombing would be resumed. The only point at issue was under what guidance it would be resumed. The Joint Chiefs pressed continuously throughout the autumn and winter of 1965–1966 for permission to expand the attacks into a program of virtually unlimited strategic bombing aimed at all North Vietnamese industrial and economic resources in addition to all interdiction targets. They did so, it might be added, despite a steady stream of memoranda from the intelligence community consistently expressing skepticism that bombing at any conceivable level (i.e., any bombing except a campaign aimed primarily at the destruction of North Vietnam's population) could either persuade Hanoi to negotiate a settlement on U.S. terms or effectively limit Hanoi's ability to infiltrate men and supplies into the South. Writing to the secretary of defense on January 18, 1966, the Joint Chiefs repeated their November statement that numerous "self-imposed restraints" had limited the effectiveness of the bombing campaign and again proposed a substantial intensification of the bombing. They declared that future air operations should be conducted in such a manner and be of sufficient magnitude to: "deny the DRV large-scale external assistance; destroy those resources already in NVN [North Vietnam] which contribute most to the support of aggression; destroy or deny use of military facilities; and harass, disrupt, and impede the movement of men and materials into SVN [South Vietnam]." That most of these tasks were beyond the capability of airpower seems to have not been considered by these senior military leaders.

Similarly, diplomatic and political considerations seemed to play no part in the recommendations of the military chiefs.[9] None of the military leaders seemed concerned at the possibility that such a large-scale bombing campaign might engender Chinese intervention or an extension of the war. Admiral Sharp argued that the air campaign should be enlarged to "drastically reduce the flow of military supplies reaching the DRV and hence the VC [Vietcong]," adding that "the armed forces of the United States should not be required to fight this war with one arm tied behind their backs." These pressures to greatly enlarge the war through a massive strategic bombing campaign against the North continued to be resisted by the president and the secretary of defense. When the bombing was resumed on January 31, the sortie ceilings and the target restrictions were maintained. The administration remained primarily interested in keeping the objectives of the bombing limited and any escalation in check. The emphasis remained on bombing interdiction routes into South Vietnam rather than pressure or strategic objectives in North Vietnam.

Resumption of Rolling Thunder, however, did not constitute a final decision on escalation of the bombing. On March 1, the Joint Chiefs sent forward a memorandum stressing the special importance of an early attack on North Vietnamese petroleum, oil, and lubricant (POL) storage areas. They had earlier singled out POL, writing the secretary in November 1965 that an attack on this target "would be more damaging to the DRV capability to move war-supporting resources within country and along infiltration routes to SVN than an attack against any other target system." While causing very little damage to the civilian economy, it would, they stated, force a sharp reduction in truck and other traffic moving men and supplies southward. Although the Joint Chiefs appeared to be learning to place their requests for increased strategic air operations against North Vietnam in terms of interfering with infiltration to the South, they were not successful at that time. McNamara rejected this recommendation not only because of the planned bombing pause but also because the Central Intelligence Agency (CIA) questioned the conclusions reached by the Joint Chiefs. The Board of National Estimates observed that, in regard to the POL system, "it is unlikely that this loss would cripple communist military operations in the South." The military chiefs, however, continued to press for a favorable decision on this target system. In addition, they continued to press for authorization to mine the approaches to the harbor at Haiphong. During the Christmas bombing pause of December and January 1965–1966, they presented fresh memoranda in this regard to the secretary of defense and disputed assessments of the CIA that even with an air campaign extended to port facilities, power plants, and LOCs, "with a determined effort the DRV could still move substantially greater amounts [to the South] than in 1965."

The Joint Chiefs requested a 25 percent increase in B-52 sorties per month. Admiral Sharp stated a requirement for an additional ten fighter squadrons and an additional aircraft carrier both to support an intensification of the air war in the North and to support additional troop levels requested in the South. The strategic concept of the air mission in SEA that USCINCPAC had previously stated (and that had not been approved) was included here again as justification.

The Joint Chiefs endorsed the USCINCPAC air war recommendations in principle. They also stated that in their view the air war against North Vietnam had two objectives: "to make it as difficult and costly as possible" for NVN to support the war in the South and to motivate the DRV to "cease controlling and directing the insurgency in South Vietnam." Once again, failure to date to achieve those two objectives was attributed to the constraints imposed by political authorities. The Joint Chiefs again urged that these restrictions be lifted and the target base be widened in order to apply increasing pressure to the DRV.[10] These were, of course, the standard arguments that "political authority" had rejected in the past, and the president rejected them once more. "Political authority" intended to keep the war limited and not to run the risk of Chinese or Soviet intervention. The promises of the military chiefs for dramatic results in the South through bombing the North simply did not ring true and were not supported by intelligence analysis or by results on the ground. Immediately after the midterm elections in November, the president adopted

McNamara's recommendation for the stabilization of the air campaign, though he did not act on the secretary's suggestion of a dramatic gesture, such as a bombing halt in the North, to stimulate a move toward the negotiating table.

At the end of 1966, however, strikes were authorized in Hanoi against a vehicle depot and rail yards. These particular air raids raised charges of civilian casualties from news sources. The net result was another round of world opinion pressures on Washington. In this atmosphere, on December 23, attacks against all targets within ten nautical miles of Hanoi were prohibited without specific presidential authorization. Thus, 1966 drew to a close on a sour note for the president insofar as the air war was concerned. He had for most of the year rejected pressure from his military leaders for a major escalation of the war in the North and had adopted the restrained approach of his secretary of defense, an approach that suited his own objectives, only to have a few inadvertent raids within the Hanoi periphery mushroom into a significant loss of support in world opinion. He was in the uncomfortable position of being able to please neither his hawkish nor his dovish critics with his carefully modulated middle course. The public and the press were becoming increasingly wary of statistics and statements that came from Washington concerning American actions in Vietnam. In January 1967, a Harris opinion poll showed that the public was just as likely to blame the United States for truce violations as the enemy. A "credibility gap" began to build. The realization grew among the American public that the war was likely to be long and costly.

Thus, at the beginning of 1967, the lines were again drawn in the United States for an internal struggle over the effectiveness of the air campaign against North Vietnam. Secretary McNamara had become disillusioned with both the results and the human costs of the bombing and held few expectations for the ability of airpower, even massively applied, to produce anything but the same inconclusive results at far higher levels of overall hostility, with increased American losses, with significant risk of Chinese or Soviet direct intervention, and with the opprobrium of world public opinion. American military leaders, on the other hand, by and large remained indifferent to any of these considerations. In fact, they were becoming even more insistent in their rationalization for why the bombing had failed. It was the fault of the civilian-imposed restraints on targets. Only this, they held, had prevented the successful interdiction of North Vietnamese infiltration to the South. And only civilian restrictions—which they regarded as unnecessary—had prevented U.S. airpower from bringing the DRV to its knees and making it lose the will to support its aggression in the South. They continued to insist that the removal of these political restrictions would bring dramatic results. They foresaw an effectiveness to a strategic bombing campaign that had never previously been achieved and that all intelligence analyses indicated would not occur. Thus did the U.S. military leadership oppose civilian control of the bombing campaign against North Vietnam. They voiced their opposition to both the specific proposals of Secretary McNamara regarding the air war and his rationale for them. The Joint Chiefs still believed that if only (what they called) "political authority" would fully unleash it from civilian control, a U.S. victory in Vietnam was still possible through airpower.

The argument within the administration concerning the conduct of the air war over North Vietnam continued unabated and with few new arguments on either side throughout 1967. There were some gradual enhancements of the military's operating authority, but the limited overall U.S. objectives were reiterated by the administration and by civilian leadership of the Department of Defense. At no time, however, does it appear that the military leaders accepted the political reasons for limitations on bombing targets developed by their civilian superiors.[11] Instead, they simply continued to reiterate, over and over again and in the complete absence of supporting data, that they could "win the war"—if only they would be allowed to do so.

The policy differences within the administration were revealed in acrimonious detail in hearings on the air war in North Vietnam before Senator Stennis's Preparedness Investigating Subcommittee of the Senate Armed Services Committee in August 1967. Members of the subcommittee, known for their sympathies for the military, reflected the military's concern that restraints on bombing in the North were unnecessary, were contrary to military advice, and were prolonging the war. The civilian officials, primarily Secretary of Defense McNamara, who appeared to be imposing these restraints "against sound military advice," were undoubtedly the targets of the investigation. Senator Stennis explained the reasons for the inquiry: "The real question is whether we are doing what we can and should do in the opinion of our military experts to hit the enemy when and where and in a manner that will end the war soonest and thus save American lives."

The subcommittee heard first from the entire senior echelon of military leaders involved in the air war. They all maintained that the bombing had been much less effective than it might have been—and could still be—if civilian leaders had heeded military advice and lifted the overly restrictive controls. When Secretary McNamara appeared before the subcommittee on August 25, he took direct issue with these views. He defended the bombing campaign as having been carefully tailored to limited U.S. purposes in Southeast Asia. The secretary argued that those who criticized the limited nature of the bombing sought unrealistic objectives, those of breaking the will of the North Vietnamese and cutting off the infiltration of war supplies to the South. The air war, the secretary contended, was not a substitute for the arduous ground war being waged in the South. On August 31, 1967, only days after the hearings, the subcommittee issued its predictable report that accepted almost all the military's criticisms and advised the administration that "logic and prudence requires that the decision be with the unanimous weight of professional military judgment."[12] The Stennis committee report starkly exposed to the public the policy rift within the administration. In an attempt to dampen the public effects of this rift, the president, in a news conference on September 1, 1967, that was devoted largely to the issue of bombing, praised the advice he had been receiving from his military leaders. Subsequent bombing decisions, however, must have been even more stinging to McNamara than this seeming repudiation by the president. On September 10, 1967, for example, North Vietnam's third port at Cam Pha, a target McNamara had counseled against bombing and had specifically discussed in his testimony, was struck for the first time. The secretary of defense and the Joint Chiefs, it appeared, continued on a now public collision course, with the president apparently leaning toward his military advisers. Shortly thereafter, the president announced that he would appoint Robert McNamara to be president of the World Bank.

The Tet offensive of January 1968 provided a graphic demonstration of Rolling Thunder's failure to affect the war in the South. The air campaign apparently had done little to inhibit the enemy's capability or willingness to plan for and carry out this assault. The reaction to Tet by the new secretary of defense, Clark Clifford, led directly to the initiation in May 1968 of negotiations with the North concerning the total cessation of bombing of the North.

Did the Johnson administration's bombing campaign against North Vietnam contribute significantly to the achievement of American political objectives in South Vietnam? Would an extensive bombing campaign as advocated by the military have made a difference in North Vietnam's ability and willingness to support the war in the South? Would such a bombing campaign have engendered more direct interference by the Soviet Union or communist China and thus resulted in a major extension of the war? Were the military chiefs correct in their insistence that a massive air campaign against strategic targets in North Vietnam would produce greater results in the South? The evidence plainly seems to indicate that the promises of the advocates of strategic bombing against North Vietnam were, at the very least, vastly exaggerated. Initially and, indeed, throughout the Rolling Thunder campaign, the objective of the bombing of North Vietnam was a limited one. When the bombing began in early 1965, the public rationale was the reduction of the flow of supplies and men from North Vietnam to the South. The targets of the bombing were directly or indirectly related to that infiltration, and the purpose of attacking them was to reduce the flow and/or to increase the costs of that infiltration. Secretary McNamara specifically reiterated that objective in his testimony before the Stennis committee in August 1967:

Our primary objective was to reduce the flow and/or to raise the cost of the continued infiltration of men and supplies from North to South Vietnam. It was also anticipated that these air operations would raise the morale of the South Vietnamese people. . . . Finally, we hoped to make clear to the North Vietnamese leadership that so long as they continued their aggression against the South, they would have to pay a price in the North.[13]

Such a rationale specifically put the bombing in a politically acceptable military idiom of interdiction. This justification gave moral credence to U.S. intervention in the war in terms of North Vietnam's own aggression against South Vietnam. The objectives of the bombing campaign, then, were the infiltration routes into South Vietnam, and the measure of its effectiveness would be its impact on the ability of North Vietnam to supply and carry out the war in the South. The effectiveness of the air attacks against North Vietnam would be measured in the South. An additional major objective was to preclude an extension of the war through Chinese or Soviet direct intervention. In stressing the limited objectives in Vietnam, the secretary of defense stated that the air war against North Vietnam had always been considered a supplement to and not a substitute for an effective counterinsurgency land and air campaign in South Vietnam.

The physical reduction of North Vietnam's support for the war in the South by airpower theoretically could be accomplished by four methods: (1) the destruction of war-related industry and war-supporting facilities such as weapons production and petroleum storage facilities; (2) general debilitation of the North Vietnamese economy and thereby its ability to support the war effort and with the implied reduction of the willingness of its people to suffer further in support of that war effort; (3) attacking the lines of communication so that supplies would be slowed, stopped, or destroyed; and (4) destruction of the North Vietnamese military so that it could no longer support the effort in the South. During the course of the war, all four methods were tried, but none proved successful in accomplishing the goal of reduced support by North Vietnam for the war in the South. During the war, a number of comprehensive studies were conducted concerning the effectiveness of the bombing campaign in stopping North Vietnamese infiltration of men and supplies to the South. Two of the most important were carried out in 1966 and 1967, at the direction of the secretary of defense, by a group of leading scientists under the auspices of a division of the Institute for Defense Analyses. Both studies strongly criticized the effectiveness of bombing as a policy tool in the war effort. The 1967 study concluded that "as of October 1967, the U.S. bombing of North Vietnam has had no measurable effect on Hanoi's ability to mount and support military operations in the South."

The studies found that the bombing had not even achieved the limited goal of reducing the flow of supplies to the communists in South Vietnam. In an unqualified dismissal of claims of the airpower enthusiasts, they stated,

> Since the beginning of the Rolling Thunder air strikes on NVN, the flow of men and materiel from NVN to SVN has greatly increased, and present evidence provides no basis for concluding that the damage inflicted on North Vietnam by the bombing program has had any significant effect on this flow. In short, the flow of men and materiel from North Vietnam to the South appears to reflect Hanoi's intentions rather than capabilities even in the face of the bombing.[14]

The debate as to the effectiveness of bombing in interdicting the flow of supplies from the North was reflected in the 1969 National Security Study Memorandum 1 (NSSM 1). The U.S. military command in Saigon (MACV) and the Joint Chiefs held that the bombing had *succeeded*, whereas the Department of State, CIA, and the Office of the Secretary of Defense (OSD) agreed that it had *failed*. The debate over the attempt by MACV to block two key roads near the passes from North Vietnam into Laos in late 1968 illustrates the differences between the two views. MACV indicated that these roads had been blocked effectively 80 percent of the time and therefore caused less traffic to get through. The OSD, CIA, and State Department agreed that enemy traffic on the roads had been disrupted. However, they pointed out that the enemy used less than 15 percent of the available road capacity and was constantly expanding that capacity through new roads and bypasses and that our air strikes did not actually block but only delayed traffic.

Besides blocking the roads, of course, the bombing destroyed material in transit on them. The MACV and the Joint Chiefs interpreted this to mean that the material destroyed could not be replaced, leading to the conclusion that the air war had denied it to the North Vietnamese and NLF forces in South Vietnam. The OSD and the CIA, however, concluded that the enemy needs in South Vietnam were so minimal and his supply of war material so ample that he could replace losses easily, increase his traffic flows slightly, and thus ship and get through just as many men and supplies to South Vietnam as he wanted to in spite of the U.S. bombing.[15] On balance, it seems clear that even though the interdiction bombing in southern North Vietnam and Laos made the North Vietnamese logistical effort more difficult, more costly, and time consuming, it did not and could not prevent Hanoi from meeting the supply needs of the communist forces in the South.

The northern half of North Vietnam, however, would seem to offer more lucrative transportation targets, particularly railroads and harbors. In 1966, approximately two-thirds of North Vietnam's imports arrived by sea and the bulk of the remaining third by rail from China. Again, in the assessment of the air war in the far North, there was a complete disconnect between the MACV and the JCS on the one hand and the CIA and the OSD on the other. The MACV and Joint Chiefs expressed the belief that if all imports by sea were denied and land routes through Laos and Cambodia were attacked vigorously, the North Vietnamese would be unable to obtain enough war supplies to continue. The OSD and the CIA, however, concluded that the overland routes alone could provide North Vietnam enough material to carry on even in the face of a limited bombing campaign.[16]

Three major factors stand out in these and other assessments as the most significant inhibitors of a successful air interdiction campaign against North Vietnam. First, North Vietnam was an underdeveloped, mostly agricultural country. This made it far less susceptible to the effects of strategic bombing. Second, the vast majority of material support for its war effort originated not in North Vietnam but in Russia and China. North Vietnam served essentially as a conduit for supplies. In order to cut off the North Vietnamese war machine, it would have been necessary to "go to the source" in China and the Soviet Union—an act that would risk nuclear war with those two countries. Third, the North Vietnamese demonstrated great resourcefulness and determination, far beyond anything the Americans envisioned or expected, at the onset of the air war in February 1965. The Americans generally overestimated the effectiveness and the results of the strategic bombing of North Vietnam.

Over time, the rationale for the bombing became a mixture of complex and often conflicting objectives, especially for the nation's military commanders. As the infiltration continued and the war in the South increased in intensity, additional rationales for the bombing were put forth. The bombing of the North, it was stated, could have a telling impact on the war only if it received a free hand and was systematically employed against the enemy's economic assets. According to current air doctrine, the air campaign should be directed toward the enemy's war-making capability, which would in turn collapse the insurgency and cause Hanoi to sue for peace. The air commanders' conviction that their conventional bombing doctrine suited the nature of the war in Vietnam was deep. They felt that the leaders of North Vietnam attached great value to their nascent industrial capability and would do whatever was in their power to preserve it.

American air leaders were influenced greatly by their experience with strategic bombing in World War II. They had planned and developed their forces on the basis that any subsequent war would be directed against a highly developed industrial nation producing large quantities of military goods to sustain mass armies engaged in intensive warfare and with a well-developed and sophisticated transportation and fuel distribution system. They seemed to view Vietnam in much the same way. They aimed to wreck the enemy economy in order to produce a prostrate foe unable and unwilling to continue its aggression in the South. They seemed to seldom pause to consider whether their perception of the war was correct or whether it conformed to the purposes of their political leaders. They either dismissed or failed to consider the president's fears of Soviet or Chinese intervention. Their perception of Rolling Thunder's military objective was that it should be designed to destroy North Vietnam's capability and willingness to fight.[17]

It is worth noting just a few of the details concerning how and why North Vietnam was such a poor choice for a U.S. strategic bombing campaign. As indicated, North Vietnam was an agricultural country with a rudimentary transportation system and little industry of any kind. The nation provided an extremely poor target for air attack. A great majority of the people were rice farmers who worked the land with water buffaloes and hand tools and whose well-being at a subsistence level was almost entirely dependent on what they grew or made themselves. The so-called modern industrial sector of the economy was tiny even by Asian standards, producing only about 12 percent of a gross national product of $1.6 billion in 1965. There were only a handful of major industrial facilities.

When North Vietnam was first targeted, the Joint Chiefs found only eight industrial installations worth listing on a par with airfields, military supply dumps, barracks complexes, port facilities, bridges, and oil tanks. Even by the end of 1965, after the Joint Chiefs had lowered the standards and more than doubled the number of important targets, the list included only twenty-four industrial installations, eighteen of them power plants, which were as important for such humble uses as lighting streets and pumping water as for operating any real factories. North Vietnam's limited industry made little contribution to its military capabilities. Its armed forces placed little direct reliance on the domestic economy for war material other than manpower. North Vietnam in fact produced only limited quantities of simple military items, such as mortars, grenades, mines, small arms, and bullets. Moreover, such arms and munitions as were produced in North Vietnam were made in small workshops, which provided poor targets. Larger, more vulnerable arsenals that might have been lucrative targets from the air were nonexistent. The great bulk of its military equipment and all the heavier and more sophisticated items had to be imported. In short, North Vietnam's industry did not provide a rewarding target for strategic air attack. Meaningful targets were few, and those that existed were critical to neither the viability of the economy nor the prosecution of the war in the South.

Thus, North Vietnam's industrial capabilities did not match well with U.S. Air Force doctrine. The idea that destroying or threatening to destroy North Vietnam's industry would pressure Hanoi into calling it quits seems, in retrospect, a colossal misjudgment. The North improved its air defenses, laid aside its economic development plans, and made necessary adjustments. Imports were increased to offset production losses, bombed facilities were in most cases simply abandoned, and large, vulnerable targets, such as barracks and storage depots, were dispersed and concealed. The North Vietnamese appeared willing to accept the loss of the small industrial base rather than reduce their support for the war in the South.[18] It valued the unification of the country greater than it valued its primitive industrial capability. It is difficult to imagine a less likely country to buckle under an air assault such as the United States undertook against North Vietnam.

Another factor contributing to North Vietnam's ability to continue aiding the war in the South is the large amount of military and economic aid received from communist China and the Soviet Union. North Vietnam transmitted many of the material costs imposed by the bombing back to its allies. Since the bombing began, it has been estimated that North Vietnam's allies provided almost $600 million in economic aid and another $1 billion in military aid—more than four times what North Vietnam has lost in bombing damage. If economic criteria were the only consideration, North Vietnam would show a substantial net gain from the bombing, primarily in military equipment. Because of this aid and the effectiveness of its countermeasures, North Vietnam's economy continued to function.[19] North Vietnam's adjustments to the physical damage, disruption, and other difficulties brought on by the bombing were sufficiently effective to maintain living standards, meet transportation requirements, and improve its military capabilities. A study by the Systems Analysis Office of the Department of Defense concluded, "Over the entire period of the bombing, the value of economic resources gained through foreign aid has been greater than that lost because of the bombing."

The study concluded that North Vietnamese standards of living might have declined but that food supplies had been maintained with only a slight decline. Overall, "the North Vietnamese are not badly off by past North Vietnamese standards or the standards of other Asian countries."

The 1969 NSSM 1 concluded, "It is generally agreed that the bombing did not significantly raise the cost of the war to NVN. This was because production facilities outside of VN were not targetable." The key consideration as far as bombing policy was concerned, then, was the fact that North Vietnam served as a funnel for the transit of military aid from other communist countries to North Vietnam and then to its forces in the South. Since the rail routes along the Chinese border were off limits to air attack because of the necessity to avoid direct confrontation with China, attention should have focused on North Vietnam's capability to transport men and supplies to the South rather than on its ability to support the war economically.[20]

The North Vietnamese transportation system was primitive and appeared to be highly vulnerable to air attack. But it proved to be highly flexible, and its capacity greatly exceeded the comparatively small demands placed on it. Because the North Vietnamese transportation system was based to a large degree on crude roads, trails, and waterways rather than on highways and railroads, it provided relatively few lucrative targets for effective air bombardment. This was particularly true of the southern half of North Vietnam and the trails through Laos. A March 1966 report by the CIA argued,

The rudimentary nature of the logistic targets in the southern part of North Vietnam, the small volume of traffic moving over them in relation to route capacities, the relative ease and speed with which they are repaired, the extremely high frequency with which they would have to be struck again—once every three days—all combined to make the logistic network in this region a relatively unattractive target system, except as a supplement to a larger program. A significant lesson from the Rolling Thunder program to date is that the goals of sustained interdictions of the rudimentary road and trail networks in southern North Vietnam and Laos will be extremely difficult and probably impossible to obtain in 1966, given the conventional ordnance and strike capabilities likely to exist.[21]

As a North Vietnamese colonel recently explained,

It [the bombing] did have an effect. It forces us to think of a new way for the Southern revolution to be stronger so as to defeat the Americans. And the North had to increase its efforts as well to defeat the US air strikes. Then the US would lose in the North and the South—on both fronts. . . . Quite frankly, having to fight on two fronts did create a lot of problems for us, but it also gave us more opportunities because we were given the chance to fight the US on two fronts.[22]

An important factor reducing the effectiveness of the bombing of the North was the resourcefulness and determination of the North Vietnamese. During the massive bombing of their petroleum facilities, for example, distribution was quickly switched from bulk to barrels and decentralized without a major reduction in capabilities. The North had also adapted well to the continuing attacks on the transportation system. North Vietnamese General Van Tien Dong proclaimed that "the central task of all parties and people" was to ensure the southward movement of men and supplies. To accomplish that goal, Hanoi mobilized its manpower to ensure that movement. An estimated total of 500,000 laborers repaired roads and bridges. They built miles of bypass roads and fords to make the bombed highway system redundant.

The bombing and the strain of supporting the war in the South caused considerable dislocation in the labor force of North Vietnam. By 1968, as many as 475,000 to 600,000 civilians, including women and children, were working to repair the damage done by the air strikes, while another 110,000 military personnel were assigned to air defense duties. It appears, however, that the North was always able to meet its manpower needs. A study by the Systems Analysis Office of the Department of Defense reported that 90 percent of the North's manpower needs were met by normal population growth. The same study found that the bombing also increased the supply of labor. Forty-eight thousand women were made available for work on roads and bridges in the countryside by their evacuation from the cities. Similarly, North Vietnam as an underdeveloped country had many underemployed who could be used to repair war damage without reducing production. The vast amount of available manpower guaranteed that this diversion would not affect rice production. It appeared that the North Vietnamese government was not likely to be hampered by aggregate manpower shortages. They continued to have adequate manpower to continue the war even at the high casualty rates they sustained in 1968.[23]

On the Ho Chi Minh Trail, travel times were often restricted to night or bad weather. Shuttling and transshipment practices were instituted. Construction material, equipment, and workers were pre-positioned along key routes in order to effect quick repairs. Imports of trucks were increased to offset equipment losses. Hanoi exploited the jungle camouflage and used the sanctuaries of eastern Laos and Cambodia to establish the Ho Chi Minh Trail to the South. Because of such countermeasures, the North Vietnamese transportation system became increasingly less vulnerable to aerial interdiction aimed at reducing the flow of men and material from the North to the South.

Did the Hanoi leadership at any point fear that it was in danger of having its main supply route to the South cut off? The North Vietnamese indicated that they saw the possibility of such a cutoff as a very serious development. That is why they constructed the strategic Truong Son Road, known to Americans as the Ho Chi Minh Trail, and developed elaborate precautions to keep it open. They stated,

> We not only had trails on land, we also had a "sea trail." In addition to the east Truong Son Road, there was a west Truong Son Road, with numerous crisscross pathways, like a labyrinth. So it would have been hard to cut it off completely. . . . We could not, and in fact did not, allow the Trail to be cut off.[24]

Coupled with the adaptability of the North Vietnamese was a tendency by the United States to overestimate the persuasive and disruptive effects of the U.S. air strikes and, correspondingly, to underestimate the tenacity and recuperative capabilities of the North Vietnamese. Because of foreign aid and the effectiveness of its countermeasures, North Vietnam's economy continued to function under American bombing. North Vietnam's adjustments to the physical damage, disruption, and other difficulties brought on by the bombing were sufficiently effective to maintain living standards, meet transportation requirements, and improve its military capabilities. Interdiction and curtailment of North Vietnamese aid to the insurgency in the South remained the primary objective of the U.S. bombing effort. Over time, however, the rationale became complex and often conflicting and ill considered. The air commanders, increasingly frustrated both with the political restrictions on bombing targets as well as with the ineffectiveness of the bombing in influencing Hanoi's willingness and ability to support the war in the South, soon adduced other objectives for the massive, ever-increasing bombing campaign. Although seldom stated explicitly in either memoranda or official statements, an implicit goal of the bombing became the punishment of the North for its support of the war in the South. Secretary of Defense McNamara gave a relatively explicit statement of the goal in 1967 at the Stennis hearings. In the list of what he considered to be the three objectives of the bombing campaign against North Vietnam, the third objective was stated as follows: "To make clear to the North Vietnamese political leadership that so long as they continued their aggression against the South, they would have to pay a price in the North."

The goal is often stated in terms of increasing the cost of the war for the North. The bombing clearly caused some damage and disruption to the domestic economy of North Vietnam. Many thousands of civilians were evacuated from the cities or diverted to repairing damage done by the air strikes. The civilian population suffered many hardships. While the total supply of goods in North Vietnam increased, individual standards of living declined. Food was rationed, consumer goods were scarce, and air raid warnings disrupted the lives of the populace and forced many to leave their homes.[25] While there is a natural desire to impose hardship on an enemy, such a goal was unsupportable on either moral or policy grounds. By the same token, the high cost of the bombing to the United States in terms of lives and material made such a policy clearly undesirable and unsupportable. Simply raising the cost of the war to the North served no policy end unless it had a payoff in terms of impeding the ability of the North to support the war in the South or increased the likelihood of the North's deciding to end its support for that war. Hence, retribution was again linked to interdiction or putting pressure on Hanoi's will.

One of the most often made justifications for the bombing of the North was the belief of some proponents of airpower that in some degree the bombing would put pressure on the Hanoi leadership to terminate the war. This was an original purpose of the sustained bombing of the North, although the public rationale was put in terms of North Vietnam's capability to continue to support the war in the South. With the relative failure of bombing to achieve the goal of interdicting the flow of supplies south, the goal of breaking Hanoi's will became more prominent. Although the reasoning is seldom explicit, the argument that the bombing would affect the will of Hanoi's leadership is generally based on three suppositions. First, the bombing would so reduce North Vietnam's capability to successfully prosecute the war that Hanoi would either sue for peace or substantially reduce the level of warfare. Second, the leadership would decide that the level of destruction visited on the North Vietnamese economy was greater than the gain from supporting the revolution in the South. Or, third, the morale of the North Vietnamese population would so deteriorate that the leadership would be forced to seek relief from the bombing through negotiations or reduced support for the forces in the South.

In practice, none of these suppositions was borne out. The bombing did indeed make support of the war in the South more difficult and costly but did not reduce North Vietnam's ability or will to prosecute it. The damage to the North Vietnamese economy was substantial, but aid from Russia and China more than offset the damage inflicted by bombing. Hanoi's political relations with its allies were in some respects strengthened by the bombing. The attacks had the effect of encouraging greater material and political support from the Soviet Union than might otherwise have been the case. While the Soviet aid complicated Hanoi's relationship with Peking, it reduced North Vietnam's dependence on China and thereby gave Hanoi more room for maneuver on its own behalf.[26]

There were some indications in late 1967 and in 1968 that morale was wavering but not to a degree that influenced the regime's policies on the war. Neither did the hardships reduce to a critical level North Vietnam's willingness or resolve to continue the conflict. The will of the North Vietnamese leadership and people was not broken, and, as far as we know, it never came close to breaking at any point during the air war. In fact, as we now know, the Hanoi government, in effect, turned this rationale for the air war—that it would break the will of North Vietnam to fight—on its head. The Hanoi government was remarkably successful in using actual and threatened U.S. bombings to mobilize people behind the communist war effort. There is substantial evidence, for instance, that the people of North Vietnam found the hardships brought on by the war more tolerable when they faced daily dangers from the bombing. The air campaign actually seemed to have hardened the attitude of the people and rallied them behind the government's war effort.

The persistence of the view that Hanoi's will could be broken by bombing seems inconsistent with what should have been known of the North Vietnamese leadership and history. Hanoi's top leadership was composed of longtime revolutionaries who were intimately involved with Vietnam's struggle for independence from the French. Their struggle, lasting more than thirty years, should have indicated a tenacity that would not easily be broken. Moreover, as both communists and nationalists, they believed that they had a mission to liberate what they considered to be the southern half of their country. Their statements during the long period of negotiations leave little doubt that they thought that time had come.

In answer to the question as to whether massive, quick strikes would have been more effective in breaking the will of the Hanoi government, the North Vietnamese responded as follows:

> Leadership requires consideration of even the worst possibility. But in our view, if you bombed the North, irrespective of the way you did it, this meant you were losing in the South. By bombing the North, in fact, you unwittingly helped us arouse hatred against yourself, the invaders, among our people, just as you helped us gain friends overseas and eventually, to bringing the American people to their senses. Thus, it did not matter to us whether your strikes were launched like "instant thunder" or Rolling Thunder, as you called it.[27]

The tendency to equate destruction of physical assets with breaking the will of the people, a precept of U.S. Air Force strategic doctrine, reflected a general failure to appreciate the fact, well documented in the historical and social scientific literature, that a direct, frontal attack on a society tends to strengthen the social fabric of the nation, to increase popular support of the existing government, to improve the determination of both the leadership and the populace to fight back, to induce a variety of protective measures that reduce the society's vulnerability to future attack, and to develop an increased capacity for quick repair and restoration of essential functions. The great variety of physical and social countermeasures that North Vietnam took in response to the bombing is now well documented, but the potential effectiveness of these countermeasures was not stressed in planning for the air war against the North. Indeed, the North Vietnamese have stated that when the United States began bombing the North, it united the people from top to bottom more than they had ever been united in supporting Ho Chi Minh's appeal.

Rolling Thunder's failure to achieve decisive results did not stem directly from the well-publicized political controls placed by "political authority" on its implementation, although these were the most obvious operational restrictions. Of equal importance was the failure of civilian and military leaders to appreciate the type of warfare being waged by the North. The absence of limited war experience and doctrine, combined with smug self-assurance concerning the capabilities of airpower, led to a misguided faith in Rolling Thunder and obscured the true nature of the Vietnam War. The restrictions on the air campaign in the North were based on the specific political objective of avoiding direct Chinese and Russian intervention in the war. This objective led to restrictions on targets such as Hanoi and Haiphong and on geographic locations, such as targets near the Chinese border. But, of course, it is difficult to assess the success of achieving a negative objective. The Chinese and the Russians did not intervene directly, but it cannot be conclusively stated that this was because of the restrictions on air raids near the Chinese border. On one occasion, two American jets strayed over the Chinese border and were shot down by Chinese fighters. Conversely, it cannot be stated clearly that if the restrictions had been lifted, the Chinese would or would not have responded. But the president, unlike his military commanders, was unwilling to take that risk. In addition, it cannot be clearly stated that the bombing encouraged Soviet and Chinese assistance to North Vietnam. Both of these powers felt that they were competing for Hanoi's favor, and both continued to supply military arms. The Chinese helped develop a somewhat sophisticated air defense system and furnished advisers to train North Vietnamese in its use.

Although less obvious than these political restraints, military controls limited Rolling Thunder's effectiveness. As already mentioned, air force bombing doctrine, based on World War II experience, equated economic viability with industrial prowess, assuming that the destruction of production centers and transportation systems guaranteed the loss of the war-fighting capacity of a modern industrial society. Thus, in addition to interdiction, the bombing campaign was also designed to wreck North Vietnam's industrial capacity. The contention was that the overall lack of technical sophistication increased the value of this miniscule industrial base to North Vietnam and that its destruction would significantly affect commercial and industrial activity in the DRV and place in serious jeopardy the viability of the North Vietnamese economy. This view persisted until the Tet offensive of 1968. The military chiefs continued to argue for attacks on oil storage facilities, cement and steel factories, and electric power plants and attacks on transportation systems. This inflexible approach to the North Vietnamese economy was almost certainly wrong. The miniscule industrial sector of the North Vietnamese economy did not significantly impinge on the capability of this largely agricultural country to pursue its strategic aims.

Another limiting factor was the desire by both civilian and military leaders to avoid civilian casualties. The Joint Chiefs did not advocate direct attacks on the civilian population. The desire to destroy North Vietnam's industrial capacity was coupled with the goal of causing minimal casualties to the civilian population. This also prevented the military chiefs from suggesting raids on targets like dams and dikes that might have had a more telling effect on the people's will and the North's capability to fight.

The military's organizational arrangements for Rolling Thunder also limited the air campaign. The multiple chain of command and the absence of a single overall air commander often led to confusion. These factors prevented military chiefs from integrating Rolling Thunder with other air efforts in Southeast Asia.[28] Air operations in North Vietnam were controlled by the overall combined commander, USCINCPAC, based in Hawaii. Air operations in South Vietnam were controlled by the air commander and the marine commander under General Westmoreland. When B-52 bombers were used, the Strategic Air Command retained control, based in Omaha, Nebraska, and flying out of Guam. The mismatch between North Vietnam and U.S. air objectives aside, one must still marvel at North Vietnam's power of recovery and overall resourcefulness. Its adjustments to the physical damage, disruption, and other difficulties brought on by the bombing were sufficient, as indicated, to allow the nation to maintain minimum living standards, to meet transportation requirements, and even to improve its military capabilities. Given that one of the purposes of the sustained bombing of the North was to break the will of the Hanoi leadership to prosecute the war in the South, it must be said that on this basis alone, the air war was a disappointing failure.

This controversy over the type of air war to be fought in North Vietnam eventually strained the relationship between the secretary of defense and the Joint Chiefs. By the fall of 1966, the Chairman of the Joint Chiefs knew that McNamara had lost faith in Rolling Thunder. Although bombing hindered the movement of men and supplies, it did not and could not significantly interfere with the quantity of supplies that reached the South. The supply routes were redundant, and the supply needs were minimal. As the Joint Chiefs remarked in August 1965, the amount of goods that North Vietnam shipped south "is primarily a function of their choosing." That appraisal remained valid throughout the Rolling Thunder campaign. Similarly, most North Vietnamese civilians did not suffer inordinately from the bombing. Evacuations contributed to keeping the number of civilian casualties small. For the typical North Vietnamese, the bombing was a nuisance rather than a danger.

In the words of one informed analyst, Rolling Thunder made a meager contribution toward achieving this nation's announced political goal of an independent noncommunist South Vietnam. Despite the bombing, the North was not persuaded, nor did it abandon the southern insurgency. Besides overestimating the importance of northern industry, American leaders underestimated their enemy's determination. To be effective, bombing the North had to eliminate or reduce the prospect of a communist victory in the South. It could not do so. As long as the communists used efficiently the supplies that they received from their allies, they had little to fear from Rolling Thunder.[29]

The bombing campaign against North Vietnam had other negative effects. Rolling Thunder often created an unfavorable impression of the United States and the war in Vietnam among American friends, allies, and others abroad. Instead of viewing the air campaign as a necessary effort to support an ally, South Vietnam, many of these countries saw the bombing of a small country by the world's greatest military power as the bullying of that small country. Some nations—some American allies—publicly denounced the bombing.[30]

The North Vietnamese stated that they perceived the bombing of the North "as a direct result of the failure of your previous strategy" and labeled the air campaign "the product of defeat on the southern battlefield." They insist that this campaign would never affect North Vietnam's initiatives in the South. Propaganda aside, this statement, which is still the conclusion of the North Vietnamese, contained a large measure of truth. The air war troubled the North Vietnamese, but from the very beginning of the conflict, Hanoi had prepared its citizens for heavy pressure. Party officials first warned of an American invasion and then a war of destruction against the North. But when citizens saw that they could withstand the punishment from the air, their morale actually improved. The party had long anticipated heavy damage to the major cities in the North. In Hanoi, streets were lined with individual bomb shelters. The now-well-known one-person sanctuaries were constructed of concrete cylinders, just large enough for an adult. According to some estimates, North Vietnam constructed more than 21 million air raid shelters.[31] Every able-bodied person was involved in the civil defense war, building shelters under the slogan "The Shelter Is Your Second Home." According to historian William Duiker, the city of Hanoi contained an average of one shelter every six to thirty feet.[32] The ruling North Vietnamese Politburo often met in the bomb shelter next to Ho Chi Minh's private home. Air raid drills were an everyday occurrence.

The party also supervised the dispersion of nonessential personnel. The city of Hanoi had a population of roughly 1 million people in 1965. After the bombing began, the population was reduced to approximately 200,000. One former member of Hanoi's Foreign Ministry remembers the evacuations:

> During the Gulf of Tonkin incident, you bombed us. Sometimes you forget about that one. I am talking about August 4 and 5, 1964 and the bombing right after. So after August 5, the children of Hanoi were ordered to go to the countryside for dispersal. My young son was among these children who were quickly moved to the countryside, because we knew that the bombing—the real bombing in earnest—could begin at any time. Our Foreign Ministry, and many other ministries, organized boarding houses in the countryside for children and spouses.

So this means that in 1963 we realized—I would say for the first time—that the bombing is coming, at some point. In August 1964, we went on alert, so to speak, and evacuated spouses and children from Hanoi, in anticipation of the bombing. And the bombing began the following February.[33]

During Harrison Salisbury's late 1966–1967 visit to Hanoi, he reported on one school set up outside the city in which students moved from class to class in trenches. Each student had a foxhole under his or her desk and was provided with a helmet in case of attack.[34] According to some government reports, more than 4 million children continued their schooling uninterrupted.[35] Most fixed industries were completely destroyed by the bombings, but their essential ingredients had also been dispersed. Oil as already indicated was stored in fifty-five-gallon tanks along minor roadways throughout the country. Small factories were entirely relocated to the countryside as well. Railroads and bridges were camouflaged, and there were permanent curfews and blackouts in the major cities.

The passive defense of the cities cut down immensely on civilian casualties. The active defense of Vietnam's skies gave the people an outlet for their rage. Beginning shortly after the Gulf of Tonkin incident, the North Vietnamese constructed a complex antiaircraft system. Using sophisticated weaponry from the Soviet Union and China, Hanoi created a practical combination of radar, defense missiles, antiaircraft guns, and surface-to-air missiles. The radar system consisted of long-range search radar and shorter-range tracking radar supported by a refined network of ground observers who reported to North Vietnamese Army control centers. When American aircraft approached within thirty kilometers, air raid sirens went off, and civil defense instructions followed on the radio.

The people were also involved in air defense. As Colonel Quach Hai Luong, a former North Vietnamese air defense commander, recently explained,

One of the enduring images of that time was of a farmer working in his rice field with his rifle slung on his back. And the industrial workers toiled in the factories with guns on their backs. Many of the artillerymen were often both farmers and factory workers. Every time the US air strikes came, the workers would leave their factories and operate the artillery, and the farmers would also leave their rice fields and in groups of three and five, would man the anti-aircraft missiles. Many people in the world cannot understand why the US planes were shot down by rifles because every village would fire at these planes.[36]

Life under the bombs required enormous sacrifice, but at no time did the ordeal come close to breaking the will of the people or leaders of the DRV. Hardships were reduced by preparation and increased aid from other socialist countries. The Hanoi government transferred many of the material costs imposed by the bombing back to its allies, which accepted them as their part in what was officially recognized as a fraternal struggle. From 1965 through the end of the war, it is estimated that socialist countries provided North Vietnam in economic aid and military support more than four times what was lost in bombing damage. If economic criteria were the only considerations, therefore, North Vietnam would have shown a substantial net gain from the bombing, primarily in military equipment. Because of this aid and the effectiveness of its own countermeasures, North Vietnam's economy continued to function. Immediate mobilization of the largely underemployed population to repair damage done by American bombing missions also reduced the hardship. By 1968, nearly 600,000 civilians were working in cleanup and rehabilitation efforts. An estimated 500,000 laborers repaired roads and railroads. In his June 30, 1968, report on the war in Vietnam, the CINCPAC, Admiral Sharp, acknowledged this fact, although he tried to put it in a good light. His report stated,

During 1967, attacks against the North Vietnamese transport system resulted in destruction of logistics carriers and their cargo as well as personnel casualties. Air attacks throughout North Vietnam destroyed or damaged over 5,200 motor vehicles, 2,500 pieces of railroad rolling stock, and 11,500 watercraft. . . . Through assistance from other Communist countries the enemy was able to replace or rehabilitate many of the items damaged or destroyed, and logistic carrier inventories thus were roughly at the same level as they were at the beginning of the year. Nevertheless, construction problems and delays caused interruptions in the flow of men and supplies, caused a great loss of workhours, and restricted movement, particularly during daylight hours. A major effect of our efforts to impede movement of the enemy was to force Hanoi to divert the efforts of 500,000 to 600,000 civilians to full-time and part-time war related activities, in particular for air defense and repair of the LOC's.[37]

It appears, in short, that North Vietnam never faced a transport or manpower shortage, even under the heaviest pressure of U.S. bombing. A study by the Systems Analysis Office of the Department of Defense reported, for example, that 90 percent of the North's manpower needs were met by normal population growth. The same study found, moreover, that bombing actually increased the supply of available labor for these purposes.[38] With such admittedly meager results, it is clear that the air war against the North contributed very little toward winning the war in the South. During the three years of Rolling Thunder, the North Vietnamese shot down more than 900 American aircraft, increasing the cost of the war dramatically to the United States in human and material terms.[39] Extensive casualties of highly trained personnel were sustained by the United States, and, especially, the American prisoners of war gave the North Vietnamese additional leverage in any negotiations.

The bombing of most of North Vietnam was halted by President Lyndon Johnson on October 31, 1968, through private negotiations in Paris with his northern adversaries and with the concurrence of his field commander, General Creighton Abrams.[40] Rolling Thunder was finished, and the air effort devoted to it was directed toward and concentrated on the Ho Chi Minh Trail. Secretary of Defense Clark Clifford, Robert McNamara's successor, no longer sought "military victory" for the United States. His goal was to negotiate an end to the war.

Relieved from the restricted Rolling Thunder campaign against North Vietnam, the air force was able to concentrate its resources to attacks on the Ho Chi Minh Trail in Laos and concentrate on interdicting North Vietnamese lines of communications that supported the infiltration of men, equipment, and supplies into South Vietnam. This operation was labeled Commando Hunt and became the largest interdiction campaign in the history of aerial warfare. It was quickly determined that fast jet aircraft were relatively ineffective in searching out and destroying single trucks and were too costly to be risked in such an inefficient interdiction operation. Consequently, the air force used slower, cheaper propeller-driven aircraft and developed gunships—C-130, C-119, and C-123 aircraft—equipped initially with Gatling guns. Eventually, 105-millimeter howitzers in the C-130 aircraft replaced the smaller aircraft. These planes could linger over the target area for extensive periods of time and could more easily locate, engage, and destroy North Vietnamese trucks along the trail. Other targets included the Ho Chi Minh Trail itself, its bridges and roads, and, finally, the terrain itself. Those missions, generally conducted by B-52s, were designed to block the trails and roads or to crater them. Often, mines were dropped after these missions to impede North Vietnamese repair operations. Defoliation operations were also conducted.

As this campaign proceeded, the North Vietnamese, of course, moved a significant amount of antiaircraft equipment to protect the trail. This antiair capability became the fourth target for the air campaign against the Ho Chi Minh Trail.[41] In this manner, Laos became second only to South Vietnam as the most heavily bombed country in history.[42] Despite optimistic reports from the air force concerning the number of trucks destroyed, the Commando Hunt operation failed as an interdiction campaign. The North Vietnamese continued to move supplies and units southward at a steady rate. They were able to expand the Ho Chi Minh Trail to meet all their supply and reinforcement requirements.[43]

This display of strategic airpower under President Johnson had not had and could not have had any great influence on the war in the South. The air campaigns clearly were ineffective as strategic instruments against North Vietnamese industry. There was little industry in that nation, and whatever industry existed was quickly destroyed. This destruction had a minimum impact on the war in the South. Similarly, the supplies from China and the Soviet Union and their movement to the South could not be stopped by airpower. The needs of communist forces in the South, both Vietcong and North Vietnamese, were minimal. American strategic bombing never broke the will of the North Vietnamese leadership. And if it had—highly unlikely—it would still have not caused fighting in the South to cease. The NLF, consisting of opponents to the South Vietnamese regime, would have continued its fight. The bombing also contributed little or nothing to the legitimacy and strength of the South Vietnamese government, the same sine qua non of success in the South.

Ngo Dinh Diem is greeted by President Eisenhower and Secretary of State John Foster Dulles upon his arrival in Washington on May 8, 1967.

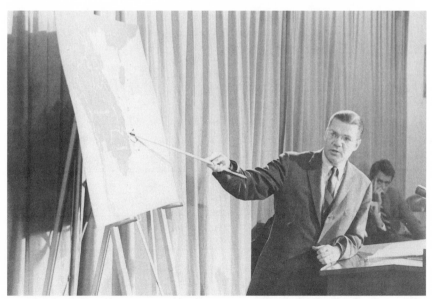

Robert S. McNamara, secretary of defense during the administrations of presidents John F. Kennedy and Lyndon B. Johnson during the Vietnam War, holding a press conference at the Pentagon, February 7, 1965.

Secretary of Defense Robert S. McNamara and Commander of U.S. troops in Vietnam General William C. Westmoreland talk with Vietnamese officers on the conditions of the war in their part of the war on Vietnam.

General William C. Westmoreland, appointed as leader of U.S. forces in Vietnam, as COMUSMACV (Commander, U.S. Military Assistance Command, Vietnam).

Helicopters of the 170th and 189th Helicopter Assault Companies await the landing of South Vietnamese troops at Polei Kieng in the Central Highlands of the Republic of (South) Vietnam, April 1969.

U.S. Air Force (USAF) tactical aircraft drop bombs on North Vietnamese targets.

U.S. forces begin to form an assault line south of Chi Lai, South Vietnam. The operation is aimed at clearing the Viet Cong/North Vietnamese from the Batangan Peninsula, 1969.

A Viet Cong soldier crouches in a bunker with an SKS rifle, waiting to leap out and attack ARVN soldiers.

Chapter Seven

The Ground War

At approximately 9:00 A.M. on March 8, 1965, a U.S. Marine Corps battalion landing team splashed ashore at Da Nang in South Vietnam. A companion battalion landed by air later the same day. Although there were already more than 20,000 American servicemen in South Vietnam when the two marine battalions arrived, this was the first time that an organized ground combat unit had been committed. The mission assigned to these two battalions was to secure the airfield and U.S. supporting installations and facilities. The orders were clear: "The U.S. Marine Force will not, repeat will not, engage in day to day actions against the Viet Cong."[1] The landing and the mission assigned these forces had been recommended by General Westmoreland. He was concerned about the ability of the South Vietnamese to protect the base from which American aircraft were conducting air strikes against the North and providing air support missions in the South. Although Ambassador Taylor supported Westmoreland's request for the marines at Da Nang, he also voiced grave reservations as to the wisdom of this course. He saw other bases as equally in need of security and foresaw that, once it became evident that U.S. forces would assume this mission, other tasks for these ground combat units would soon follow. Despite these reservations, the ambassador was informed that the marines were on the way.[2]

The landing of U.S. ground combat units in South Vietnam represented a watershed event in the history of the U.S. involvement in Vietnam. It was a major decision made without much fanfare, deliberation, or planning. Whereas the decision to bomb North Vietnam was the product of a year's discussion, this decision to introduce the marines apparently was made with little discussion at the highest levels of the Johnson administration. With the commitment of just these two battalions in March, the administration would begin to slide down a slippery slope of surprising steepness. By December, nearly 200,000 U.S. combat troops would be deployed in South Vietnam, and more than 1,500 Americans would already have died there.

As Ambassador Taylor had predicted, the policy of using these forces only for base security was short lived. The marines hardly had their feet dry when several proposals were brought forward to get U.S. troops actively engaged in the ground war. The first of these came from Army Chief of Staff General Harold K. Johnson following his trip to Vietnam from March 5 to March 12. The purpose of his trip was to examine what more could be done within South Vietnam, and General Johnson proposed the deployment of a full U.S. division for the security of various bases. On March 17, General Westmoreland sought an additional marine battalion to secure Phu Bai, a base north of Da Nang. In forwarding Westmoreland's request, the Joint Chiefs of Staff also recommended that an additional battalion be deployed to Da Nang. In addition, on March 20, the Joint Chiefs proposed a plan that called for the deployment of a three-division force, two American and one Korean.[3]

The president met with his advisers on April 1 and 2, 1965, to review the whole panoply of military and nonmilitary measures that might be undertaken in both South and North Vietnam. But the main focus of the discussions was clearly on action within South Vietnam, and the principal concern of the policymakers was the prospect of additional deployments of U.S. ground forces to South Vietnam and the mission to be assigned to these forces. Ambassador Taylor, while agreeing to the introduction of the additional marines, opposed the introduction of a full U.S. division without further examination of the probable effectiveness of such a unit and of the missions it should be assigned. Other advisers, according to President Johnson, who left them unidentified, opposed any significant U.S. involvement in the ground war in South Vietnam.[4]

The president's decisions were published as National Security Action Memorandum (NSAM) 328 on April 6, 1965. Approval was given for the deployment of two additional marine battalions, one to Phu Bai and one to Da Nang, and for an 18,000- to 20,000-man increase in U.S. logistical and support forces. Of perhaps more significance, however, NSAM 328 sanctioned a change in mission for U.S. ground forces in Vietnam although in very cautious language: "The President approved a change of mission for all Marine battalions deployed to Vietnam to permit their more active use under conditions to be established and approved by the Secretary of Defense in consultation with the Secretary of State."[5]

This decision, although it did not clearly define the new mission, was a pivotal one. It marked the president's acceptance of the reality that U.S. troops would engage in offensive ground operations against an Asian foe. To be sure, the language indicated a desire to proceed slowly and carefully. But missing from NSAM 328 was any concept of a unified, coherent strategy for the use of American ground forces in this new mode.

Ambassador Taylor, among others, had raised the question as to whether Western troops could fight effectively in Vietnam. The president apparently agreed that before devising a strategy for the use of these forces, it would be necessary to experiment to see how they would perform in this new environment. NSAM 328, therefore, implied that a limited number of troops would be tested in offensive ground operations *before* a strategy was devised for using those forces.

But efforts were made to make the change as imperceptible as possible to the American public. The memorandum, signed by McGeorge Bundy, stated that the president wished to avoid premature publicity for these decisions and that

> the actions themselves should be taken as rapidly as practicable, but in ways that should minimize any appearance of sudden changes in policy. . . . The President's desire is that these movements and changes should be understood as being gradual and wholly consistent with existing policy.[6]

Thus, the change in mission, an important step toward involving American forces in offensive ground combat in South Vietnam, was kept from the American people. It crept out almost by accident two months later in a State Department press release on June 8 to the effect that "American forces would be available for combat support together with Vietnamese forces when and if necessary."[7]

Editorial comment the next day saw the significance in this seemingly innocuous statement:

> The American people were told by a minor State Department official yesterday that, in effect, they were in a land war on the continent of Asia. . . . There is still no official explanation for a move that fundamentally alters the character of the American involvement in Vietnam. . . . It [the country] has been taken into a ground war by presidential decision when there is no emergency that would seem to rule out congressional debate.[8]

The same day, the White House blandly denied that such a decision had been made. George B. Reedy, press secretary to the president, read the following statement at a press conference: "There has been no change in the mission of U.S. ground combat units in Viet-Nam in recent days or weeks. The President has issued no order of any kind in this regard to General Westmoreland recently or at any other time."[9]

The president's decisions of April 6, 1965, did not cause the pressures for an increased buildup of American forces to abate. From April 8 on, Ambassador Taylor was bombarded with messages and instructions from Washington testifying to an eagerness to speed up the introduction to Vietnam of U.S. ground combat forces far beyond anything that had been authorized in NSAM 328. Ambassador Taylor's annoyance at these mounting pressures was transmitted to Washington. Communications between Washington and Saigon became more strained, and Ambassador Taylor's annoyance soon changed to open protest. Taylor indicated his need to have a clearer statement of U.S. purposes and objectives before he could present the case for increased American deployment of combat forces to the South Vietnamese government. In his cable to Washington, the ambassador stated, "Before I can present our case to GVN [government of South Vietnam] I have to know what the case is and why. It is not going to be easy to get ready concurrence for the large scale introduction of foreign troops unless the need is clear and explicit."[10]

In order to smooth ruffled feathers and to restore some sense of common purpose, a conference was hurriedly convened in Honolulu on April 20. This conference brought together most of the key personalities responsible for U.S. policy in Vietnam: Chairman of the Joint Chiefs of Staff General Wheeler, Secretary of Defense McNamara, General Westmoreland, Admiral Sharp, Ambassador Taylor, and Assistant Secretaries William Bundy of the Department of State and John McNaughton of the Department of Defense. Again, the majority of these individuals represented the Department of Defense. Ambassador Taylor's resistance to a buildup of U.S. forces was overcome at this conference. An increase of U.S. forces to a total of thirteen battalions and 82,000 men was agreed on. The Honolulu conference also marked the relative downgrading of air pressure against North Vietnam in favor of more intense activity in the South. The president's advisers agreed that henceforth targets in South Vietnam would have first call on air assets. The key to success, it was now stated, was not to put unacceptable pressure on the enemy in the North but to frustrate his strategy— "to break the will of the DRV/VC [Democratic Republic of North Vietnam/ Vietcong] by denying them victory."[11]

Although it may not have occurred to the decision makers at that time, this reiteration of the American objective of frustrating North Vietnam's strategy in South Vietnam was a clear repudiation by the United States of "winning militarily." It should have been clear to the participants at the Honolulu conference that "winning militarily" was not the stated objective. The Honolulu conference recommendations in effect postulated an enclave strategy—that is, operations centered on coastal areas with the purpose of protecting the population and denying the resources of these areas to the enemy. This strategy, first proposed by General Harold K. Johnson in March, was tenaciously advocated by Ambassador Taylor throughout this period. Taylor saw many advantages to it:

> The . . . role which has been suggested for U.S. ground forces is the occupation and defense of key enclaves along the coast such as Quang Ngai, Qui Nhon, Tuy Hoa and Nha Trang. Such a disposition would have the advantage of placing our forces in areas of easy access and egress with minimum logistic problems associated with supply and maintenance. The presence of our troops would assure the defense of these important key areas and would relieve some GVN forces for employment elsewhere. The troops would not be called upon to engage in counter insurgency operations except in their own local defense and hence would be exposed to minimum losses.[12]

Thus, the enclave strategy envisaged denying the enemy victory because he would be unable to seize decisive urban areas held by U.S. forces despite whatever successes he might enjoy throughout the rest of the country. Realizing his inability to gain a final victory, the enemy would be moved to a negotiated settlement of the conflict. In addition, U.S. forces would be limited in number, could be brought in and supplied with ease over sea lines of communications controlled entirely by the U.S. Navy, and could be withdrawn with equal ease should the situation so dictate. American casualties could be kept light. Beyond the enclaves, the South Vietnamese army, freed from the requirement of defending bases, would be expected to continue to prosecute the war against the enemy's main forces and could provide security to the villages and hamlets of South Vietnam outside the larger cities in the rural portions of Vietnam.[13]

But as Ambassador Taylor also pointed out, the enclave strategy was "a rather inglorious static defensive mission unappealing to them [U.S. forces] and unimpressive in the eyes of the Vietnamese." It was perceived by the military commanders as a negative strategy, yielding the initiative to the enemy and designed to frustrate rather than to defeat him. The U.S. military had been trained in offensive warfare for employment on the plains of northern Europe. A defensive strategy, however well it fit American political objectives, was not contemplated seriously by American military commanders. Although "frustrating the enemy" was the objective, the American military commanders continued to interpret this as "defeating the enemy." This confusion of the mission for American ground forces continued throughout the war. Like the "defensive" enclave strategy, "frustrating the enemy" was seen as a negative defensive mission unsuited to a combat force designed for offensive ground operations in order to defeat the enemy.

Although security was no longer the only authorized mission of U.S. units, it remained their primary one, and they consolidated and developed their coastal base areas. Patrol perimeters were pushed out, and an active defense was conducted, although failure to solve knotty problems concerning control and coordination between U.S. and Vietnamese forces prevented offensive operations in support of the Vietnamese for some months. The relative quiet in the war in the South ended in May. Before the month was over, the South Vietnamese were decimated in a series of battles at Ba Gia, near Quang Ngai city. In early June, two Vietcong regiments again defeated the South Vietnamese at Dong Xoai, inflicting heavy casualties. Although U.S. troops were nearby in both cases, they were not committed to prevent the South Vietnamese defeats.[14]

On June 7, 1965, shortly after the defeat at Ba Gia, General Westmoreland forwarded to the commander in chief of the U.S. Pacific Command (CINCPAC) "a broad review of force requirements . . . in light of the changing situation in Southeast Asia and within RVN [Republic of South Vietnam]." Describing the South Vietnamese army as near collapse, reluctant to assume the offensive, with desertion rates inordinately high, and with its steadfastness under fire coming into doubt, Westmoreland saw "no course of action open to us except to reinforce our efforts in SVN [South Vietnam] with additional U.S. or Third Country forces as rapidly as is practicable during the critical weeks ahead."

In addition, he added, even greater forces should be prepared for deployment if required "to attain our objectives or counter enemy initiatives." These forces would not be involved in a security mission or an enclave strategy, however. As General Westmoreland saw it, "I am convinced that U.S. troops with their energy, mobility, and firepower can successfully take the fight to the VC. The basic purpose of the additional deployments . . . is to give us a substantial and hard hitting offensive capability on the ground."[15]

In his cable, Westmoreland requested a buildup to a total of thirty-five maneuver battalions with a further nine battalions to be prepared for deployment if needed at a later date. In subsequent communications, the U.S. commander spelled out his concept for employing these forces. Sweeping away the last vestiges of the enclave strategy, Westmoreland described his plans for assuming the offensive and defeating the enemy. He saw the war developing in three distinct phases as follows:

Phase I. Commitment of U.S. (and other Free World) forces necessary to halt the losing trend by the end of 1965.

Phase II. U.S. and Allied forces mount offensive actions to seize the initiative to destroy guerrilla and organized enemy forces. This phase would be concluded when the enemy had been worn down, thrown on the defensive and driven back from the major populated areas.

Phase III. If the enemy persisted, a period of a year to a year and a half following Phase II would be required for the final destruction of enemy forces remaining in remote base areas.[16]

General Westmoreland's recommendations to the president stirred up a hornet's nest in Washington. His request for reinforcements on a large scale, accompanied by a desire to put the troops on the offensive throughout the country, did not contain any of the comfortable restrictions that had been part of the strategies debated up until that time. In fact, it presaged a virtual American takeover of the war. In General Westmoreland's request, there was little or no mention of South Vietnamese forces or any program to utilize those forces or to make them more effective. There was also no mention of a converse strategy of protecting the population of South Vietnam against communist intrusion. The specter of major U.S. military forces engaged in ground combat on the Asian mainland had indeed become a possibility, indeed, a recommendation of the field commander. The implications for the United States in terms of lives and money could not be ignored.

In American senior military colleges, students are taught that an estimate of the situation that states that "there is only one course of action open to us" is inadequate and should be viewed with suspicion. Clearly, there was more than one course of action open to the United States. The "enclave" strategy was not mentioned in this faulty "estimate of the situation," nor was there any mention of a pacification program or any mention of building up the South Vietnamese government or army or of using American forces to protect the population of South Vietnam. But Westmoreland's request was taken at face value both by senior U.S. political and by military leaders. Before making any decision to deploy more American forces, however, President Johnson again wanted to examine all the options. The secretary of defense was dispatched to Saigon to examine General Westmoreland's request, to develop alternatives, and to determine the force requirements for the immediate future and for 1966. But in a fait accompli, General Westmoreland was given authority on June 26 to commit U.S. ground forces anywhere in the country when, in his judgment, they were needed to strengthen South Vietnamese forces. Thus liberated from the restrictions of the coastal enclaves, the first major operation by U.S. forces under this new authority was conducted on June 27 in War Zone D northwest of Saigon.[17]

In Saigon, General Westmoreland indicated to Secretary McNamara that a buildup to forty-four American battalions (now dubbed Phase I forces and totaling 175,000 men) would be needed in South Vietnam by the end of 1965. However, he also made it clear that this force and the new offensive strategy would prevent defeat only long enough to prepare the way for additional

forces to allow him to seize the initiative from the Vietcong in 1966. He foresaw the necessity of some twenty-four additional American combat battalions, plus associated combat support and support units by the end of 1966
(Phase II forces totaling 100,000 men). This force would enable him to take
the offensive that year and, with "appropriate" but unstated additional reinforcements (Phase III), to have defeated the enemy by the end of 1967.[18]

Here again, there seemed to be a confusion of objectives. The American
objective, clearly stated on several occasions, was, first, to develop an independent noncommunist South Vietnam and, second, to convince North Vietnam that over time it could not be successful in its attempts to defeat South
Vietnam and unify the country. The American military commanders quickly
translated this into the objective of "defeating the enemy," a traditional objective with which they felt comfortable. But defeating the enemy was not an
American objective and did not necessarily translate into a "stable noncommunist South Vietnam."

In his memoir, *In Retrospect*, Secretary of Defense McNamara characterized these discussions with General Westmoreland in Saigon in 1965 as "superficial." Looking back, he states,

> I clearly erred by not forcing—then or later, in Saigon or in Washington—a
> knock-down, drag-out debate over the loose assumptions, unasked questions,
> and thin analyses underlying our military strategy in Vietnam. I had spent
> twenty years as a manager . . . forcing organizations to think deep and realisti-
> cally about alternative courses of action and their consequences. I doubt if I will
> fully understand why I did not do so here.[19]

McNamara reported Westmoreland's requirements to the president on July
20. He recommended that Westmoreland's Phase I request be met with the understanding that additional troops would be needed in 1966 and also recommended asking Congress for authority to call up 235,000 reservists. McNamara's report engendered perhaps the only full-scale examination of U.S.
objectives and strategy for Vietnam at the highest levels of the administration
until after the Tet offensive of 1968.

President Johnson met with various advisers and congressional leaders almost continuously during the period July 21–July 27, 1965. The president's
advisers were divided and for the first time expressed their concerns. Ambassador Taylor and his deputy, U. Alexis Johnson, while recognizing the seri-
ousness of the situation, were less than sanguine about the prospects for success if large numbers of U.S. troops were brought in. Both men were
concerned with the effect of the proposed buildup on the Vietnamese. Although not directly opposed to the use of U.S. forces to assist the South Vietnamese, they wanted to proceed slowly to prevent the loss of Vietnamese au-

thority and control in the conduct of the war. But, as Ambassador Taylor put it, these reasons "did not seem to us sufficiently important to warrant rejecting the proposed troop augmentation."[20]

Undersecretary of State George Ball, both in meetings with the president and in memoranda that he submitted, directly opposed the buildup. In his view, there was absolutely no assurance that the United States could attain its political objectives in Vietnam by providing additional ground forces. He saw the risk of a struggle of unknown outcome with high but indeterminate costs and felt the United States should not embark on such a course.[21] Secretary of State Dean Rusk disagreed strongly with the views expressed by his undersecretary. In a rare written memorandum to the president and later during discussions on this issue, he indicated that he felt it absolutely necessary for the United States to live up to its commitments in South Vietnam:

> The integrity of the U.S. commitment is the principal pillar of peace throughout the world. If that commitment becomes unreliable, the communist world would draw conclusions that would lead to our ruin and almost certainly to a catastrophic war. So long as the South Vietnamese are prepared to fight for themselves, we cannot abandon them without disaster to peace and to our interests throughout the world.[22]

But clearly, the requirement for American troops was based on the unwillingness—or inability—of the South Vietnamese to fight for themselves.

Others, such as Assistant Secretary of State William Bundy and Clark Clifford, fell somewhere in between. They wanted to deploy just enough additional forces to prevent defeat so that it would be possible to work toward a diplomatic solution. Of the congressional leaders consulted, only Senator Mike Mansfield expressed any opposition. As the majority leader of the Senate saw it,

> Whatever pledge we had was to assist South Vietnam in its own defense. Since then there has been no government of legitimacy. We owe this government nothing, no pledge of any kind. We are going deeper into war. . . . We cannot expect our people to support a war for three-to-five years. What we are about to get is an anti-Communist crusade, on and on. Remember, escalation begets escalation.[23]

President Johnson in the end agreed with and accepted the arguments of his secretary of state. As he later indicated,

> If we ran out on Southeast Asia, I could see trouble ahead in every part of the globe—not just in Asia but in the Middle East and in Europe, Africa and in Latin America. I was convinced that our retreat from this challenge would open the path to World War III. . . . I knew our people well enough to realize that if we

walked away from Vietnam and let Southeast Asia fall, there would follow a divisive and destructive debate within our country. . . . A divisive debate over "who lost Vietnam" would be, in my judgment, even more destructive to our national life than the argument over China had been. It would inevitably increase isolationist pressures from the right and from the left and cause a pulling back from our commitments in Europe and the Middle East as well as in Asia.[24]

President Johnson, on July 28, 1965, approved the deployment to South Vietnam of the Phase I forces totaling 175,000 troops (later raised to 219,000). He refused to call up the reserves and made no decision about the deployment of Phase II forces (no decision was required at the time). In announcing these increases in U.S. forces to South Vietnam, the president stressed the continuity of the U.S. commitment to the defense of South Vietnam and indicated that he foresaw no quick solution to the problem there.[25]

Whatever they may have thought personally of the wisdom of this momentous decision of July 1965, all the participants realized that a major threshold had been crossed. A new course had been taken, the end of which was not in sight. As General Westmoreland understood, "Explicit in my forty-four battalion proposal and President Johnson's approval of it was a proviso for free maneuver of American and allied units throughout South Vietnam. Thus the restrictive enclave strategy with which I had disagreed from the first was finally rejected." And as Johnson later stated, "Now we were committed to major combat in Vietnam."[26]

Accompanying this change from enclave defense to offensive "search-and-destroy" operations, as they came to be called, was also a subtle but extremely significant change in emphasis. As has been pointed out, instead of the limited objective of simply denying the enemy victory and convincing him that he could not win, the thrust of U.S. policy was now directed toward providing sufficient forces to defeat the enemy in the South. The decision to build up U.S. forces and to use them in an offensive strategy left the U.S. commitment to the defense of South Vietnam open ended. The amount of force required to defeat the enemy depended entirely on the enemy's response to the U.S. buildup and his willingness to increase his own commitment to the struggle. Thus, the force approved by President Johnson in July 1965 was recognized as sufficient only to prevent the collapse of South Vietnam while the stage was being set for further U.S. troop deployments.

But the acceptance of the goal of defeating the enemy rather than merely denying him victory opened the door, as George Ball had foreseen, to an indeterminate amount of additional force. Although U.S. forces could maintain the tactical initiative in South Vietnam through their great mobility and firepower, the enemy maintained the strategic initiative throughout by his willingness to increase his commitment of force to the struggle. Thus, the pace and level of the fighting would be dictated by the enemy and not by the United States. The size of U.S. forces required to "defeat" the enemy depended entirely on the enemy's response to the U.S. buildup and his willingness to increase his own commitment to the struggle. Under the political guidelines under which the U.S. entered the war, Vietcong and North Vietnamese units were not vulnerable to U.S. ground forces until they crossed the border into South Vietnam. Likewise, enemy units could escape pursuit and engagement with U.S. units by crossing over the borders into Cambodia or Laos or beyond the Demilitarized Zone (DMZ) into North Vietnam. Thus, the enemy could enter the battle when he chose and could withdraw from the battlefield when he chose.

Success in this kind of war did not depend on the ability of American forces to defeat the enemy in South Vietnam. It depended instead on how long the North Vietnamese were willing to feed the pipeline with men and material. If they were willing to pay the price, the enemy could keep large numbers of American forces tied up indefinitely and inflict casualties on them. As long as the president continued to insist on his political guidelines of not spreading the war to Cambodia and Laos, the war could become an open-ended struggle, a protracted war of attrition. As it turned out, the president insisted on these geographic restrictions, and the North Vietnamese were willing to pay a very high price.

Finally, the acceptance of the buildup of U.S. forces and their use in an offensive role throughout Vietnam was an explicit expression of a total loss of confidence in the South Vietnamese government and army and a concomitant willingness on the part of U.S. commanders to take over the major part of the war effort. The paradox arose of the Americans fighting on behalf of a government and army that they often treated with disdain, even contempt. The South Vietnamese, on whose behalf the United States had entered a land war in Asia, were dealt with as if they really weren't worth saving. Thus, there grew a naked contradiction between the political objectives of the war and the actual situation of virtually ignoring the South Vietnamese government and army in the formulation of American strategy. There was usually little coordination or cooperation between U.S. and South Vietnamese forces. Sharing information with the South Vietnamese, it was felt by American commanders, ensured the compromise of that information.

American involvement in an Asian ground war was now a reality. From this point forward, the United States pursued the dangerous illusion of a military victory without any evaluation of the costs of that victory in casualties, material, or money. No further proof of the monumental implications of the decisions made in the summer of 1965 is required beyond the fact that, by the end of 1967, the time General Westmoreland estimated was required to defeat the enemy, the United States had 107 battalions and a total of 525,000 men in Vietnam while pursuing a bombing campaign against the North without a victory in sight and without any agreed-on strategic concept as to how to achieve such a "victory."

General Westmoreland, the U.S. commander in Vietnam, had indicated that he saw no alternative to a strategy of attrition. But this strategy could not be successful as long as the North Vietnamese controlled the pace of the war. General Westmoreland had adopted a strategy that could not succeed within the political guidelines insisted on by the administration. From this time forward, he continued to request through the Joint Chiefs release from the geographic restrictions on his military operations. But these were recommendations to enlarge the war and recommendations that the president was never willing to approve. As historian Barbara Tuchman later recognized, the attrition strategy in any case was futile

> in the first place because the North Vietnamese and Viet Cong are fighting for their country and for a cause and therefore have a stronger motive for enduring than we have. . . . It is indefensible in the second place because it is destroying the land and welfare and lives of the people we are supposed to be fighting for.[27]

The North Vietnamese realized this as well. They saw the deployment of American troops as an admission of U.S. failure in the "special war," the war of Vietnamese against Vietnamese, with American advisers guiding the South Vietnamese. The deployment of U.S. troops signaled to North Vietnam what they already knew: that the Diem regime and its successors had been repudiated by the South Vietnamese people. American troops were needed to keep the South Vietnamese people from placing the National Liberation Front (NLF) in power in South Vietnam.[28] The theme of the Vietcong, that the Saigon government lacked legitimacy and was a puppet of the United States, rang true among many of the rural peasantry of South Vietnam.

The North Vietnamese viewed the introduction of American troops as an indication of the failure of American attempts to prop up the South Vietnamese government. According to North Vietnamese General Nguyen Din Uoc, the enemy also recognized the contradictions in the American strategy:

> We could always be able to put more people in the field in Vietnam than Westmoreland could. . . . It seemed to us he had no real strategy. Rather, he seemed to be only a battle commander who just relied on numbers of troops to achieve victory. . . . When we heard that Westmoreland's "strategy" was the so-called "strategy of attrition," and when we fully understood what this meant, then we were sure we would prevail. Why? Because this so-called strategy worked to our benefit. We have more people. Our people are determined, because they are

fighting in our own homeland. We are not mercenaries, like the U.S. troops. And our troops were hardened veterans—we fought the French and knew our way around whereas most of the U.S. troops were "green," as we say, not experienced in any kind of war, let alone war in a country like Vietnam. We knew about Dien Bien Phu. Some of us were there. Westmoreland should have read some books about Dien Bien Phu. If he had, he might have designed a different strategy.[29]

General Uoc also claimed that by the time the United States had more than 70,000 troops in the South, North Vietnam had still not sent any organized army units there. He claimed that before this point, it might have been possible to head off the war, "to discuss, to find some way out of the conflict. But once the troops were sent and the fighting began, then I think there were no more chances. . . . Once the troops have been sent, the war must follow."

What were North Vietnamese objectives once American combat forces joined the war? According to recent discussions with former North Vietnamese senior officials, a military victory over the United States was never an option. As Luu Doan Huynh stated,

In our history, we have had to fight against big countries many times, and each time the pattern is more or less the same: we fight for a while and then we must talk in order to find a resolution. A military victory has never been an option. . . . Early in 1965 . . . we decided our objectives would be fight in order to defeat the U.S. air war, to exhaust the U.S. troops in the South and to weaken the determination to fight of both American politicians and soldiers. This became our objective. . . . Ultimately, we would try to get the U.S. to withdraw its troops from Vietnam through negotiations. But we believed that the prerequisite conditions for withdrawal were as I have just stated: defeat the air war, exhaust the troops, and erode your aggressive will.[30]

The North Vietnamese, therefore, claim that northern troops came into the picture in the South only after the United States bombed the North and brought troops into the South—in other words, after it was clear that the United States was escalating the war. Then the North began to support the "southern resistance" with regular regiments. In 1965, they claim, the NLF in the central highlands received three regiments from the North. Those three regiments fought against the United States in the November 1965 battle in the Ia Drang Valley. After that, many more regiments were sent. General Dang Vu Hiep stated,

Our policy was really nothing more than retaliation. . . . If you escalate, then I must also escalate, and so on. You know, at the time there was a saying in the South: every time you bomb the North, then the South will step up its

retaliation. . . . That is how it worked. This is why we "escalated" the war—
in retaliation.[31]

On the U.S. side, although General Westmoreland had proposed a tactical
concept of operations for the forces that were to be deployed to South Vietnam, an overall strategic plan was required to clarify the national purposes
and objectives that these additional forces were meant to serve. President
Johnson, in his message to the American people announcing the deployments,
had indicated that these forces were to resist aggression in South Vietnam and
to "convince the communists that we cannot be defeated by force of arms or
by superior power." General Westmoreland, as has been mentioned, had a
more ambitious objective: to defeat and destroy enemy forces and drive them
from South Vietnam.

Therefore, in order to establish a basis for future force requirements and for
overall conduct of the ground war, the military chiefs set out to develop their
own strategic concept for U.S. military operations in Southeast Asia. By the
end of August 1965, they had developed a concept that contained their basic
assumptions and goals, and they pressed this concept on the civilian leadership with single-minded intensity in the years to come. The Joint Chiefs saw
three equally important military tasks to be accomplished in Vietnam:

1. To cause the DRV to cease its direction and support of the Viet Cong insurgency;
2. To defeat the Viet Cong and to extend GVN control over all of South Vietnam;
3. To deter Communist China from direct intervention and to defeat such intervention if it should occur.[32]

This third objective, deterring communist China from direct intervention,
was a thread that had run through the debate over bombing North Vietnam in
1965. The Joint Chiefs consistently mentioned the possibility of direct Chinese intervention as an additional justification for troop deployments and as
an important reason for a reserve call-up to reconstitute the U.S. strategic reserve as these deployments proceeded. The president and his civilian advisers consistently used this possibility to limit military action against North
Vietnam. National intelligence estimates just as consistently discounted the
probability of such intervention.

The North Vietnamese have indicated that they, too, were concerned about
the possibility of Chinese intervention. They, of course, welcomed Chinese
aid, and, in particular, the Chinese provided North Vietnam with a sophisticated missile air defense system. But the North Vietnamese used the possibility of Chinese intervention as a deterrent to the United States. The Chinese

made it clear in an editorial in the *Peoples Daily* on February 15, 1965, that warned that if the United States crossed the seventeenth parallel with ground troops, the war would expand all the way from Vietnam to Korea. In that way, a message was sent to the United States. The message was, according to the North Vietnamese, "If you don't touch me, I won't touch you." Chinese preparations, they state, were based on deterrence but were not a bluff and were related to the Chinese notion of North Vietnam as lying within its own zone of security and influence. The North Vietnamese wanted to fight alone; they did not look forward to another Chinese intervention. But it was a credible threat, they felt, in response to any American invasion of the North.[33]

The military tasks recommended by the Joint Chiefs to achieve their self-imposed objectives were extremely ambitious and went far beyond anything recommended by General Westmoreland. Aggressive and sustained military action, the military chiefs stated, would allow the United States to hold the initiative in both North and South Vietnam. North Vietnam's war-supporting power would be progressively destroyed and the Vietcong defeated. To achieve this, they visualized that the following military actions would be required:

to intensify military pressure on the DRV by air and naval power; to destroy significant DRV military targets; to interdict supporting LOCs in the DRV; to interdict the infiltration and supply routes into the RVN; to improve the combat effectiveness of the RVNAF; to build and protect bases; to reduce enemy reinforcements; to defeat the Viet Cong. . . . The physical capability of the DRV to move men and supplies through the Lao corridor, down the coastline, across the DMZ, and through Cambodia must be reduced . . . by land, naval and air actions. . . . Finally . . . a buildup in Thailand to ensure attainment of the proper U.S.-Thai posture to deter CHICOM aggression and to facilitate placing U.S. forces in an advantageous logistical position if such aggression occurs.

The secretary of defense, of course, did not approve this ambitious program, which raised such controversial and far-reaching policy issues as blockading North Vietnam, involving U.S. ground forces in Laos and Cambodia, and building up U.S. forces in Thailand. But he did not reject it either. Indicating that an overall approval was not required at that time, the secretary merely agreed that "recommendations for future operations in Southeast Asia should be formulated" as the occasion necessitated.[34]

Left with no other guidance from their civilian superiors, the Joint Chiefs continued to formulate recommendations for future operations along the same lines. Throughout the war, their recommendations continued to take the form of requests for additional American troops in South Vietnam and for expanded operational authority outside South Vietnam. Since Secretary

McNamara or a higher civilian authority had failed to provide them with any national objectives, missions, or strategic concepts other than the very general ones of "resisting aggression" or "ensuring a noncommunist South Vietnam," the military leaders virtually were forced to adopt their own concept for conducting the war and to continue to press for its approval.

By November 1965, it appeared that the infiltration of units from North Vietnam had increased substantially and had outpaced the buildup of American forces. Moreover, with its augmented forces, the enemy was showing an increasing willingness to stand and fight in large-scale engagements. The implications of this enemy buildup for the future were made abundantly clear to newly arrived U.S. forces. As mentioned, U.S. forces were engaged in bloody fighting in the Ia Drang Valley in mid-November in which more than 300 U.S. soldiers were killed. There was also significant Vietcong action against newly arrived American forces north of Saigon.[35] The Americans had thrown down the challenge, and the North Vietnamese and their southern supporters quickly accepted it.

The North Vietnamese saw their deployment of troops to South Vietnam as only a natural and required response to American escalation. After having defeated the hated Diem puppet regime largely through indigenous resistance in South Vietnam, they saw the entrance of American forces into the struggle as an attempt by these foreign forces once again to deny them the fruits of their victory and to deny once again the unity of Vietnam under an indigenous and popular regime. They claim that the use of North Vietnamese forces against the Americans at the Ia Drang Valley was the first use of North Vietnamese regular forces in South Vietnam.

Be that as it may, General Westmoreland pointed out to Washington on November 22, 1965, that the enemy buildup rate was double that planned for American forces in Phase II. He requested forces in addition to those already planned as being "essential to meet the immediate threat" and indicated that even the forces he was now requesting (which would raise Phase II forces to approximately 154,000 and bring total U.S. troop strength in Vietnam to nearly 375,000 by mid-1967) would not match the enemy buildup. Reaching the level of force required to take the offensive, General Westmoreland indicated, "will ultimately require much larger deployments." But, as he pointed out, "certain physical restrictions and the time required to establish a suitable logistics base limit the rate of buildup in RVN CY 66."[36] In this regard, General Westmoreland himself advocated a gradual buildup required by the necessity to establish a suitable logistics rate—a significant restriction on the number of American combat troops that could be deployed. Thus, the necessity of a strategy of "gradualism" was recognized and broached by the field commander. As General Westmoreland explained, physical limitations within South Vietnam made a gradual buildup of fighting forces necessary.

The costs of the policy the administration had adopted in July 1965 were made apparent by the North Vietnamese in November. Willing to match or exceed the American buildup, the North Vietnamese clearly demonstrated to American leaders the open-ended nature of the troop commitment to South Vietnam that the United States had made by its entry into the ground war. As North Vietnamese officials explained, "Our objectives . . . would be to fight in order to . . . exhaust the U.S. troops in the South and to weaken the determination to fight of both American politicians and soldiers. . . . Ultimately we would try to get the U.S. to withdraw its troops from Vietnam through negotiations."[37]

Faced with the dilemma of increasing the number of American forces, the president once again sent Secretary of Defense McNamara to Saigon to study the situation. McNamara spent two days in Saigon, November 28–30, 1965, and returned to report his grim findings to the president. He stated that present plans for deployment of Phase I and Phase II forces would not be enough. In order to "provide what it takes in men and materiel . . . to stick with our stated objectives," McNamara recommended additional troop deployments to bring total U.S. maneuver battalions to seventy-four and total U.S. personnel in Vietnam to approximately 400,000 by the end of 1966, with the possible need for an additional 200,000 in 1967. Even these deployments, the secretary of defense warned, "would not guarantee success." Instead, he foresaw that "even with the recommended deployments, we will be faced in early 1967 with a military standoff at a much higher level, with pacification still stalled, and with any prospect of military success marred by the chance of an active Chinese intervention."[38]

McNamara, of course, did not indicate which "stated objectives" were being pursued, those of the president or those of the Joint Chiefs.

The prospect that now faced the president was not a pleasant one. Before approving such a large commitment of American forces, Johnson again sought other alternatives. As has been mentioned, by the summer of 1965, the bombing of North Vietnam had been relegated to a secondary role in U.S. military strategy. From the time of the president's decision in July to send substantial numbers of American troops to engage in combat in South Vietnam, the Rolling Thunder campaign in the North was seen by American civilian leaders as useful and necessary but also as a supplement to rather than a substitute for action in South Vietnam. But the bombing was also seen by these leaders as a negotiating option for the United States, a bargaining chip that could be given up in return for a reduction or cessation of North Vietnam's military efforts in the South. There had been a five-day bombing pause in May 1965 to see if the North Vietnamese government would respond with a gesture of its own. But that pause had been hastily arranged and was not widely publicized before its initiation so that no adequate diplomatic preparation had been made. In addition, its brief span (May 13–May 18) seemed to have precluded a meaningful response.

McNamara had suggested to the president in July that, subsequent to the deployment of the U.S. forces contemplated in Phase I, another, longer bombing pause might be appropriate. Now McNamara brought the issue up again, indicating that a three- or four-week pause might be useful before any great increase in troop deployments to Vietnam.[39] The president was at first deeply skeptical of the value of such an initiative, and this skepticism was shared by Dean Rusk, McGeorge Bundy, Ambassador Henry Cabot Lodge (who had replaced Taylor in July), and the military commanders. However, with the prospect of heavy new troop deployments, the weight of opinion slowly changed in favor of a bombing pause as "worth the risk." The bombing pause that occurred—for thirty-seven days, from December 25, 1965, until January 31, 1966—was accompanied by a widespread American diplomatic campaign to persuade Hanoi to reciprocate by making some gesture toward peace. But the bombing pause had another, unannounced objective: that of creating a public impression of U.S. willingness to take extraordinary measures in a search for a peaceful solution in South Vietnam before increasing the U.S. military commitment there. As Secretary of State Rusk frankly stated in a cable to Ambassador Lodge,

> The prospect of large-scale reinforcement in men and defense budget increases of some twenty billions for the next eighteen month period requires solid preparation of the American public. A crucial element will be clear demonstration that we have explored fully every alternative but that aggressor has left us no choice.[40]

The American diplomatic initiatives met with no success, and Hanoi used the bombing pause to rush men and supplies into South Vietnam. The president, on January 31, ordered the bombing resumed.

The decision on additional major U.S. troop deployments to Vietnam now had to be faced. President Johnson met with the top South Vietnamese leadership for the first time in Honolulu on February 7–8, 1966. Here the discussions focused primarily on pacification and the nonmilitary measures that could be pursued in South Vietnam. President Johnson indicated that he expected to see results from these programs—to see "coonskins on the wall."[41] At first, the buildup of American forces was limited by the speed with which units could be gotten ready to move and the availability in Vietnam of facilities to receive and support them.[42] Once these problems had been surmounted, as they were by early 1966, the barrier then became either the level at which reserve forces would have to be called up or the time it took to form and train new units. The need for new units became pressing as General West-moreland's requests for numbers of men and rates of deployment began to exceed the capabilities of the services to provide them from existing forces. But President Johnson, anxious to preserve the facade of normality and reluctant to put the country on a war footing, resisted a reserve call-up. This issue, then, became a major concern of military and political leaders during the next two years of American involvement in Vietnam.

By April 10, 1966, President Johnson had approved a plan for the subsequent buildup of U.S. forces that did not require a reserve call-up; it projected U.S. strength in South Vietnam at the end of 1966 to be seventy battalions and 383,500 men. By the end of June 1967, total U.S. strength in South Vietnam was scheduled to be 425,000. During the next three months, adjustments in these deployment capabilities raised the totals to seventy-nine maneuver battalions by the end of 1966 and eighty-two battalions by June 1967. Even this ambitious plan, called Program 3 (not to be confused with Phase III), nevertheless involved fewer men than General Westmoreland's original recommendations. Even before these figures had been published by the Department of Defense, the military commanders (on August 5, 1966) submitted new troop requirements for 1967. They considered the additional forces to be "rounding-out forces" to give a balanced additional capability. If the request were approved, troop strength in Vietnam would be raised to ninety maneuver battalions and 542,588 men by the end of 1967.[43]

Secretary McNamara did not question these new requirements. He gave the following guidance to the Joint Chiefs:

> As you know, it is our policy to provide the troops, weapons, and supplies requested by General Westmoreland at the times he desires them, to the greatest possible degree. The latest revised CINCPAC requirements . . . are to be accorded the same consideration: valid requirements for SVN . . . will be deployed on a schedule as close as possible to CINCPAC/COMUSMACV's [Commander U.S. Military Assistance Command Vietnam] requests. Nevertheless, I desire and expect detailed line-by-line analysis of these requirements to determine that each is truly essential to the carrying out of our war plan.[44]

By "our war plan," of course, McNamara on this occasion meant the war plan developed by the Joint Chiefs and the military commanders in the Pacific. It was these military officials who, in the absence of direction from higher authority, were developing U.S. strategy in Vietnam and setting force requirements. The secretary of defense had limited his role and that of his department to merely examining these requests of the military commanders to make sure they could be supported without a reserve call-up. Up to that time, the civilian Department of Defense officials had largely abnegated any role in the strategic or policy direction of the ground war and had, in fact, turned it over to the military commanders to win according to their own definition of winning, limited only by certain geographic constraints imposed to prevent the war from spreading to Cambodia and Laos and possibly involving China or the Soviet Union.

The perennial problem of calling up reserve forces to support proposed U.S. deployments and, just as importantly in the eyes of the Joint Chiefs, to reconstitute a strategic reserve in the United States that had been seriously depleted by the Vietnam buildup continued to be a contentious issue. The military chiefs, in their review of the 1967 force requirements, provided the secretary of defense with their analysis of the U.S. worldwide military posture in the light of these force requirements. Assuming that there would be no call-up of reserve forces and no change in rotation policy (a one-year tour for U.S. personnel) and that resources for the proposed deployments would be taken from the active force structure, the impact of meeting the 1967 requirements would be devastating. Without a reserve call-up, the Joint Chiefs indicated, the services could not fully respond to the stated force requirements on the time schedule prescribed. Providing these forces on a delayed schedule, in fact, would

> further impair the U.S. military posture and capability to maintain forward deployments to deter aggression worldwide. It would further reduce the capability to reinforce NATO rapidly, to provide forces for other contingencies, and to maintain a sufficient rotation and training base. . . . Of particular note in the case of the Army, equipment withdrawals from the Reserve components have substantially weakened the Army's reserve structure.[45]

It seemed that now, at last, the Joint Chiefs were telling the secretary of defense that it would no longer be possible to carry on the war in Vietnam in accordance with their strategy without a concurrent call-up of large numbers of reserves. With all these facts and recommendations in hand, Secretary McNamara again departed for Saigon to confer with the field commander and get a better feel for what was really needed. On his return, on August 10, 1966, McNamara revealed with striking clarity that many of the premises under which the United States had committed major combat forces were, in his mind, becoming questionable. In his report to the president, the secretary of defense agreed that the military situation had gotten somewhat better in 1966, but he saw little cause for optimism in the long run. In fact, McNamara seemed somewhat disheartened, as he noted that he could "see no reasonable way to bring the war to an end soon."

Based on these observations, the secretary now recommended changing the emphasis of U.S. strategy. Rather than defeating the enemy by offensive action, as had been consistently recommended by the military commanders, McNamara's solution was to return to a rather defensive posture "by getting ourselves into a military posture that we credibly would maintain indefinitely—a posture that makes trying to 'wait us out' less attractive to the North Vietnamese/Viet Cong." To achieve this, the secretary recommended a five-part program far different from the war plan envisaged by his military commanders:

1. Barring a dramatic change in the war, we should . . . level off at the total of 470,000 [U.S. ground forces].
2. An infiltration barrier should be constructed across the neck of South Vietnam near the 17th parallel and across the infiltration trails in Laos;
3. Stabilize the ROLLING THUNDER program against the North at present levels;
4. Pursue a vigorous pacification program;
5. Increase the prospects for a negotiated settlement of the war [McNamara here suggested several possible actions].

Even if these steps were taken, however, McNamara foresaw no great probability of success in the near future. The solution, as he saw it at that time, was to prepare openly for a longer war in order to "give clear evidence that the continuing costs and risks to the American people are acceptably limited, that the formula for success has been found, and that the end of the war is merely a matter of time."[46]

The dangerous illusion of seeking to achieve a military victory was finally recognized and expressed officially by the secretary of defense. This remarkably somber and pessimistic document gave an answer, finally, to the demands of the military chiefs for an approved strategic concept for U.S. operations in Vietnam. That answer, however, was a clear "no" to their proposals to defeat North Vietnamese forces through major increases in U.S. forces in South Vietnam and expanded bombing in the North. But more than just a "no," McNamara's concept provided an alternative strategy and criteria for success as well as new assumptions about the meaning of "winning" against which future military recommendations would be measured. The Joint Chiefs, as could be expected, disagreed with McNamara's strategic alternative. They reiterated their previously developed but unapproved strategic concept of maximum pressure on the enemy at all points free of most political restraints in order to defeat the enemy in the shortest possible time and at the least cost in men. They again made a twofold case for calling up the reserves: first, that the United States could not meet force requirements and simultaneously fulfill its commitments to NATO and other threatened areas without mobilization and, second, that the achievement of U.S. war objectives "in the shortest time with the least cost" could not be done without mobilization.[47]

President Johnson, with the specter of reserve mobilization constantly on his mind, was not enchanted with the prospect of a costly major force increase. After a series of conferences with the president, McNamara informed the Joint Chiefs formally, on November 11, 1966, that a new deployment program, Program 4, had been approved with an end strength of U.S. military personnel of 470,000 to be reached by June 1968 (as opposed to the original request for some 542,000 by the end of 1967). In explaining the reasoning behind the Program 4 decisions, McNamara posed the strategic dilemma and seemed to resolve it finally:

> We now face a choice of two approaches to the threat of the regular VC/NVA forces. The first approach would be to continue in 1967 to increase friendly forces as rapidly as possible, and without limit, and employ them primarily in large scale "seek out and destroy" operations to destroy the main force VC/NVA units. . . .
>
> The second approach is to follow a similarly aggressive strategy of "seek out and destroy," but to build friendly forces only to that level required to neutralize the large enemy units and prevent them from interfering with the pacification program. It is essential to this approach that such a level be consistent with a stable economy in SVN, and consistent with a military posture that the U.S. credibly would maintain indefinitely, thus making a Communist attempt to "wait us out" less attractive.
>
> I believe it is time to adopt the second approach for three reasons: (1) if MACV estimates of enemy strength are correct, we have not been able to attrite the enemy forces fast enough to break their morale and more U.S. forces are unlikely to do so in the foreseeable future; (2) we cannot deploy more than 470,000 personnel . . . without a high probability of generating a self-defeating runaway inflation in SVN, and (3) an endless escalation of U.S. deployments is not likely to be acceptable in the U.S. or to induce the enemy to believe that the U.S. is prepared to stay as long as it is required to produce a secure noncommunist SVN.[48]

Thus, the secretary of defense finally seemed to have adopted an overall strategic concept for the conduct of the war in Vietnam. But it was not a concept for "defeating" the enemy and "winning" the war, and as such it was not a concept advocated by or even acceptable to the military leaders, from the field commanders to the Joint Chiefs. The civilian decision makers in the Department of Defense were beginning to question the illusion of military victory advocated and followed by the nation's military leaders. That illusion had led to programs that were increasingly expensive in money and lives and were depressingly barren of tangible results. But although the illusion of quick military victory had largely dissipated, other than this recommendation of the secretary of defense, there was no formal reevaluation at the national level at this time concerning overall American objectives in South Vietnam.

America's initial strategic concept emerged from the realization that the military and political situation in South Vietnam in the spring and early summer of 1965 was irretrievably lost unless the United States committed substantial combat forces and unless Hanoi could be persuaded to cease its support of the Vietcong. American military leaders saw no alternative to Americanizing the war and defeating the enemy on the ground. The way to accomplish this, traditionally, was to bring the maximum power to bear on the enemy and on his war-making capability.

Although not questioning this strategy or explicitly advocating a different one, many political leaders sought to limit U.S. involvement. So the military initially was denied the resources it advocated for a rapid and maximum application of power against the enemy in North and South Vietnam and their contiguous areas, laying the groundwork for future charges that "gradualism" and "political restraints" had prevented victory. But even the gradual application of American power, a policy that frustrated the desire of the military for quick and decisive results, soon began to prove too costly to an administration determined to keep the economy on a peacetime footing and determined not to mobilize reserve forces. Further, this strategy could not, in the face of a matching North Vietnamese buildup, produce tangible results for a president interested in "coonskins on the wall." Thus, during this period, other alternatives were sought that would relieve the pressure on U.S. resources, especially manpower, yet that would contribute to the military effort. Among these were a barrier plan proposed by McNamara, attempts to obtain the commitment of additional Free World forces to supplement American troops, and heightened diplomatic activity aimed at engaging the North Vietnamese in negotiations. The turn of the year saw the policy debate over basic U.S. tactics in South Vietnam continue as it became increasingly clear that the nature of the objectives, the political bases of resolution, the desirable magnitude of the presence, and the ground and air strategy to be pursued were still not crystallized or carefully delineated within the administration. The civilians in the Defense Department continued to stress the theme of establishing security and stabilizing troop and bombing levels for the long haul, frustrating North Vietnam's strategy over time. The military authorities continued to pursue the illusion of military victory and to insist on their strategic concept designed "to defeat externally directed and supported communist subversion and aggression." They attacked the premise that the restoration of economic stability in South Vietnam was of overriding importance and regarded the ceiling of 470,000 men as inadequate and restrictive.

Thus, the secretary of defense, the Joint Chiefs, and the field commander were still not agreed on their understanding of the country's strategy and objectives in South Vietnam. This tended not only to aggravate a communications problem that had always hindered political-military planning but also to place the military on the defensive. The divergence between Washington policy and the military direction of the war was to assume great importance before the gap was closed. For the time being, however, ambiguity and uncertainty continued. The costs of the war were also being brought to the attention of the American people with increased emphasis. American casualties announced on March 10, 1967, were the highest for any week of the war: 232 killed in action, 1,381 wounded in action, and four missing in action, a total of 1,617 American casualties in one week. The realization grew among the American public that the war was likely to be long, costly, and indecisive.

The underlying controversy within the Pentagon over the ground strategy to pursue in Vietnam was soon brought into the open again. On March 18, 1967, General Westmoreland submitted to CINCPAC an analysis of his additional force requirements projected through June of 1968. Westmoreland indicated that although he had not strongly objected to the 470,000-man ceiling established earlier, reassessment of the situation had made it clear that that force, although enabling the United States to gain the initiative, did not permit "sustained operations of the scope and intensity required to avoid an unreasonably protracted war." Thus, General Westmoreland indicated, the minimum essential force needed to exploit success and to retain effective control of areas being cleared of enemy influence was an additional two and one-third divisions with a total of twenty-one maneuver battalions. He considered the optimum force to be four and two-thirds divisions, which, with supporting forces, would total some 200,000 men in addition to the 1967 ceiling of 470,000.[49]

After developing more detailed justification for these figures, the Joint Chiefs formally reported to the secretary of defense on April 20, 1967, that additional forces were needed to achieve the objectives *they* considered the United States to be pursuing in Vietnam. The request of the Joint Chiefs reaffirmed the basic objectives and strategy that had been contained in each troop request since 1965 but that had now become a point of issue within the administration. The military leaders repeated the view that the U.S. national objective in South Vietnam remained the attainment of a stable and independent noncommunist government. They indicated that the military missions necessary to achieve that [basically political] goal were the following:

(a) Making it as difficult and costly as possible for the NVA to continue effective support of the VC and to cause North Vietnam to cease direction of the VC insurgency;
(b) To defeat the VC/NVA and force the withdrawal of NVA forces;
(c) Extend government dominion, direction and control;
(d) To deter Chinese Communists from direct intervention in SEA.

They then listed the three general areas of military effort that they felt were necessary in pursuit of those missions:

1. Operations against the Viet Cong/North Vietnamese Army (VC/NVA) forces in SVN while concurrently assisting the South Vietnamese Government in their nation-building efforts;
2. Operations to obstruct and reduce the flow of men and materials from North Vietnam (NVN) to SVN;
3. Operations to obstruct and reduce imports of war-sustaining materials into NVN.

The military leaders believed that the American effort continued to be inadequate in each of these areas. In South Vietnam, insufficient forces prevented the establishment of a secure environment for the people. (This, in any case, should not have been an American responsibility. Where *was* the South Vietnamese army and government?) In North Vietnam, an expanded bombing campaign was required to reduce infiltration of men and supplies to the South, and in the third area, relatively little effort had been permitted. Therefore, in addition to the deployment of additional ground forces to South Vietnam, the Joint Chiefs strongly recommended increased effort against the enemy's strategic supply lines into North Vietnam. Again, the Joint Chiefs reiterated their belief that a reserve call-up and extension of terms of service were "the only feasible means of meeting the additional FY [fiscal year] 1968 requirements in the stipulated time frame." And in another plea for an approved strategy for the conduct of the war and freedom from civilian control, something they had been seeking since the first troop deployments in 1965, the military leaders recommended that their "military strategy for the conduct of the war in Southeast Asia . . . be approved in principle."[50]

Thus, the issues were squarely posed for the president. On April 25, 1967, General Westmoreland returned to the United States, ostensibly to address the Associated Press annual convention in New York. He and General Wheeler met with the president on April 27. Westmoreland indicated to the president that if the troops he requested were not provided, the war would not necessarily be lost but progress would certainly be slowed. He admitted that it was likely that the enemy would also add more troops, although he felt we had reached the crossover point where "attritions will be greater than additions to the [enemy] force." General Westmoreland concluded by estimating that with 565,000 men, the war could well go on for three years, but with a total of 665,000 as he had requested, it could be over in two years. General Wheeler repeated to the president his concern about the possibility of military threats in other parts of the world.[51]

In the Defense Department, meanwhile, the search for alternatives to West-moreland's troop request was intensive. The strategic concept on which the request was based was attacked directly by the civilians in the Defense Department, who preferred the strategy stated by McNamara in November 1966. They argued that a limit to the number of U.S. forces had to be imposed, thereby "stabilizing" the ground conflict. The Joint Chiefs, of course, fought back, declaring that this position would not permit early termination of the war on terms acceptable to the United States, provided little capacity for initiating new actions or "maintaining momentum," and presented "an alarming pattern" of realignment of U.S. objectives and intentions in Southeast Asia.[52]

The search for alternatives continued. In mid-July, the president sent Maxwell Taylor and Clark Clifford to the Far East, ostensibly to visit allies and to explain American policy. Their real purpose of trying to induce nations that had contributed token ground forces to the effort in Vietnam to commit more troops was no secret. These efforts, characterized in the press as the arm-twisting of reluctant allies, met with little or no success; indeed, President Marcos of the Philippines refused to meet with the president's representatives. This reluctance by Korea, Thailand, Australia, New Zealand, and the Philippines to feel a great deal of concern about the situation in Vietnam had a profound effect on Clifford. He was later to indicate that this trip and the reaction of these nations caused him to begin to question American policy in Vietnam.

In the meantime, analysts in the Defense Department had concluded that a total of 51,249 troops in maneuver battalions could be deployed to Vietnam without changing the policy of a one-year tour in Vietnam, without calling up reserves, and without deploying NATO-reinforcing units in the United States. In his budget message to Congress on August 3, 1967, President Johnson disclosed plans to dispatch "at least 45,000" additional troops to South Vietnam in that fiscal year, bringing the total authorized troop strength in the war zone to 525,000 American forces. This was Program 5, officially published by the Defense Department on August 14. The press and the public greeted this announcement with a certain resignation bordering on apathy.[53]

The arguments about strategy went on throughout the summer. But once again, what should have been a fundamental argument as to American purposes in South Vietnam was reduced to one crucial factor—the single issue of what force buildup could be supported without mobilizing the reserves. When the president began to search for the elusive point at which the costs of Vietnam would become unacceptable to the American people, he always settled on mobilization, the point at which reserves would have to be called up to support a war that was becoming increasingly distasteful to the American public. This constraint, with all its political and social repercussions, not any argument about strategic concepts or the "philosophy" of the war, dictated American manpower policy.

The Joint Chiefs again failed to get agreement on their strategic concept for fighting the war. Indeed, a change in concept or in objectives was not even mentioned in the decision to allocate additional limited ground forces to the war. But the forces allocated, in numbers far below that deemed necessary by the military to pursue their tactical concept, would necessarily force a change in the way the war was pursued on the battlefield. The illusion of military victory faded into the distant future. On this occasion, Secretary McNamara apparently felt more strongly than he had in the past that the course to be pursued in Vietnam be reviewed and approved at the highest level. The secretary of defense forwarded a personal memorandum to the president on November 1, 1967, that spelled out his feeling that the continuation of the present course of action in Vietnam "would be dangerous, costly, and unsatisfactory to our people." In his memorandum, McNamara suggested alternative moves toward "stabilization of our military operations in the South . . . and of our air operations in the North, along with a demonstration that our air attacks on the North are not blocking negotiations leading to a peaceful settlement."

McNamara concluded his unusual memorandum with three recommendations, strikingly similar to the ones he had made in August 1966. First, he suggested that the United States announce that it would not expand air operations in the North or the size of combat forces in the South beyond those already planned. Second, he proposed a bombing halt before the end of 1967. Finally, he favored a new study of military operations in the South aimed at reducing U.S. casualties and giving the South Vietnamese greater responsibilities for their own security.[54]

President Johnson gave McNamara's memorandum long and careful consideration. He had already addressed the alternative strategy advocated by the Joint Chiefs. At a White House luncheon on September 12, the president had asked his military advisers to recommend additional actions within existing policy limitations that would increase pressure on North Vietnam and accelerate the achievement of U.S. objectives in South Vietnam. Here, again, however, the military chiefs showed neither flexibility, imagination, nor creativeness. In their reply, on October 17, 1967, the Joint Chiefs indicated, in rather a resigned tone, that they considered the rate of progress to have been and to continue to be slow largely because U.S. military power had been constrained in a manner that had significantly reduced its impact and effectiveness. Military operations had been hampered in four ways, they argued:

a. the attacks on enemy military targets had been on such a prolonged, graduated basis that the enemy had adjusted psychologically, economically, and militarily, e.g., inured themselves to the difficulties and hardships accompanying the war, dispersed their logistic support system, and developed alternative transport routes and a significant air defense system; b. areas of sanctuary, containing important military targets, had been afforded the enemy; c. covert operations in Cambodia and Laos had been restricted; d. major importation of supplies into North Vietnam by sea had been permitted.[55]

Pessimistically, the Joint Chiefs indicated that progress would continue to be slow as long as these limitations on military operations continued. The military leaders then listed a series of steps they believed should be taken. Their recommendations included removing restrictions on the air campaign against all militarily significant targets in North Vietnam, mining North Vietnam's deep-water ports and North Vietnam inland waterways and estuaries north of twenty degrees north, extending naval surface operations north of twenty degrees north, increasing air interdiction in Laos and along North Vietnamese borders, eliminating operational restrictions on B-52s in Laos, expanding ground operations in Laos and Cambodia, and expanding and reorienting covert programs in North Vietnam. Significantly, none of these recommendations was directed toward strengthening an army or a government of South Vietnam, which, since 1964, had been incapable of providing security to its people. The Americanization of the war was complete.

The president reviewed the recommendations of the Joint Chiefs. Many of them had already been rejected previously and would not now be approved. And so it finally appeared that the military chiefs had accepted the political restrictions imposed on them by the commander in chief. On November 27, 1967, in response to another presidential request to recommend military action in Southeast Asia over the next four months, the military chiefs reiterated their pessimistic analysis: "There are no new programs which can be undertaken under current policy guidelines which would result in a rapid or significantly more visible increase in the rate of progress in the near term."[56]

Thus, the president was aware of how widely the secretary of defense's proposals varied from the recommendations of his military leaders. Surprisingly enough, however, it does not appear that the military leaders threatened or even contemplated resigning to dramatize their differences with and opposition to the limitations on the conduct of the war insisted on by the president and his civilian advisers. President Johnson was aware of the possible political effects of such a military defection, and he had temporized in order not to push his loyal military leaders to such a point. Although he never approved the strategy that the Joint Chiefs continued to recommend, he never completely ruled it out either. He allowed the military chiefs a gradual increase in their combat forces and held out the possibility of greater combat authority in the future. He was successful in pointing out the political limitations that prevented his meeting all of their requests while never finally rejecting those requests.

But now the alternatives seemed clear. The president pondered McNamara's proposals over the next few weeks, consulting administration officials, close personal friends, and members of Congress. President Johnson, on December 18, 1967, wrote a personal memorandum for the permanent files giving his view of McNamara's proposals. The president had concluded that a unilateral bombing halt would "be read both in Hanoi and the United States as a sign of weakening will," although he agreed with Secretary of State Dean Rusk that we should "strive to remove the drama and public attention" from the bombing of North Vietnam. The president went a long way toward approving McNamara's concept of ground strategy. Although he considered that the announcement of a so-called policy of stabilization would have undesirable political effects, he also indicated that he could see no basis at the moment for increasing U.S. forces above the current approved level. Finally, the president accepted McNamara's suggestion that military operations in South Vietnam be reviewed with a view to reducing U.S. casualties and accelerating the turnover of responsibility to the South Vietnamese government. Shortly before, President Johnson had announced that McNamara would soon leave his post as secretary of defense and would be appointed president of the World Bank.[57] Although the Joint Chiefs may have been placated by the removal of McNamara and were hopeful that their strategy would be approved by his successor, the president in large part had agreed with McNamara's proposed ground strategy.

The president had discussed the McNamara proposals with, among others, General Westmoreland, the ground commander in Vietnam. Westmoreland had been summoned home along with Ambassador Ellsworth Bunker in mid-November to appear on television and before Congress in order to stress the progress being made in Vietnam. In a major address to the National Press Club on November 21, 1967, Westmoreland indicated,

It is conceivable to me that within two years or less, it will be possible for us to phase down our level of commitment and turn more of the burden of the war over to the Vietnamese Armed Forces who are improving and who, I believe, will be prepared to assume this greater burden.[58]

Thus, with the president's apparent intention to study turning over more of the war to the Vietnamese while sending no more American ground forces to Vietnam and with General Westmoreland's specific and public enunciation of this policy, the debate about strategic concepts within the administration seemed to have come to a consensus. American forces in Vietnam would be stabilized at 525,000, and the Vietnamese would be forced to carry a larger share of the load. This strategy promised a limit on the American commitment to Vietnam while putting emphasis on the essential role of the South Vietnamese in defending their nation. The illusion of an American military victory on behalf of its hapless South Vietnamese allies finally seemed to have been abandoned both by the president and by American military leaders.

Chapter Eight

The Tet Offensive

The United States entered 1968 in a mood of cautious optimism concerning the course of the war in Vietnam. Although the press and the Congress were becoming increasingly skeptical about the extent and the success of the American effort, the president and his principal advisers remained optimistic. Only Secretary McNamara, among the president's closest advisers, had expressed doubts about the course of the American effort, and his doubts had led to his departure from the cabinet. How shallow and tenuous American military gains might be, however, was disclosed in General Westmoreland's year-end assessment of the military situation. This assessment, which was furnished on January 26, 1968, and was little noticed in the excitement that followed, gave an optimistic view of the military situation but was much less sanguine about political progress. General Westmoreland reported, "The GVN [government of South Vietnam] is not yet a ready and effective partner with its own people. The Viet Cong infrastructure remains basically intact; and corruption is both corrosive and extensive."[1]

But, as had been true throughout the war, American progress depended almost totally on what Hanoi would do, what resources North Vietnam would devote to the war, and what strategy it would pursue. And Hanoi had long since begun to implement a new strategy that would, within a month after the new year began, dash American optimism and put the Johnson administration and the American public through a profound political catharsis. The massive Tet attack on the cities and towns of South Vietnam would engender in Washington the most soul-searching debate of the entire war.

By July 1967, the North Vietnamese have indicated, they had decided upon a major revision in strategy from that of protracted war to what came to be known as "general offensive, general uprising." From Hanoi's standpoint, the war in the South was not going well. Their forces had not won a significant battle in two years. Hanoi needed a decisive victory in order to create the military, political, and psychological conditions that would destroy both the political foundations of the Saigon regime and political support for the war in the United States. Large-scale attacks across South Vietnam, they felt, would precipitate a general uprising, destroying the Saigon government and making it psychologically and politically impossible for the United States to continue to pursue the war. Negotiations to end the war could then follow.

A general military and diplomatic offensive was first discussed at the Thirteenth Party Plenum held in Hanoi from January 23 to 27, 1967. As the Vietnamese explained it recently,

> A decision was taken at the Plenum which was designed to open a new stage of struggle; that is, to continue the armed struggle while preparing for the conditions favorable to peace negotiations. The resolution said that the success of the military and political struggle in South Vietnam must be the decisive factor for victory on the battlefield, and that this victory will serve as the foundation for success in the diplomatic field. That is: we can only win at the negotiating table what we have already won on the battlefield.

However, diplomatic struggle does not merely reflect the success of the armed struggle. The resolution said that in light of the then present-day world conditions and the nature of the present war, diplomatic struggle plays an active role, full of initiative. This new line was reflected in two statements (in January and December 1967) by Foreign Minister Nguyen Duy Trinh of the Democratic Republic of North Vietnam (DRV), stating the DRV's readiness to hold talks with the United States following unconditional cessation of bombing and other acts of war against the DRV.[2]

Operationally, Hanoi's plan was to distract and overextend United States forces through massive attacks on the frontiers, far from the populated areas. Having thus diverted attention by these large, costly, but deceptive battles, the major attacks would be directed by specially trained forces against the government administrative structure in the towns and cities. With the collapse of the government and the expected general uprising of the population, the United States would be faced with a fait accompli—a crumbling government and army in South Vietnam. The United States would have no recourse but to enter into negotiations, leading to a coalition government and the withdrawal of American forces.

As the North Vietnamese recently indicated, in planning for the offensive, they allowed for three possibilities:

1. *Very Big Victory.* This would compel the U.S. to enter negotiations, to seek an end to the war and to withdraw U.S. troops.
2. *Big Victory.* This would be a major setback for the U.S. military position. However, the U.S. would still be able to increase its troop strength and stabilize the situation. Fighting would continue.
3. *Limited Victory.* The U.S. would increase its troop strength, and even expand the war to the North, Cambodia, and Laos.[3]

By July, the North Vietnamese claim that they had developed concrete plans and began to make preparations. As early as October, the communist plan was put into effect with a series of bloody battles in remote areas along the borders of South Vietnam. Determined North Vietnamese forces attacked the marine base at Con Thien near the Demilitarized Zone (DMZ). Then communist forces struck Loc Ninh and Song Be, farther south along the Cambodian border. Beginning November 3 and continuing for twenty-two days, the North Vietnamese fiercely attacked Dak To in the central highlands. December saw the fighting spread to the Mekong Delta. In January, the enemy moved in strength against the marine outpost at Khe Sanh near the DMZ. Two North Vietnamese divisions were soon identified in the vicinity, the 325th Division and the 304th Division, elite units that had participated in the triumph at Dien Bien Phu. Faced with this massive enemy buildup, General Westmoreland decided to hold Khe Sanh rather than withdraw. He felt that this base guarded the approaches to Quang Tri City and the two northern provinces of Quang Tri and Thua Thien. In addition, the apparent determination of the enemy to take the base argued for holding it in order to tie down large North Vietnamese forces that otherwise could move against the populated areas. In any case, this border fight fit General Westmoreland's predilection for fighting on the frontiers and away from the populated areas. He believed that in these areas, fires were more effective because they were not restricted by political constraints or by the presence of civilians. He defended this strategy in a cable to the Chairman of the Joint Chiefs of Staff:

When we engage the enemy near the borders we often preempt his plans and force him to fight before he is fully organized and before he can do his damage. Although such fighting gets high visibility in the press, it has low visibility to the people of South Vietnam since it is not being fought in their front yard.

The similarities between Khe Sanh and Dien Bien Phu, in terms of both terrain and enemy action, quickly attracted the attention of the American press and public. The president followed the action closely and had a terrain model of the battle area constructed in the White House Situation Room. Having decided to defend Khe Sanh, General Westmoreland simply could not permit the position to be taken. The Korean marine brigade was shifted from the South to the Da Nang area to relieve American marines so that they could shift northward if necessary. Operation Niagara, a reconnaissance and fire-power program in support of the outpost, was begun, with Westmoreland personally directing B-52 strikes in support of the beleaguered outpost.[4]

The North Vietnamese have indicated the major thrust would be in the urban centers because they knew that U.S. forces would be located mainly in the peripheral areas, such as the central highlands and Khe Sanh, thus leaving the urban areas vulnerable to attack. As the Vietcong began extensive infiltration of South Vietnam's cities, indications of their plan began to reach U.S. officials. An intelligence summary prepared in Saigon on December 8 accurately predicted a "general counteroffensive and general uprising" designed to lure allied units to the border areas, allow the communists to control the country's armed forces and local administration, and force the Americans "to withdraw from South Vietnam in a short period of time." Indeed, the attack order for the communist offensive had been captured by American forces on November 19, 1967. The order stressed that strong military attacks would be used "in coordination with the uprisings of the local population to take over towns and cities." In releasing this document on January 5, however, the U.S. press release cautioned that the document could not be taken as conclusive evidence that such an order had been given and might represent merely an internal propaganda document "designed to inspire the fighting troops." Washington intelligence analysts were inclined to think the coming campaign was to be merely a continuation of past communist strategy.[5]

Although an attack was felt to be imminent, it was initially inconceivable to the American command and to the South Vietnamese that military action would come during the Tet holidays. Tet is the Vietnamese holiday celebrating the arrival of the Chinese lunar New Year. But it is much more than that. It has been described as "a combination All Souls' Day, a family celebration, a spring festival, a national holiday, and an overall manifestation of a way of life." In North Vietnam as well as in South Vietnam, it is the nation's most important and most sacred holiday, universally cherished by every religious group and social class. The unique and peaceful nature of the Tet holiday had been stressed throughout the course of the Vietnam War. Beginning in 1963, the North Vietnamese had proclaimed annual battlefield cease-fires for Christmas, New Year's Day, Buddha's birthday, and Tet. The Saigon government and the United States followed suit beginning with Christmas 1965. These recurrent holiday truces quickly became expected in Vietnam, although the U.S. command complained of massive communist violations and supply movements during the truce periods. Very few Americans were aware that the greatest feat of arms in Vietnam's history was considered to be the epic surprise attack by Nguyen Hue (Quang Trung) on the Chinese garrison in Hanoi during Tet of 1789.[6]

By early January, General Westmoreland felt that in view of the obvious enemy buildup, the annual Tet cease-fire should be canceled. However, the South Vietnamese demurred. The army, as well as the rest of the nation, looked forward to the traditional respite. It was agreed, however, that the cease-fire would be limited to a thirty-six-hour period (1800, January 29, to 0600, January 31) rather than the forty-eight hours previously scheduled. By January 24, both Ambassador Bunker and General Westmoreland, in a joint message to the president, indicated that it was undesirable to have any truce in Quang Tri, the DMZ, and at least part of North Vietnam. The president agreed that the cease-fire would not apply in the I Corps area, the DMZ, or North Vietnam south of Vinh. President Thieu of South Vietnam concurred but indicated that he would withhold public announcement of these exceptions until six hours before the cease-fire began. But the Vietnamese announcement never came. Saigon was in a festive mood on the eve of Tet. For the city dwellers, the war seemed remote. At least half the Army of the Republic of South Vietnam (ARVN) had departed for their homes to celebrate Tet. President Thieu was celebrating at his wife's hometown of My Tho in the Mekong Delta.[7]

According to the lunar calendar, the Year of the Monkey was to begin on Tuesday, January 30. In a virtually unnoticed action, however, the North Vietnamese government announced that the celebration would begin one day earlier. Thus, the families of North Vietnam were able to celebrate the important first day of Tet together in peace, prior to the anticipated retaliatory American air raids. In the early morning hours of January 31, 1968, the North Vietnamese launched a series of simultaneous and coordinated attacks against the major population centers in III and IV Corps Tactical Zones (CTZ). Attacks had been launched against the major cities of I and II CTZ the previous night. During the period January 30–31, thirty-nine of South Vietnam's forty-four provincial capitals, five of its six autonomous cities, and at least seventy-one of 245 district towns were attacked by fire and ground action. The offensive was aimed primarily at civilian centers of authority and military command installations. At 9:45 A.M. on Tuesday, January 30, the U.S. and Saigon governments canceled the Tet truce, which by then had become meaningless. In Saigon, the enemy attack began with a sapper assault on the American embassy, rapidly followed by assaults on Tan San Nhut Air Base, the Presidential Palace, the Republic of Vietnam Armed Forces Joint General Staff headquarters compound, and other government installations. Large enemy forces infiltrated into Hue and captured the Imperial Citadel and most of the city. Hue was in enemy hands despite heavy reinforcement by the U.S. and South

Vietnamese forces until February 25. The fighting continued throughout the country and gradually tapered off by February.

There is no doubt that the American command had not anticipated the true nature of the Vietcong attacks. General Westmoreland acknowledged,

> The extent of this offensive was not known to us, although we did feel it was going to be widespread. The timing was not known. I frankly did not think they would assume the psychological disadvantage of hitting at Tet itself, so I thought it would be before or after Tet. I did not anticipate that they would strike in the cities and make them their targets.[8]

Few U.S. or GVN officials believed that the enemy would attack during Tet. Neither did the Vietnamese public. A second major unexpected element was the number of simultaneous attacks mounted. American intelligence had given the enemy a capability of attacking virtually all the points that he did in fact attack and of mounting coordinated attacks in a number of areas. He was not, however, granted a specific capability for coordinated attacks in all areas at once. More important, the nature of the targets was not anticipated. Underlying these specific problems was a more basic one: most commanders and intelligence officers at all levels did not visualize the enemy as capable of accomplishing his stated goals as they appeared in propaganda and in captured documents. Prevailing estimates of attrition, infiltration, and local recruitment; reports of low morale; and a long series of defeats had downgraded the American image of the enemy.

The communist leaders had made a radical departure from their strategy of prolonged war. They sought decisive objectives that were considered sufficiently important to justify paying a very high price. Their purposes in thus changing their strategy were twofold. Their first goal was to destroy GVN military and political control, generate a spontaneous uprising or create the impression of spontaneous uprisings against the GVN, and cause the disaffection of units of the ARVN. To these ends, Vietcong forces conducted the initial assaults, while North Vietnamese forces were retained for follow-up attacks and exploitation. In these objectives, however, the enemy failed. Throughout the country, there was no instance in which the population welcomed the Vietcong, and there were no defections from political or military ranks. Indeed, the ARVN fought valiantly in almost every case, although it was caught in a "pre-Tet" posture, with half its personnel on leave and with security relaxed.

The second purpose of the communist attack was psychological. The attacks apparently were designed "to discourage the United States, to shake the faith of the people of South Vietnam in the ability of the United States and their own Government to protect them, and to impress all concerned with the strength and popular support of the Viet Cong." This would leave Hanoi in a position of strength from which it could negotiate a cease-fire and the eventual withdrawal of American forces. Ambassador Bunker indicated that, based on this analysis, he considered the "primary purpose of the operation to be psychological, rather than military." In this psychological objective, the communists were more successful, both in South Vietnam as well as in the United States. General Westmoreland reported the unfavorable psychological effects on the Vietnamese people to include

> added fear and respect of Communist capabilities, more fence-straddling by the uncommitted, and greater war weariness. . . . From a realistic point of view, we must accept the fact that the enemy has dealt the GVN a severe blow. He has brought the war to the cities and the towns and has inflicted damage and casualties on the population.[9]

On the other hand, Westmoreland pointed out some of the more favorable psychological factors. "There is anger at the Communist violence and atrocities," he reported. Thus, although it soon became apparent to the American command in Saigon that the enemy had suffered a severe military defeat and had paid a high price for the change in strategy, losing large numbers of high-quality troops, the question remained whether he had secured in spite of his losses a decisive psychological victory both in Saigon and in the United States. The public, the media, and the government in the United States were shocked by the unexpected attacks.

In the aftermath of the offensive, President Johnson was anxious to send whatever additional forces were needed by his field commander in Vietnam in order to prevent a politically damaging defeat. Faced with this fact and with communist threats in Korea, Berlin, and possibly elsewhere in the world, the Joint Chiefs of Staff saw Tet as an opportunity, perhaps one last opportunity, to force the president's hand and to achieve their long-sought goal of the removal of restraints on military action in Vietnam, Laos, and Cambodia as well as a mobilization of reserve forces. Emphasizing the gravity of the situation in Vietnam, the Chairman of the Joint Chiefs, General Earle Wheeler, after a visit to Saigon and consultations with the field commander, recommended that 206,000 additional men be added to the American military through mobilizing the reserves. Some of these troops would be sent to Vietnam, but most would be used to reconstitute the strategic reserve in the United States to guard against contingencies in other parts of the world, although this was not made completely clear in the chairman's report to the president.

By stressing the dangers inherent in the Vietnamese battlefield, General Wheeler hoped to persuade the president, who would not endure a defeat, and a new secretary of defense, Clark Clifford, who was known for his support of American strategy in Vietnam, that the time had come for, indeed necessitated, drastic action. Although the critical underlying issue was mobilization in order to reconstitute the strategic reserve, this aspect of the troop request was subordinated to the field commander's apparent needs. Once the strategic reserve had been reconstituted and the nation put on a virtual war footing, resources and authority would finally be available for achieving the illusory military victory in Vietnam to which the military still clung. The Joint Chiefs, therefore, saw Tet not as a repudiation of past efforts in Vietnam but as an opportunity to attain their basic objective of military victory by eliminating the hated civilian control and restrictions on military operations that they felt had hampered military efforts to date.[10]

The choices that the Chairman of the Joint Chiefs presented to President Johnson were not attractive. Accepting General Wheeler's request for troops would mean a total U.S. military commitment to South Vietnam, a further Americanization of the war, a large call-up of reserve forces, and a need to put the economy on a war footing to meet vastly increased expenditures—all in an election year and at a time of growing dissent, dissatisfaction, and disillusionment about the purpose, conduct, and cost of the war and all of this accompanied by no guarantee of military victory in the near future. On the other hand, to deny the request for troops or to attempt again to cut it to a size that could be sustained by the thinly stretched active forces would signal that an upper limit to the U.S. military commitment in South Vietnam finally had been reached, that the illusion of military victory had been discarded, and that an end to the war satisfactory to the United States had become remote or even unlikely.

But elements were now at work in the body politic of the United States that made this choice an inevitable one for a beleaguered president. Decisions that had been avoided in past years could no longer be avoided. The political reality that faced President Johnson in 1968 was that more of the same in South Vietnam, with an increased commitment of American lives and money and its consequent impact on the country, accompanied by no guarantee of victory in the near future, had become unacceptable to major elements of the American public. After the shock of the Tet offensive, the military reports of success no longer rang true. The impression grew that significant progress had not been achieved. The American people finally recognized the possibility of military victory as illusory and remote, and the cost had become too high in political, economic, and military terms. The illusion of military victory by the United States seemed finally to have been put aside by the American people.

The Tet offensive provided dramatic evidence that the progress toward a military victory had been illusory and that an alternative policy had to be found. It was a time for reassessing American purposes and policies in Vietnam not only within the administration but also within the whole political process of the nation. The existing policy was shown not to be producing the results expected in a reasonable time or at an acceptable cost. It was seen that the costs—political, materiel, and human—of obtaining satisfactory results in Vietnam within a reasonable period of time would be more than the nation was willing to pay. The public could not see a triumphant end to the war. In his book *Big Story*, Peter Braestrup charged that the press, by concentrating on the attacks and by failing to report the follow-up and subsequent North Vietnamese and Vietcong casualties, gave the American people a distorted image of the results of the Tet offensive.[11]

Nevertheless, it was apparent to all that in order to produce quicker or more decisive results, the commitment of resources would have to be increased vastly, and the whole nature of the war and its relationship to the United States would be changed. There was strong indication that large and growing elements of the American public had begun to believe that the cost had already reached unacceptable levels and that the objective was no longer worth the price. It was brought home to President Johnson finally that the policy being pursued in Vietnam, no matter how he had tried to limit it, would no longer be supported by the American electorate. The political reality—recognized by the president—was that without necessarily renouncing the former policy, a new and less costly strategy had to be found. All of America seemed to yearn for the magic solution, the way to peace with honor.

Since the beginning of hostilities involving major U.S. forces in Vietnam, there was a core group of dissidents protesting the war and the draft that supported it. But largely, these groups were on college campuses and were non-political, disorganized, and small with little overall leadership. They seemed to be peripheral to the war effort that initially had the support of the vast majority of the American people. Indeed, Lyndon Johnson was remarkably successful in keeping the Vietnam war "above politics." However, the Tet offensive of 1968 raised the issue of American policy in Vietnam and renewed antiwar sentiment. It seemed to reinforce the feeling among the American people that the war was bogged down and that a military success would not be found in the near future. Demonstration against the war increased on campuses and in the streets.

Shortly after the battles at Tet, the challengers to the president in both parties began to speak up. The Vietnam War became the major issue of the still embryonic presidential campaign. This issue dominated all other policy concerns. One man came to the conclusion that, however hopeless the odds, the incumbent president and his war policies must be challenged by something more than street and campus demonstrations. On November 30, 1967, Senator Eugene McCarthy announced his candidacy for the Democratic nomination for president, thus becoming the leader of an insurgency that was to deeply divide the Democratic Party.[12] The results of the New Hampshire Democratic primary held on March 12, which McCarthy had entered reluctantly under pressure to rally his support insofar as it existed, came as a shock. McCarthy, the peace candidate, had made a surprisingly strong showing. With the president's vulnerability on Vietnam demonstrated, Senator Robert Kennedy, his political opponent on Vietnam and other issues, on March 16 announced that he would be a candidate for the Democratic presidential nomination.

For President Johnson, the threat was now real. McCarthy, even in the flush of a strong showing in New Hampshire, could not be reasonably expected to unseat the incumbent president. But Kennedy was another matter. His candidacy gave the peace movement instant credibility and respectability. The president now faced a long and divisive battle for nomination within his own party against a very strong contender, with the albatross of an unpopular war hanging around his neck. Lyndon Johnson had become a wartime president, an appellation he had tried so hard to avoid, and the country now hungered for some movement toward peace in Vietnam. The war in Vietnam had become a partisan political issue. After consultations with his friends, political advisers, and cabinet members, the president, in a speech to the American people on March 31, 1968, announced four major decisions that were to have a profound effect on American political life and on the conduct of the war in Vietnam: (1) he would make only a token increase in the size of American forces in South Vietnam in response to the call of the military for major reinforcements and reconstitution of the strategic reserve, (2) he would make the expansion and improvement of the South Vietnamese armed forces the first priority of the continuing effort in Vietnam, (3) he would stop the bombing of a major portion of North Vietnam in order to move toward peace, and (4) he would not accept his party's nomination for another term as president.[13]

Unexpectedly, the North Vietnamese accepted the president's offer to negotiate only "the unconditional stopping of the bombing and other acts of war against North Vietnam." After a period of disagreement as to the venue of the negotiations, it was agreed by both sides that they would meet for negotiations in Paris. These particular negotiations concluded successfully with some "conditions" on October 31, several days before the election that brought Richard M. Nixon to the presidency.

To the North Vietnamese, then, the Tet offensive appeared to be a triumph. Nguyen Khac Huynh concluded that

> the main significance of the Tet offensive lies in the fact that it was a decisive blow which brought to light the bankruptcy of the U.S. local war, and thus broke the will of the U.S. aggressors and compelled them to de-escalate and proceed

toward their withdrawal from South Vietnam. . . . We still believe that this was the event that forced the U.S. to begin to think about ending the war—ending their involvement in Vietnam. . . . We achieved the second possibility (Big Victory) or perhaps a bit more.

The Tet offensive should also be viewed in terms of its context and total impact. . . . Whatever one may say about the various aspects of the Tet offensive, it was launched at the most appropriate moment, when the U.S. government was beset with huge internal, economic and external difficulties, and when its will to fight, its staying power, had already been seriously eroded. This good timing was coupled with the nature of the widespread surprise attacks on all the urban centers in South Vietnam, which were then considered quite stable, thanks to U.S. intervention. Thus did the Tet offensive produce satisfactory political and diplomatic results from the point of view of the DRV and NLF [National Liberation Front]. The U.S. had to change its strategy, come to the negotiating table, and sit down with us to discuss in earnest a solution to end the war.[14]

March 1968, then, represented a de facto turning point in American military policy toward Vietnam. The president's objective—an independent noncommunist South Vietnam—remained the same. But after years of military effort, after years of pursuing the dangerous illusion of military victory, after years of political anguish in pursuit of that illusion, after years of increasing American forces in Vietnam and thus Americanizing the war, these decisions marked the limit of U.S. commitment of its military forces. The request of military leaders for a large increase in American forces would, in large part, be denied. The administration finally began to develop a strategy for attaining its objective that it hoped would not place an unlimited burden on the national and military resources of the nation that, it was hoped, would lower American battle casualties and could, over time, hold public acceptance. The decisions at Tet to limit U.S. troop levels and to place more reliance on the South Vietnamese represented a long-overdue rationalization of the American effort in Vietnam and a return to the basic principles that had been used to justify American intervention in Vietnam in the first place. It finally became clear to American leaders that the road to ending the war in Vietnam depended as much on South Vietnamese political and military development as it did on American arms. This realization, which had been recognized in 1964 and 1965 prior to the American takeover from an obviously failing South Vietnamese government and army, made it possible for the United States to return to the original purpose for which American forces had initially been sent to South Vietnam, that of preventing the loss to communism of the South Vietnamese government.

American forces, in almost the number then deployed, would continue to provide a shield behind which the South Vietnamese forces could rally and attempt to become effective in order to win the support of the people of South Vietnam. More weapons and equipment would be made available to the South Vietnamese, and pressure would be applied to allow, indeed require, progress in this long-neglected area. Clark Clifford, the successor to Robert McNamara as secretary of defense, gave notice finally to the South Vietnamese government that its open-ended claim on American resources and manpower had come to an end and that it would be expected to shoulder an increasing share of the war in the future.

Thus, the eventual outcome of March 1968, that of limiting the further increases of American manpower in Vietnam and improving Vietnamese forces to the point where they could take over more of the effort, represented opposite sides of the same coin. The dangerous illusion of some sort of military victory by the United States was dead. Hanoi's unexpected acceptance of Johnson's offer of negotiations became the major avenue for achieving American purposes in Vietnam. Although not explicitly stated at this time, the first steps on the road to American disengagement from Vietnam had begun. At the end of the Johnson administration, the cumulative totals of Americans killed in action in Vietnam since 1961 stood at more than 31,000. South Vietnamese casualties were close to 90,000.

Chapter Nine

The American Economy: Guns and Butter?

Lyndon Johnson would not be a wartime president. The legislation creating the Great Society and the money to make it effective was his great passion, his overriding concern. This is a major reason he refused to mobilize American reserve forces for the war. He would not put the American economy on a war footing. As late as 1966, President Johnson declared in his budget message to the Congress,

> We are a rich nation and can afford to make progress at home while meeting obligations abroad—in fact, we can afford no other course if we are to remain strong. For this reason, I have not halted progress in the great and vital Great Society programs in order to finance the cost of our efforts in Southeast Asia.[1]

In other words, the president felt that the nation could afford both guns and butter, and he was determined to have both.

And, of course, the nation could have had both if the necessary planning to pay for the war had been accomplished—with additional economic measures. The country was enjoying a period of economic prosperity, and the president focused on implementing major domestic programs in health, education, welfare, and civil rights—the Great Society. The administration was determined to continue economic growth so as to ensure a budget that could accommodate the envisioned expansion of domestic programs while at the same time containing the perceived growth of communist influence in Southeast Asia.

But this meant that the budget process had to be carefully controlled. It was not. As the administration pushed forward its domestic programs, the escalation of the Vietnam conflict was not transmitted to Johnson's budget planners or economic advisers. Vietnam planning and execution was almost completely outside the budget process. Escalation in Vietnam resulted in the addition of a billion dollars to the defense budget with no provisions for paying the larger bills that such escalation required. As escalation was planned and took place, the domestic budget planners remained in the dark. President Johnson initially felt that the war would be a short one and that the American economy could absorb the costs of a growing war and thereby escape overheating and the inflationary price increases that could result. He was bent on preserving the programs of the Great Society unchecked by the financial costs of paying for a war in Southeast Asia. But there was a growing realization in the administration over time that there would be no short-term solution to the Vietnam issue. A major commitment of manpower and finances would be needed over a long period.

The president consciously kept the functioning domestic portions of his administration from gaining a full appreciation of the costs associated with pursuing both a burgeoning domestic and foreign agenda. He deliberately excluded his economic and domestic advisers from his deliberations with the secretary of defense concerning the increasing expenditures in Vietnam over time. Consequently, his domestic advisers' recommendations concerning the expansion of domestic programs did not include the effects of increasing expenditures for the military. Conversely, the president, in considering Defense Department expenditures, did not want to place the economy on a war footing. Therefore, neither side of the government planned expenditures in coordination with the other. Johnson knew that such coordination would lead to increasing pressure to reduce either the military programs or the scope of the programs of the Great Society. Neither reduction was acceptable to the president. So military budget figures were considered independently of domestic budget requirements, and they were considered separately by Congress. Military policy was divorced from any specific overall economic policy.[2] Thus, for many reasons, domestic budget planners did not get a true idea of the military demands on American resources and finances.

The 1966 budget submitted to the Congress bore no relationship to reality. It actually forecast a decline in the defense budget. Preparation of this budget had begun in 1964 and was presented to Congress in 1965. At the time it was presented, the administration was beginning to carry out a major air offensive against North Vietnam and was planning for the introduction of American combat troop units into South Vietnam. But these were to be done with little discussion or publicity within the administration and the American public and were simply not addressed in the fiscal year 1966 budget. A budget supplement of $700 million for the Department of Defense was introduced in December and was passed by Congress with some reluctance.

The subsequent budget process was similarly bifurcated. Operating civilian agencies came up with their own budgets, but these were not integrated with the defense budget, which indeed often remained unknown to the president's economic advisers. There was a complete lack of overall economic coordination. The budget process as conducted in the Johnson administration was not well prepared to handle the effect on the civil programs associated with the military escalation taking place in Vietnam. President Johnson consciously kept the domestic functioning parts of his Great Society from gaining a full appreciation of the costs associated with simultaneously pursuing both growing domestic and growing foreign agendas. The president tried to have it both ways.

The first immediate effect of the military escalation was a rise in the consumer price index in the second quarter of 1965. But there was little concern in Washington at that time. The American economy, many economists felt, was growing and was prone to inflation. Expanding war expenditures in that sort of economy gave little slack, thus laying the ground for an overheated economy and inflation. Within the next few years, the failure to honestly account for the military costs associated with the military escalation in Vietnam was fairly devastating to the American economy. From 1965 to 1970, interest rates rose steadily, and inflation became long term. The budget deficit grew, and the trade surplus declined to a deficit. The U.S. surplus in its international balance dwindled rapidly in the final months of 1967. It seemed that the war, the Great Society, or the economy had to give. Given the president's stake in his Great Society programs as well as his pledge not to lose Vietnam, the economy was the element that suffered. The long-term result was that much of Johnson's domestic agenda was weakened because of a lack of financial resources. He hoped that continued economic prosperity would make it possible to afford both guns and butter. But he made little effort to accomplish that end. The situation was summed up succinctly by the Reverend Martin Luther King Jr. In several speeches in 1966 and 1967, he said, "The programs of Great Society have been shot down on the battlefields of Vietnam."[3]

During the busy days of March 1968, the economy again concerned President Johnson. The deficits and inflation in the United States generated uncertainties in international money markets and made the dollar particularly vulnerable to attack. The Tet offensive and its aftermath with the prospect of a large increase of American forces in Vietnam and consequently a large increase in American expenditures threatened a serious outbreak of speculative fever. The United States had lost $327 million to the speculators by March 14, and the president had to take action.[4] Over the weekend of March 16–17, treasury secretaries and heads of central banks from seven major nations hastily assembled to meet secretly in Washington. They established a new "two-tier" international gold exchange wherein gold could no longer be bought in the free market.[5]

For a time, the crisis had been averted, but the underlying problem that had given rise to it had not been resolved. Any great increase in outlays by the United States in Vietnam without cuts in expenditures for the Great Society or without increases in taxes could quickly result in renewed speculation, the downfall of the dollar, and a renewed international financial crisis. The national economy was very much on President Johnson's mind as he pondered his course in Vietnam.[6]

THE CLIMATE OF OPINION

In 1968, the Democrats gathered in Chicago to nominate Hubert Humphrey, President Johnson's vice president, as their candidate for president. But the 1968 Democratic convention was less notable for its politics than for its televised display of social unrest and national disunity. The country seemed to be at a boiling point. Two American icons, Martin Luther King Jr. and Robert Kennedy, had recently been assassinated. Every day, young American draftees were dying in a war that for many had already lost its meaning. War protesters gathered in Chicago determined to send a message to the Democratic Party and its nominee. But the mayor of Chicago, Richard Daley, was unsympathetic. He posted 12,000 police officers on the streets and called in the Illinois National Guard. Television cameras transmitted to American homes young Americans being beaten in the streets by angry police. The bloody riot resulted in police arresting more than 500 people in clashes that injured more than 100 police and 100 demonstrators.

The negotiations in Paris with the North Vietnamese resulted in a cessation of American bombing in the North on October 31, 1968. This, however, seemed too late to help the campaign of Hubert Humphrey. On Election Day, the Democratic candidate, although closing rapidly, was defeated by the Republican candidate by a small margin, being nosed out by half a million votes—less than a 1 percent difference.[7]

Chapter Ten

The Nixon Presidency

The new Nixon administration, when it came into office in 1969, apparently was determined to end the war in Vietnam, a war that had caused so much turmoil in American politics before and during the presidential campaign. The new president and his national security adviser, Henry Kissinger, felt that the war could be won by both military action and negotiation. However, the administration did not seem initially to have a specific plan for ending the war. The president finally tried almost every action that the Joint Chiefs of Staff had recommended for years as promising victory—the bombing of Hanoi, the mining of Haiphong Harbor, and the invasion of Cambodia and Laos. None of these actions seem to have been part of a well-thought-out strategy, and none made a military victory closer. Nor did any of them seem to influence the demands of North Vietnamese negotiators in Paris. The illusion of a military victory soon died quietly within the Nixon administration. President Nixon states in his memoirs,

I began my presidency with three fundamental premises regarding Vietnam. First, I would have to prepare public opinion for the fact that total military victory was no longer possible. Second, I would have to act on what my conscience, my experience, and my analysis told me true about the need to keep our commitments. . . . Third, I would have to end the war as quickly as was honorably possible.[1]

The president and his national security adviser continued to seek a breakthrough in the negotiations. The meetings that led to agreements reached in 1968 between Hanoi and the United States concerning stopping the bombing of North Vietnam were continued. The initial U.S. proposals for ending the war were unacceptable to the North Vietnamese negotiators. Their intransigence and their negotiating positions remained unchanged throughout. The unyielding position of the North Vietnamese was that political and military issues could not be separated, that all American troops must be withdrawn unilaterally from South Vietnam, that President Thieu must be removed from office, and that a coalition government including members of the National Liberation Front (NLF) should be established in the South. The American position was that military and political issues should be separated, that the withdrawal of American and North Vietnamese forces from South Vietnam should proceed, and that then the two Vietnamese sides could settle their political issues. Later, the United States added the release of prisoners of war to its negotiating agenda.[2]

The objective of the Nixon administration, narrowly elected in the expectation that it could bring peace in Vietnam, quickly became the development and implementation of a strategy for Vietnam that would result in the reduction or ending of American troops and casualties in Vietnam and eventually to the freeing of American prisoners held by the North Vietnamese/Vietcong. From the first, the president and his national security adviser fully expected that an acceptable solution to Vietnam would be achieved rather quickly through secret negotiations with the North. They also expected that by improving relations with the Soviet Union and the People's Republic of China, they could persuade these two communist nations to put pressure on the Democratic Republic of Vietnam to agree to terms favorable to the United States. Under the Vietnamization program announced by Nixon and ostensibly agreed to by President Thieu at a conference on Midway Island in June 1969, the goal would be the gradual but total withdrawal of American forces while turning the war over to an improved Army of the Republic of South Vietnam (ARVN) and a government capable of conducting the war and surviving by itself. If South Vietnamese forces could be strengthened sufficiently, U.S. troop withdrawals might gradually end American involvement.[3] In addition, the withdrawal of American forces and the consequent reduction of American casualties might win public support in the United States and would convey the image of a confident South Vietnam, indeed even giving the Saigon government a reasonable chance to survive and therefore perhaps giving Hanoi an incentive to negotiate seriously.

America's search for an agreement with North Vietnam was to be pursued through negotiations. The American ground forces in Vietnam would be reduced through the policy of Vietnamization and the war turned over to an improved ARVN and government capable of defending its territory and its people. This policy was designed to reduce the American military commitment in materials, money, and especially lives, thus maintaining American domestic support of the administration's actions while gradually phasing out American military forces as the South Vietnamese government and the ARVN tried to become effective, win the support of its people, and meet its own defense requirements. American equipment in profusion would be transferred to the ARVN to help it achieve this improved capability. But again, the conventional, not the antiguerrilla capabilities of the ARVN would be stressed.

However, withdrawing American forces unilaterally while attempting to negotiate mutual withdrawal of forces was not a strong negotiating position for the United States. The administration "was walking a fine line between withdrawing too fast to convince Hanoi of our determination and withdrawing too slowly to satisfy the American public."[4] Strengthening the ARVN was again a military, not a political, option. There seemed to be no programs to strengthen the government of South Vietnam or to try to make it competent, effective, and corruption free. And there was no new evidence that the South Vietnamese government and the ARVN would rise to this challenge and be able to accomplish by themselves what they had not been able to accomplish with massive American assistance.

Indeed, the North Vietnamese as well as the South Vietnamese saw the policy of Vietnamization for what it was—an effort to withdraw American forces from the South and to leave the government and army there with enough capability and equipment to last for a period of time.[5] After some time, after an "honorable peace," the nation would be unified by unremitting North Vietnamese conquest. As Colonel Quach Hai Luong of Vietnam described Vietnamization, "If before we had to fight two forces—both Saigon and US forces—then with Vietnamization we only had to deal with one and a half. And the result was that the Saigon forces could not endure."[6]

The Nixon administration, like the Johnson administration before it, soon came to the realization that it did not control events and did not control the pace of the war. Although it could give the South Vietnamese government military equipment and supplies, it could not give it what it had needed since 1964—a genuine, indigenous political competence or legitimacy. Complete American withdrawal from the war and the survival of the South Vietnamese government remained contradictory objectives as the South Vietnamese president recognized. The ultimate tragic result for South Vietnam of future American troop withdrawals, even with American airpower available, might have been predicted as inevitable.[7] And in the political realm, the NLF announced that a national congress had met in a "liberated area" in the South and had formed a Provisional Revolutionary Government (PRG), a legal government for the South that would take the place of the NLF at the Paris talks.[8]

During the first months of his presidency and as a signal to both Hanoi and Moscow, Nixon ordered bombing attacks against North Vietnamese sanctuaries in neutral Cambodia, a step advocated by General Abrams, the American commander in Vietnam. His recommendation had been rejected by the

Johnson administration. But he indicated to Nixon that intelligence had identified the North Vietnamese/NLF headquarters in Cambodia (the Central Office for South Vietnam [COSVN]) and that these bombing missions could destroy it and thus "will have an immediate effect . . . on future military
offensives which COSV may desire to undertake."9 Nixon intended by this
action to demonstrate to the leadership in Hanoi that he was prepared to take
measures that Johnson had refused to take, thus forcing North Vietnam into
negotiating on his terms. At Nixon's insistence, great lengths were taken to
keep the bombing in Cambodia secret from the American public, as the president felt that he had not been elected to widen the war.10

By the fall of 1969, General Abrams and the Joint Chiefs agreed that the
bombings, dubbed MENU, had failed in their primary mission: the destruction of COSVN. To avoid these bombings, North Vietnamese forces moved
further into Cambodia. A coup in Cambodia removed the neutralist Prince Si-
hanouk from power and installed his American-oriented prime minister, Lon
Nol, in his place. Although there is no direct evidence that the United States
was involved in this coup or had any reason for seeking it, this nation quickly
recognized the new government and offered military assistance. Nixon decided to take advantage of the change in Cambodian leadership by approving
General Abrams's recommendation that American ground forces enter Cambodia to eliminate the North Vietnamese headquarters still purported to be
there.11

The extension of the ground war to Cambodia in April 1970 provoked a domestic and congressional challenge to the president's authority greater than
any since the beginning of the war. The most visible and dramatic were street
and campus demonstrations, which seemed to have greatly influenced the
president's decision to withdraw troops from Cambodia by June 30; the most
significant in the long run in their impact on the Vietnam War were the related
reactions in Congress and among the general public. Spontaneous protests
and demonstrations broke out in communities and on college campuses
throughout the United States. These demonstrations resulted in student deaths
at Kent State and Jackson State universities in angry confrontations between
students and young National Guardsmen and police.12 The nation was
shocked at these deaths. The Senate voted to terminate the Tonkin Gulf Resolution of 1964. Restrictive amendments to cut off funds for military operations in Cambodia after June 30 and to withdraw American forces from Vietnam by 1971 were introduced. American troops were withdrawn from
Cambodia by June 30, and the protests gradually abated.13 But President
Nixon faced a hostile and determined opposition in Congress and a revived
domestic antiwar movement in the nation. The Cambodian incursion had not
been militarily decisive or even significant. "Winning the war militarily" in

South Vietnam was far from the minds of most Americans. As Kissinger saw it, "We were caught between an enemy unwilling to compromise and an antiwar movement in the Congress refusing either to admit that Hanoi might be implacable or to countenance military action that might have induced Hanoi to alter its terms."[14] But as Kissinger should have surmised, there was no military action that might induce the North Vietnamese to alter their goals. They were more interested in the unification of Vietnam then they were in achieving peace.

As 1970 came to an end, American forces in Vietnam had been reduced by some 200,000. It was time, perhaps, to determine the effectiveness of Vietnamization. An all-Vietnamese operation was planned in Laos. Designated as Operation Lam Son 719, its purpose, other than to check out ARVN's improved capabilities, was to cut temporarily the Ho Chi Minh Trail in Laos and for a time to disrupt enemy logistics capabilities to support an expected North Vietnamese attack in the northern part of South Vietnam later in the year.[15] American ground forces as well as advisers would not participate. The Senate, in the Cooper-Church Resolution, sought to prohibit American ground forces from operating in Cambodia and Laos. Although the House had rejected this resolution, the president was reluctant to challenge this war-limiting attitude in the Congress. He was also deeply concerned about the potential of public and antiwar protests against the sending of American troops into Laos, as had happened in Cambodia.[16] The South Vietnamese would have the benefit of American air support, to include helicopters and American artillery that could reach targets in Laos from within the borders of South Vietnam.

After preparations along Route 9 within South Vietnam by American forces, South Vietnamese forces entered Laos on February 7, 1971. Initially, they proceeded well against light opposition. However, the North Vietnamese were determined to protect their supply line and reinforced this area. Despite significant American airpower support, cautious South Vietnamese leadership soon halted the operation. Although reinforced ARVN forces reached the town of Tchepone, a supply crossroad on the Ho Chi Minh Trail, a timid President Thieu quickly terminated the operation thereafter. The ARVN lost little time in reversing its direction, and most South Vietnamese forces were out of Laos by March 25. The Laotian operation was at best a costly draw and at worst an unmitigated disaster. The operation not only failed to cut the Ho Chi Minh Trail but also exposed the ARVN's deficiencies. The entire operation raised serious questions about the success of Vietnamization.[17]

These operations in Cambodia, Laos, and the northern part of South Vietnam formed a backdrop to a spring season of peace demonstrations. There had been many and varied antiwar actions across the country in the first months of the year. During the third week of April, Vietnam Veterans Against the War (VVAW) began a series of poignant protests in the nation's capital that, as two historians of the movement characterized them, "carried the weight of tested patriotism, seeming to arise from the Vietnam conflict itself." On April 19, veterans laid wreathes at Arlington National Cemetery and on subsequent days conducted candlelight marches, staged mock search-and-destroy missions, attempted to turn themselves in as war criminals to Defense Department officials, and picketed the Supreme Court to demand that it rule on the war's constitutionality. Some, like Lieutenant John Kerry, testified before the televised hearings of the Senate Committee on Foreign Relations. On April 23, 700 VVAW members marched from their encampment on the Mall to the Capitol, where each in turn announced his name and then threw his war medals over a makeshift fence to the other side—back to the government that had sent them to war. These demonstrations were well covered by the media, and other demonstrations followed.

The majority of the public was now, however, more than ever turned off by street and campus protests. These demonstrations were unpopular with the majority of the American people. But these demonstrations, frequently covered by the media, contributed to a general perception of national malaise and crisis in the United States that made ending the war even more urgent.

THE APRIL OFFENSIVE AND LINEBACKER I

As the United States continued to build up the South Vietnamese armed forces and to reduce American forces, the North Vietnamese army completed its reorganization and rebuilding. The peace negotiations in Paris between Henry Kissinger and Le Duc Tho, the North Vietnamese representative, remained stalled. For their part, the North Vietnamese believed, as they had before Tet, that a shift of the military balance in their direction would serve to influence the negotiations in their behalf. At the end of March 1972, American military manpower in Vietnam stood at 95,000, down from more than 540,000 three years before. The war in the South seemed ominously quiet, although guerrillas still harassed the population in some areas and North Vietnamese forces remained active along the borders. This led some observers to believe—and to declare—that the North Vietnamese had ceased their long-standing nationalistic and revolutionary goal of unifying Vietnam and that the United States had effectively frustrated this and had therefore "won" the war. That judgment was premature. Subsequent to Nixon's visit to China and in the early morning darkness of Good Friday, March 30, 1972, the North Vietnamese army launched its long expected and largest attack of the Vietnam War up to that time. The army engaged in a conventional military attack by

North Vietnam across the border between the two nations as well as across the borders from Laos and Cambodia.[18] The attack apparently was designed to capture and hold territory in South Vietnam and possibly cause deterioration in the ARVN. Quang Tri province, the northernmost province of South Vietnam, was quickly lost by one of Thieu's inept political generals, and the South Vietnamese troops in I Corps began streaming south in panic. The great majority of American combat troop units had been withdrawn from Vietnam by that time, and those remaining did not take part in the battle. Only American advisers remained in South Vietnamese units. These advisers were crucial to the battle, however, as they provided a conduit for South Vietnamese units to American airpower. In many cases, their advice, courage, and mere presence bolstered the morale and fighting spirit of scared and tired South Vietnamese soldiers. In this offensive, the ARVN fought well when it received competent leadership, but it was American tactical airpower that was decisive.[19] Since the North Vietnamese were engaged in a conventional attack, their logistics train was vulnerable, and American tactical airpower was able to take advantage of that vulnerability. North Vietnamese units that crossed the Demilitarized Zone and the western border were quickly cut off from their supplies and were forced to retreat. The North Vietnamese conventional attack was vulnerable to American airpower as their guerrilla operations had not been. In addition, President Nixon, in an operation called Linebacker, resumed bombing areas of North Vietnam and also ordered the long-delayed mining of Haiphong Harbor.[20] A change in South Vietnamese military leadership, combined with massive American tactical airpower in support of South Vietnamese ground forces, stopped the attack and reversed the retreat of South Vietnamese forces. Eventually, the border was restored in most areas with great losses inflicted on North Vietnamese forces. In these battles, American advisers and their link to American tactical airpower had made a significant difference. This was a lesson that the South Vietnamese and American leadership quickly absorbed.

Like Lyndon Johnson before him, Nixon was immovably committed to the goals for which the United States had long struggled in Vietnam, and he was impervious to the peace movement's arguments about the war's immorality and folly. He was attentive, however, to the political costs that dissent exacted: the erosion of support for him and the war, the division within his own bureaucracy, the constriction of his military options in Vietnam, and the growing challenge from an emboldened Congress to his control of foreign policy. This domestic dissent led to two measures in Congress that aimed to reduce U.S. military activity in Vietnam and Southeast Asia. Two Democratic senators, John Sherman Cooper and Frank Church, sponsored legislation that would halt all U.S. military activity in Cambodia and Laos. The legislation was passed by the Senate on December 29, 1970. Senators John McGovern and Mark Hatfield proposed an amendment that would cut off all funds for the war and require the complete removal of American forces from Vietnam by the end of 1971.[21] Both these amendments were defeated but gave promise of coming up again in the future and with increasing support.

NEGOTIATIONS

President Nixon felt that, while continuing to pursue other military options, he would have to end the war by utilizing the ongoing negotiations with the North Vietnamese in Paris. Early in his administration, the president stated, "Since I had ruled out a quick military victory, the only possible course was to try for a fair negotiated settlement that would preserve the independence of South Vietnam. . . . I was prepared to take most of my first year in office to arrive at a negotiated agreement."[22]

It seems that Nixon was initially optimistic concerning negotiations with the North Vietnamese. He saw them lasting for one year. These negotiations actually were to last some four years and were to end in an agreement that would not "preserve the independence of South Vietnam." At the first meeting of the negotiators in Paris on August 4, 1969, the president, through his national security adviser, Henry Kissinger, made a proposal that political questions be separated from military questions and that the United States and North Vietnam settle the military questions by mutual withdrawal from the South, leaving the political settlement to the two Vietnamese sides. The North Vietnamese quickly rejected this proposal. Their long-held position, which they repeated consistently, was that the United States must withdraw its forces fully and immediately from South Vietnam and must force President Thieu of South Vietnam to step aside for a coalition government. The NLF delegation in Paris further announced that a national congress had met in a "liberated" part of South Vietnam and had formed the PRG of South Vietnam. This, they proclaimed, was the "legal government" of South Vietnam and would take the place of the NLF at the negotiations.[23] Although the public talks continued with South Vietnamese and PRG present, Kissinger quickly undertook secret private negotiations with Le Duc Tho, the North Vietnamese negotiator. Aside from a few National Security Council aides, only Kissinger, the president, and Ambassador Bunker would be aware of this separate negotiating track. Until January 1972, the State Department, the Joint Chiefs, the Central Intelligence Agency, and the Defense Department were kept ignorant of these negotiations. Although President Nixon and Kissinger assured President Thieu that he would be fully informed and consulted concerning these private discussions, especially those affecting South Vietnam, this was not to be the case. The private negotiations and the conclusions reached were kept secret from most of the Nixon administration as well as from the South Vietnamese.[24] A lengthy private meeting took place on February 21, 1970, but these private negotiations between Kissinger and Le Duc Tho remained deadlocked. From the beginning, the North Vietnamese continued to insist on the removal of South Vietnamese President Thieu and the establishment of a coalition government in the South. The United States refused to abandon President Thieu and insisted on the withdrawal of North Vietnamese forces from South Vietnam to match the American force withdrawal. The American negotiators also insisted on the release of all American prisoners of war held by the North Vietnamese and the Vietcong. Kissinger insisted that the United States would remain in South Vietnam, at least with a small residual force, as long as these prisoners were held.

The North Vietnamese, of course, continued to insist that there were no North Vietnamese forces in the South and later indicated that in any case these troops had a right to be there, as Vietnam was one country and their troops were not "foreign." The only foreign forces in South Vietnam, they insisted, were American forces, and they continued to insist on the withdrawal of all of them. They also seemed to be obsessed with the removal of General Thieu as president of South Vietnam. Throughout the fruitless negotiations, neither side would move from these opposing positions.

At this private meeting on February 21, 1970, Le Duc Tho provided Kissinger with the facts of life and with their determination as seen by the North Vietnamese:

> We have won and you have failed. . . . If our generation cannot win then our sons and nephews will continue. We will sacrifice everything but we will not again have slavery. This is our iron will. We have been fighting for 25 years, the French and you. . . . But you have read our history. We fought against the French for nine years. We were empty handed. . . . Yet we won victory.[25]

Perhaps Dr. Kissinger and his aides did not realize at that time that they were listening to more than a statement of Vietnamese communism. More important, they were listening to a statement of Vietnamese nationalism.

Madame Nguyen Thi Binh, the NLF representative at the negotiating sessions, finally seemed to have broken the deadlock. On September 17, 1970, she linked the fate of American prisoners of war to American troop withdrawals. She indicated that a cease-fire could then be implemented and that American prisoners could be released on the withdrawal of American forces.[26] The grim outcome of the spring offensive along with the realization that Nixon most probably would win the forthcoming American election seems to have convinced the North Vietnamese that it was time quickly to conclude a negotiated settlement. North Vietnam dropped its refusal to consider a military cease-fire in advance of a political settlement.[27]

The American president also seemed ready to compromise at this time. The American people were deeply tired of what seemed to be an interminable war, and Congress reflected their view. Congress was beginning to put political pressure to accelerate American troop withdrawals and disengage from the war, and the antiwar movement in the United States became more vocal, as there seemed to be no progress in the negotiations. President Thieu's legitimacy in South Vietnam, such as it was, was waning as he ran for president of South Vietnam unopposed. Consequently, in a nationwide talk on January 25, 1972, President Nixon proposed a new peace initiative. The president indicated that the United States would accept a cease-fire. As Kissinger later stated, "That North Vietnamese forces would remain in the South was implicit in the standstill proposal; no negotiations would be able to remove them if we had not been able to expel them with force of arms."[28] It seemed that the American side was willing to abandon its objectives in Vietnam in return for the withdrawal of American forces and the release of American prisoners. The president was reluctant to challenge Congress on war-limiting legislation. The American people, as represented by their Congress, no longer seemed to be interested in "winning" the long war.

Although negotiations were halted for periods during the American incursion into Cambodia, the South Vietnamese operation in Laos, and the North Vietnamese Easter offensive in April 1972, they quickly began again subsequent to each of those incidents. The Americans and the North Vietnamese agreed on October 12, 1972, to a preliminary peace agreement. Finally, Hanoi had separated military from political questions and no longer demanded Thieu's removal as a precondition for agreement. The agreement between the American and North Vietnamese negotiators stated, inter alia, that there would be "an Indochina-wide cease fire, withdrawal of U.S. forces, release of prisoners, no further North Vietnamese infiltration, the right to supply the South Vietnamese forces up to existing levels, and . . . the recognized continuation of the existing political structure in Saigon, eligible for U.S. economic and military aid."[29]

The cease-fire in place, of course, would leave North Vietnamese forces in areas they controlled in the South. With North Vietnamese forces remaining in strength while all American forces departed, the South Vietnamese government and the ARVN would be left to defend itself with its own resources, something it had never previously shown the capability of doing. Clearly understanding this, President Nixon promised President Thieu, in a letter on November 14, his "absolute assurance" that he would "take swift and severe retaliatory action "in the event the Communists renewed their aggression."[30] Although Kissinger was dispatched to reiterate this promise to the prime ministers of Thailand and Laos, this Nixon pledge was never mentioned to the Congress or to the American people, nor was it written in any other official document. The president felt that the American public would support the reintroduction of American airpower if the agreement were to be breached by the North. Thus, he foresaw a continuation of the war using American airpower to defend South Vietnam. But this was a flawed promise that would not be kept. Nixon's own personal difficulties in the Watergate affair as well as the attitude of Congress would keep America from reentering the Vietnam War once it withdrew its ground troops and obtained the release of its prisoners of war. After Hanoi had announced the terms of the agreement, Kissinger also announced to the public on October 26 the breakthrough in the negotiations, stating that "peace was at hand."[31] The American election would be held just twelve days later. Nixon won the election by a landslide against his Democratic opponent, Senator George McGovern. Clearly, the American people preferred Nixon's "peace was at hand" over McGovern's policy of unilateral withdrawal of American forces. McGovern had cosponsored the McGovern-Hatfield Amendment, which aimed at ending the Vietnam War by cutting off all funds by the end of 1970, later extended to December 31, 1971. The amendment was finally defeated in the Congress in 1970, but McGovern continued to advocate this approach in the presidential campaign. Although he lost the presidential campaign in a landslide, the pattern was clear. As long as the war continued, opponents in the Senate would continue to introduce amendments to end the war by cutting off funds. Sooner or later, if the war continued, one of the efforts in Congress to cut off funds for the war in Vietnam likely would pass.

And peace, it appeared, was not immediately at hand. Kissinger's optimistic announcement, while it might have bolstered his president's electoral prospects, apparently had not anticipated the depth of South Vietnamese opposition to his agreement. First, the South Vietnamese leadership was aghast that this important agreement had been reached without their government in the South knowing anything about it. Second, they were not happy with the provision that left North Vietnamese troops in South Vietnam. "Mutual withdrawal" had disappeared from the document. It appeared that the United States had given in on almost every issue except President Thieu's immediate elimination. The South Vietnamese government was upset with apparent American duplicity in the preceding months. President Thieu and his government refused to agree to the negotiated agreement, just as they had refused to agree with President Johnson concerning the halting of the bombing of North Vietnam some four years earlier. The South Vietnamese president requested that Kissinger return to the negotiations and table some sixty-nine changes in the agreement requested by the South Vietnamese government. The American negotiators also faced a restive Congress that was again considering a legislative end to the war by withdrawing American forces and stopping American expenditures in defending South Vietnam.

When the South Vietnamese recommended changes were presented in Paris on November 20, the North Vietnamese negotiators, of course, were not now interested in making changes to a document to which the Americans had agreed and which finally guaranteed the removal of all American forces from Vietnam. Negotiations on these changes continued but were, in general, fruitless. Indeed, the North Vietnamese in these talks reverted to a harder line, withdrawing concessions to which they had previously agreed. In frustration, on December 13, both sides agreed to recess the negotiations.[32]

LINEBACKER II—THE "CHRISTMAS BOMBING"[33]

All of the president's advisers felt that some military response was necessary to move North Vietnam from its intransigence. It was expected that Congress would act to cut off funds for operations in Vietnam, probably no later than January. The option chosen by President Nixon was a massive bombing attack against North Vietnam, an option that had not achieved measurable results in the past. On this occasion, however, B-52s were to be used for shock action, and previously forbidden targets in the North were to be attacked. Nixon is reported to have told Admiral Moorer, Chief of the Joint Chiefs, the following: "I don't want anymore of this crap about the fact that we couldn't hit this target or that one. This is your chance to use military power effectively to win this war, and if you don't, I'll consider you responsible."[34] At this point, by winning this war, President Nixon meant merely to get the North Vietnamese to agree to the terms of a negotiated settlement. South Vietnamese objections to the negotiated treaty no longer seemed to be of great concern to the American president.

Linebacker II, as the new operation was called, began on December 18. American B-52s and other aircraft flew nearly 3,000 sorties over North Vietnam during the next eleven days, excluding Christmas Day. These sorties were largely over the heavily populated corridor that stretched sixty miles from Haiphong to Hanoi. This was the most concentrated air offensive of the war against North Vietnam and led to an immediate worldwide uproar. There had been no presidential announcement or explanation of any kind. The adverse congressional and domestic editorial reaction was also unprecedented.

American military losses were not inconsequential. Twenty-six American aircraft were shot down, including fifteen B-52s. Ninety-three crew members were lost, thirty-one of them captured. The North Vietnamese characterized the Linebacker II offensive as "the Dien Bien Phu of the air." Western observers state that the United States was on the verge of suffering a major defeat in Linebacker II.[35] The United States had run out of targets, and the North Vietnamese had exhausted their supply of antiaircraft missiles by the time the bombing was stopped on December 30. The peace negotiations began again in Paris on January 8, 1973. The North Vietnamese, replying to an American message, had indicated their willingness to talk again as soon as the bombing ended. The peace agreement, formally signed in Paris on January 27, 1973, seven days after President Nixon's second inauguration, scarcely differed from the draft agreed on in October. President Thieu of South Vietnam, after a great deal of pressure from the United States, had finally been persuaded that he could not, as he stated it, "allow himself the luxury" of resisting America. "We have finally achieved peace with honor," Nixon announced. But all the peace agreement had accomplished was to allegedly stop the conflict pending a political solution. The Saigon government had gained a "decent interval" in which to improve and resist the challenge of North Vietnam and the North Vietnamese troops remaining in the South. But the struggle ahead would be waged without American involvement. America's role in South Vietnam ended with the return of its prisoners held in the North.

The inevitable failure of American policy in Vietnam was assured by Congress, which in June 1974 voted to block funds for any U.S. military activities in Indochina. That this occurred without any evident political backlash indicated that the American people also had had enough. With the final withdrawal of American forces and the return of U.S. prisoners of war from North Vietnam, the Vietnam War was over for the United States. Nixon's unwritten promise to President Thieu that the United States would return with airpower if North Vietnam violated the armistice was worthless. By the spring of 1975, when Thieu needed to call on that promise, Nixon had resigned to avoid impeachment, and Congress had voted to cut all expenditures in Vietnam.

In the end, America's Linebacker II operation against North Vietnam seems to have contributed little to the ending of the war. The return to negotiations was an American initiative, and the treaty between the two powers was quite similar, indeed almost identical, to what had been agreed on in October. While the bombing of Hanoi clearly cheered American prisoners of war confined there and while it is cited by air force officials as a demonstration that a concentrated bombing campaign earlier would have brought significant results, the bombing did little or nothing to extract further concessions from the

North Vietnamese. Little if any change was made to the agreements reached the previous October. All American forces were withdrawn from South Vietnam, and all known American prisoners of war were released to joyous reunions with their families.

For the Vietnamese, the war continued in the South, with each side trying to control more territory. Finally, in 1975, with the collapse of the South Vietnamese government and army in the wake of a major conventional North Vietnamese offensive, the 2,000-year-long war for Vietnamese unity ended. That goal and that dream of the North Vietnamese leadership for which their nation had sacrificed so much, the unity and freedom of Vietnam, was finally achieved.

Chapter Eleven

Conclusion

How did the United States and the North Vietnamese become enemies? The beginnings of this enmity seemed to emanate from the Vietnamese defeat of the French colonial forces arrayed against Vietnam. The Geneva Convention of 1954 met just as the French fortress of Dien Bien Phu fell. The conference produced what actually turned out to be a military truce between two wars. It confirmed the independence of Laos and Cambodia. But under intense Chinese pressure, Ho Chi Minh, Vietnam's leader, agreed to a temporary partition of Vietnam at the seventeenth parallel pending nationwide elections in 1956 to unify the country. The French finally were to depart. After thirty-four years of effort and hundreds of thousands of casualties, Ho Chi Minh had still not achieved his dream of a unified, independent Vietnam. He could not—would not—accept a permanent partition of his nation. But for a time, he concentrated on consolidating his power in the North.

The United States did not subscribe to the Geneva agreements. It fairly quickly became the protector of the new nation of South Vietnam against the forward march of communism, much as it had protected South Korea in 1950. The Republic of Vietnam, America's new anticommunist ally in Southeast Asia, was an invention of the Geneva Accords of 1954. A Vietnamese nationalist to rule South Vietnam who had no connections to the North or to the French was difficult to find, but Secretary of State John Foster Dulles finally settled on a Vietnamese Catholic, Ngo Dinh Diem. Aware of his weakness, Diem had no intention of implementing the elections of 1956 promised by the Geneva agreements. The South Vietnamese government, of course, had not signed those accords because it had not previously existed. Diem began to build a government in the South. But he became more and more arbitrary and isolated and less amenable to American advice and counsel. By 1958, guerrilla forces in the South began to attack government installations and officials. These cadres found a reception among the people of the South who had no great loyalty to a remote and distant Saigon government. The Central Intelligence Agency characterized these antigovernment cadres as indigenous southern opponents of Diem. But President Dwight D. Eisenhower and Secretary of State Dulles characterized them all as communist and supplied American aid and advisers to Diem in order to combat them.

President Kennedy, Eisenhower's successor, was also inclined to support President Diem. Beginning in late 1961, he increased the number of American advisers but he balked at committing American combat forces to shore up the Diem regime. President Diem and his government could not deal effectively with the mounting threats to his regime caused by factions alienated by his autocracy. He took harsh measures against rebellious Buddhists, thus alienating many of his generals. But his collapse would have been impossible without American complicity. Henry Cabot Lodge, the U.S. ambassador in Saigon, encouraged Diem's senior officers to stage a coup d'état. Once in motion, the plot spiraled out of control, and Diem and his brother were assassinated. Kennedy, shocked by Diem's murder, would also be assassinated three weeks later. But Diem's death marked a fresh phase in the Vietnam conflict. America's responsibility for Diem's death haunted U.S. leaders during the years ahead, prompting them to assume a larger responsibility and thus a larger burden in Vietnam.

Diem's successors were worse than he was. There were seven military coups in the following year, and South Vietnam, the artificial nation, was on the verge of collapse. The realization grew in Washington that an ally on whose behalf the United States had steadily increased its commitment was in a state of political and military collapse. Washington felt that something had to be done. Attention focused initially on positive action against North Vietnam. The controversial Tonkin Gulf incident on August 4–5, 1964, precipitated the first U.S. aerial reprisal against North Vietnam and provided President Lyndon Johnson, Kennedy's successor, with a broad congressional resolution of support. Throughout the remainder of 1964, recommendations were made by the Joint Chiefs of Staff to continue retaliatory raids against North Vietnam and to increase American force levels in South Vietnam through the deployment of combat units. These recommendations were resisted by the president.

Throughout the war, American leaders severely underestimated the resistance, determination, nationalism, and conviction with which North Vietnam and its allies in the South would fight. They misjudged the devastating effect that the enemy's weaponry and guerrilla tactics would have against modern American technology and the enemy's willingness to die for what they believed. "Winning the hearts and minds" of the people became a slogan for the pacification effort, but rather meager resources were devoted toward this important part of the war, and the South Vietnamese government was never pushed to become effective in this important area. American and South Vietnamese forces often neglected the real war for the loyalty of the rural population of South Vietnam, although the National Liberation Front, the name adopted by the southern insurgency, concentrated on this area. As the North Vietnamese repeatedly stated, they were fighting a "people's war," a war in which political actions and military actions were combined to reach the final objective.

Many Americans, including much of the nation's political and military leadership, saw the war as a naked aggression of one sovereign communist nation against another sovereign noncommunist nation. Harry G. Summers Jr., in his widely quoted book *On Strategy: A Critical Analysis of the Vietnam War*, takes this view and insists that the United States pursued the wrong objective in Vietnam. Instead of concentrating on defeating the Vietcong and North Vietnamese forces in the South, he insists, we should have attacked the source of the aggression in North Vietnam.[1] The North Vietnamese, of course, dispute this view. They indicated in recent conversations that North Vietnam went to war to defend its historic drive for unity and national independence. As Colonel Quach Hai Luong, a North Vietnamese historian stated,

> When the war in Vietnam had occurred, the US perceived that it was becoming involved in a limited war where there was distinction between North and South Vietnam, whereas the Vietnamese did not make that distinction. The perceptions were different because the Americans saw two countries where the Vietnamese saw only one. Therefore all our strategies during the war were based on this perception of Vietnam as one country. According to our perception, Vietnam was one country that was divided. . . . So our strategy was concerned with how to protect and appreciate this unified Vietnamese nation. We did not want any other country to come and intervene in our country. Therefore the basis of our strategy was to protect our independence and maintain national unity. . . . For us, we are not familiar with "civil war." . . . We call it a people's war because this war includes all kinds of forces: the official army, militia, and civilians.[2]

American opposition to North Vietnam, these leaders indicated, was based on the belief that if Vietnam gained its unity, this would lead to the spread of communism throughout Southeast Asia. This, of course, was President Eisenhower's misguided "domino theory," accepted uncritically by his successors. This perception, these North Vietnamese leaders stated, was wrong. They insisted that they did not take instruction from China or the Soviet Union. There was no intention of a threat to other nations as postulated by the "domino theory." "Our objective," Colonel Quach Hai Luong stated,

> was a people's revolution, independence, and unification independent of the USSR and China. . . . Vietnam was not simply following what the USSR and China wanted, we were not their puppets. . . . The reason I am saying this is to emphasize that Vietnam accepted assistance from the USSR and China, . . . but Vietnam was also very proud of its people and its national revolution. Vietnam was not a puppet nor was it oppressed.[3]

The war in Vietnam, from the North Vietnamese point of view, was not an aggression and was not an invasion of the South by the North. There was only one Vietnam. Temporarily divided by the Geneva Convention of 1954, the North Vietnamese looked forward to the unification of their nation as promised by that document. But the South Vietnamese government, an invention of the Geneva agreements and designed to disappear in two years, was now supported, armed, and advised by the United States. In fact, it had become in North Vietnamese eyes an American puppet. The elections to unify the country that were promised at Geneva were not held. The North Vietnamese leadership saw that the United States had replaced the French and opposed the national unity that they had won on the battlefield against France. The line set up by the Geneva Accords in 1954 had become an international boundary not intended by that document. The promises of the Geneva Accords were not kept, and the war for national independence and unity had to be resumed by North Vietnam, now against the "puppet" Diem regime rather than against the French. The Americans, in North Vietnamese eyes, had been substituted for the French and supported the corrupt and unpopular Diem regime. They hoped to defeat that regime before the Americans could intervene with major ground force. In this, they were not successful. Thereafter, each modification, each change in American strategy, was seen by North Vietnam as an admission of the defeat of the previous strategy.[4] They saw each American escalation as a signal that they were winning the war. As Colonel Quach Hai Luong recently stated, North Vietnam saw the bombing of the nation by the United States as an admission of the failure of the advisory effort not because the advisers lacked expertise

> but [because] they were given a difficult task that not many people could undertake because they had to help a government and army that were weak and inexperienced. Furthermore, the government that they were asked to help was immoral which repressed the Vietnamese people. Therefore the advisors could have expertise but they could not save such a situation. Therefore, if the US wants to draw lessons from the advisory effort, then first you must consider who

you are helping and how. We perceived the US bombing of North Vietnam as a direct result of the failure of your previous strategy; therefore you had to bomb the North. You bombed the North because this was a passive action . . . and I want to reiterate that you changed your strategy because the old one failed. Your new strategy toward the South was to introduce more troops which resulted in the Americanization of the war and Americans directly became involved with the war.[5]

The North Vietnamese leadership saw the takeover of the ground war in South Vietnam likewise as an indication that the American air war against North Vietnam had failed. They were willing to fight the Americans in a war of attrition, knowing full well that their tenacity and will would outlast that of the United States. And finally, the North Vietnamese saw the policy of Vietnamization as the ultimate admission of the failure of American strategy. The North Vietnamese viewed the Vietnamization program as they had viewed all previous changes in American strategy. It was an indication that a failed American strategy was being replaced by a new strategy that was also bound to fail. As Colonel Luong pointed out, "The Vietnamization of the war was like all other US strategies that were constantly changed, which indicated to us that we had increasing chances of a victory."[6]

So the North Vietnamese never saw themselves in any danger of being defeated militarily by American forces either through the bombing of North Vietnam or through combat operations in South Vietnam. Losing militarily was never an option that they contemplated or faced. The unification of Vietnam was not a pressing issue for the peasants of either country. But the more efficient North Vietnamese government was able to call on its people for greater sacrifices than was the government of South Vietnam, which looked to the Americans for protection and support even to the very end.

The question posed at the beginning of this book was, "Could the United States have won militarily in Vietnam at a reasonable cost in men and materiel and without the threat of intervention by Russia and China?" Actually, the question can be restated as, "Could the United States have defeated Vietnamese nationalism by military means?" The answer clearly is that it could not. Indeed, "winning militarily" was never the national goal of the Johnson or of the Nixon administration. The conclusion of this book is that the prevention of the unification of Vietnam could not have been accomplished by American military action and, indeed, that this unity, promised by the Geneva Accords, was made inevitable by the willingness of the North Vietnamese to sacrifice in order to achieve it. As stated previously, the United States after World War II followed two major foreign policy objectives: that of anticolonialism and that of anticommunism. When the nationalist leader was a communist, the choice was clear. He was a communist and must be opposed by the United States. In Vietnam, the choice the United States made was obviously incorrect. Ho Chi Minh and the North Vietnamese nation were the nationalist leaders. But by being a communist, Ho, in American eyes, gave up his role as the nationalist leader of Vietnam. He was naturally a member and agent of the monolithic communist conspiracy that threatened Southeast Asia, America, and the rest of the free world. As former secretary of defense McNamara admitted at a conference with Vietnamese leaders in Hanoi, "I believe we also greatly underestimated the nationalistic element and aspect of Ho Chi Minh's movement. We saw him first as a communist and only secondarily as a Vietnamese nationalist."[7] South Vietnam was an artificial creation of the Geneva Convention of 1954 and was designated to disappear two years later. It never possessed the legitimacy that is a requirement of nationhood. From 1965 forward, that government was preserved by force of American arms. When those arms were removed, the fate of the so-called nation of South Vietnam was inevitable and predictable. It had no claim to Vietnamese nationalism. In any case, the North Vietnamese would never have given up the struggle to unify the country. There was no way that American forces could "win" militarily. For whom would they be winning?

The American objective remained constant throughout, "an independent noncommunist South Vietnam." An independent noncommunist South Vietnam could not be achieved by American arms alone, no matter how many battles were won, no matter how many American troops were involved, no matter how many air strikes were conducted, and no matter how many North Vietnamese and Vietcong troops were killed. There actually were many American programs designed to strengthen the South Vietnamese government. However, most American actions were devoted to strengthening the South Vietnamese army, not necessarily the government. The major goal of the United States in Vietnam remained that of preventing the loss of South Vietnam to communism by force. The United States initially feared both the international and the domestic consequences of such a loss. Vietnam was seen as a test of U.S. military commitments to its allies around the world. Vietnam was also seen as a clash of wills between communism and the system of alliances established by the United States during the Cold War. Vietnam was the testing ground where the challenge of communist wars of national liberation would be met. The cost of aggression would be shown to be too high for the communists to pay, the "domino effect" in Southeast Asia would be frustrated, and the principle that armed aggression would not be allowed to succeed would be validated. Most books and commentary on the Vietnam War fail to address the domestic political considerations that affected wartime policy. The president is often not a free agent and must always keep in mind those political considerations. Domestically, the successful defense of South

Vietnam was seen to be essential to the political well-being of the United States. In his memoirs, President Johnson justified American policy in Vietnam in these terms: "A divisive debate about 'who lost Vietnam' would be, in my judgment, even more destructive to our national life than the argument over China had been."[8] The Democrats and, in particular, President Harry Truman, had been politically chastised by their Republican adversaries as "having lost China to the communists," and therefore being soft on communism. Richard Nixon had been in the lead on this castigation of the Democrats. No one was more anticommunist than he. Although patently ridiculous, this politically motivated charge stuck. The Democrats were clearly not willing to be accused by their political opponents of "losing" another country to communism. President Johnson and the great majority of his advisers concluded that the alternative to defending South Vietnam would not be peace but an expanded area of conflict. With the loss of Vietnam, according to Eisenhower's domino theory, which was accepted uncritically by his successors, communism would spread throughout Southeast Asia, other U.S. commitments would be called into question, and the nation would be split by a vicious internal debate between the parties, a debate that had already begun. President Johnson has been quoted as saying as early as 1963, "I am not going to be the president who saw Southeast Asia go the way China went." He was not going to be the president to be accused of "losing" another country to communism. He was not going to be the first president, indeed, was not going to be the first Democratic president, to lose a war. This domestic political consideration was foremost in his mind. President Johnson's policy objectives translated into doing the minimum amount militarily to prevent a South Vietnamese defeat while convincing Hanoi that it could not succeed in its aggression. There was no intention—no objective—of defeating North Vietnam militarily. The long-term goal was a political settlement that would "allow the South Vietnamese to determine their own future without outside interference." The possibility that a majority of the population of South Vietnam might determine that it wished to join North Vietnam and form a unified nation under the communist Ho Chi Minh, a possibility held forth by the provisions of the Geneva agreements, never occurred to the Americans, nor would it have been acceptable to them. In pursuing his objective, President Johnson also was not going to run the risk of a direct military confrontation with the Soviet Union or China. Avoiding provocation of those two communist nations became an equally important objective in keeping the war limited. To the president and his secretary of defense, then, this meant a war for limited purposes using limited resources in a geographically constricted area to achieve a diplomatic purpose. The allocation of American manpower, resources, and materiel would not be allowed to reach the point where the war would unduly affect the civilian economy or interfere with the burgeoning programs of the Great Society. Operations would be restricted geographically so as not to incite Soviet or Chinese intervention. The objective would not be to win militarily, either in North or in South Vietnam, but rather to convince the North Vietnamese (and their inferred Soviet and Chinese sponsors) that the cost of continuing the war in South Vietnam would be, over time, prohibitive to them and that they could not succeed. The president's policy seemed to be a classic application of limited war theory. Military force was to be applied in ways that would provide signals to the enemy, signals of American resolve that would convince the North Vietnamese that they could not win and that a diplomatic settlement would be desirable. The president's strategy, then, was defensive in nature and, in effect, left the decision as to when to end the war in the hands of the North Vietnamese. The administration saw the conflict in South Vietnam simply as a communist aggression on the Cold War model— a challenge to a free nation by expansionist international communism. The questionable legitimacy and the inefficiency of the fledgling South Vietnamese government and the anticolonial tradition, nationalist credentials, history, and determination of North Vietnam were overlooked. Thus, the enemy was much too simply described, and the Saigon government had ascribed to it by Washington capabilities and qualities that it never possessed.

The president's principal military advisers, from the beginning, saw the White House's limited political objective as essentially negative and ineffective. This no-win approach, they felt, yielded the initiative to the enemy and ultimately placed primary reliance on the fragile and undependable South Vietnamese armed forces. If the United States was to go to war, the Joint Chiefs felt that a more ambitious objective was necessary, that of defeating the enemy both in North and in South Vietnam. They advocated the classic doctrine that victory depended on the rapid application of overwhelming military power through offensive action to defeat the enemy's main forces. Twice since the end of World War II, the United States had been involved in conflicts where the objective had been to "not lose" rather than to defeat the enemy and win a military victory. In Greece, our advice and material support allowed the Greek forces to eliminate the insurgency in their nation without the use of American troops. In Korea, however, after several changes in objectives based on military circumstances, the war evolved into a mission of restoring the nation and "not losing" rather than defeating the enemy. Political and resource constraints limited American military action finally to a defensive role: that of preserving the independence of South Korea. The American military chafed under these political constraints and by the no-win strategy in Korea and were determined not to repeat in a future war this no-win scenario. The military's determination to go beyond limited political

goals in Korea played a large part in President Truman's removal from command of General MacArthur. During the Vietnam War, the military preference
for overwhelming force frequently trumped the hearts and minds aspect of
counterinsurgency. Prominent anthropologists such as Gerald Hickey, who
went to Vietnam as a University of Chicago graduate student and remained
throughout the war as a researcher for the RAND Corporation, found that
their deep knowledge of Vietnam (valuable for counterinsurgency) was frequently ignored by U.S. military leaders who increasingly adopted a conventional war approach as the conflict progressed. The failure to use historical
and anthropological studies in Vietnam raises a number of issues that even
now plague anthropological research in a military context and prevents the
military, with some exceptions, from effectively utilizing anthropological
study in the many places around the world where U.S. armed forces may be
deployed. Throughout American engagement in Vietnam, the Joint Chiefs opposed the political restrictions on the use of American force in North and
South Vietnam. They complained about what actually was effective civilian
control. The field commander adopted a ground strategy that could not succeed within the political limits placed on him, and he continuously sought to
have those political limits removed. The military chiefs in Washington continued to request additional American troops for South Vietnam, increased
bombing of North Vietnam, and expanded authority to strike by air and
ground in Laos, Cambodia, and North Vietnam. They felt that any U.S. effort
to "win" the war in the South was thwarted by the availability to enemy
troops of crucial sanctuaries and supply routes in Laos and Cambodia, where
they would refit, reequip, and escape destruction by American ground and airpower. Further, the constraints on the use of airpower in North Vietnam, they
felt, allowed the enemy to adjust to the bombing campaign so that its pressure
did not become unacceptable.

Of equal consequence and concern to the military chiefs was the fact
that the White House decision not to call up U.S. reserve units depleted
American active forces outside of Vietnam to the point where the nation
might not be able to respond to other overseas military contingencies. In
fact, as the war developed, the debate within the administration concerning the level of American effort in South Vietnam came to revolve around
this one crucial issue of mobilization. When the president searched for
the elusive point at which the political costs of the effort in Vietnam would
become unacceptable to the American people, he always settled on
mobilization—that point at which significant members of reservists would
have to be called up to provide enough manpower to support the war. President Johnson saw reserve mobilization as the threshold at which the nation would see itself as being on a war footing. His top priority continued

to be the passage by Congress of the social programs of the Great Society. He would not be a wartime president.

This debate behind closed doors concerning the limited strategy advocated by the president and his civilian advisers and the more forceful strategy advocate by the military chiefs continued throughout Johnson's presidency. Fundamental differences between military and civilians at the national level concerning the war in Indochina were never resolved. There was no agreed, coherent strategy to achieve American objectives and, indeed, no agreement as to those objectives. Decisions concerning the allocation of American resources to Vietnam were made on the basis of what was the minimum additional effort that could be made while maintaining congressional support for (or acquiescence in) the administration's war policy and for the programs of the Great Society. There was to be minimum disruption of American life. As late as 1966, President Johnson declared to the Congress, "I believe we can continue the Great Society while we fight in Vietnam." Concerning Vietnam, the Joint Chiefs continued to resist the civilian political controls on the military and to pursue the illusion of military victory, even though that was not the nation's objective. As H. R. McMaster has indicated in his book *Dereliction of Duty: Lyndon Johnson, Robert McNamara, the Joint Chiefs of Staff, and the Lies That Led to Vietnam*, "The Chiefs and the administration had started down divergent paths."[9] In the American system of government, there can only be one winner in such a situation.

Within the army itself, the strategy of "attrition" through large unit operations as practiced by General Westmoreland was criticized by many for failing to take into account "pacification" programs designed to win the South Vietnamese populace over to the side of its government. Many felt that the strategy of attrition raised American casualties and that a strategy to protect the South Vietnamese populace would be a more effective use of American soldiers. Although the army strived mightily to meet the personnel demands of the field commander, many in the top echelons of that service felt that these troops were not being used effectively and efficiently.

Perhaps the most glaring and costly mistake of the Johnson administration was this failure to establish clear, understandable, specific, and limited objectives for the military and to agree on a unified military strategy for conducting the war. Although the political objectives—to resist aggression and to contain communism in Southeast Asia by defending South Vietnam, thereby ensuring an independent noncommunist South Vietnam—were promulgated and understood at every level, neither President Johnson nor Secretary of Defense McNamara provided specific strategic objectives to their military leaders other than that very general one. Therefore, military leaders were, in effect, able to develop their own strategy and objectives, and they developed ambitious ones indeed, often in conflict with the unstated desires of their superiors to keep the war limited both in materiel, manpower, and geographic reach.

The consequences should have been predictable—confusion, contradiction, frustration, and eventually being worn down by a more dedicated enemy who ignored casualties and would not give up. Different leaders voiced different strategies and objectives at different times, often without clear purpose and never with official approval. To illustrate, in July 1965, the administration's stated objective was "to deny the enemy victory in South Vietnam and convince him he could not win." This objective was soon stated by the Joint Chiefs to be defeating the enemy and driving him out of South Vietnam. One month later, the Joint Chiefs complicated that objective with the following tasks: (1) to compel Hanoi to cease and desist in South Vietnam, (2) to defeat the Vietcong and restore government control in South Vietnam, and (3) to deter China from intervening and to defeat intervention if it should occur. Adding to the confusion were the "military missions" of increasing the cost for the North Vietnamese to wage war, defeating the Vietcong and North Vietnamese army, forcing the withdrawal of North Vietnamese forces from the South, and raising the morale of the South Vietnamese.

In many respects, confusion and ambiguity became a strategy in themselves. President Johnson apparently believed that the best way to preserve harmony and to encourage continued support from his military leaders was to keep the strategic concept ambiguous or undefined. He avoided a debate on strategy and never arrived at a final decision with regard to the conduct of the war. Although there had been superficial discussions of strategy and objectives in the early years of the Johnson presidency, these almost always involved military measures. Outside the Department of Defense, the civilian advisers to the president, with few exceptions, saw Vietnam as a military problem and were quite willing to sit back and let the military handle it. The military services were quick to step into the gap, each with its own program. But these programs were American programs that basically ignored the South Vietnamese government and its often inept army and that called for American resources and operational authority far beyond what political leaders were prepared to undertake.

President Johnson made at least eight separate decisions concerning increasing U.S. manpower levels in Vietnam in 1965–1968. The issues addressed and the decisions that were made were always tactical and short term in nature. The only alternative policies examined involved different force levels or alternative bombing campaigns. Although Johnson was determined to wage a limited campaign with limited resources for limited political purposes as opposed to military victory, these operational and resource constraints were not made specific to his military chiefs. He continued to buy time for his domestic programs and to buy the support of his military chiefs by temporizing, by avoiding decisive action, and by getting agreement at the lowest level of intensity he could to meet the current situation in Vietnam, to not derail his legislative program, and to maintain the support of the American people.

Approximately every six months, the president would query the Joint Chiefs as to how faster progress could be made in Vietnam. The answer was always the same: (1) bomb Hanoi, (2) mine Haiphong Harbor, (3) invade Laos and Cambodia to cut the Ho Chi Minh Trail, and (4) mobilize the reserves. And the president would always refuse to lift those restrictions. He would then ask how faster progress could be made within his political limitations. And the parochial answer from the military was always the same: (1) give the army more men, (2) give the air force more men, (3) give the navy more men, and (4) give the marines more men.

The president would ask how many more men could be provided within the time limits required and without calling on the reserve forces. The services would study their training base to discover how many draftees and volunteers could be trained in that period of time, and the answer would be added up and presented to the president. He would approve this number and announce that he had met the field commanders' request. Finally, in November 1967, the Joint Chiefs told the president that faster progress could not be made under current political restrictions. By that time, the United States had some 485,000 military personnel in South Vietnam with no agreed-on national strategy on how to use them.

Political science provides no clear prescription for "nation building," for the development of a viable democratic political system in a traditional society emerging from colonial rule, with limited physical and administrative resources, and in the midst of a bitter civil war. Certainly there is no agency of the U.S. government charged with such a task. Therefore, there must be some doubt as to what could have been accomplished along such lines by an outside power in an alien society even if a clear realization of the true political problem had been present. And, as mentioned, there was little or no historical or anthropological knowledge of either North or South Vietnam on the part of the military commanders or civilian policymakers. So it was not surprising that the American response was a traditional military one. The military defeat of the enemy seemed an achievable goal, and the United States escalated and reescalated in pursuing that illusion. For the nation's military leaders, the defeat of the enemy became an end in itself, as it had been in more conventional American wars.

There was some recognition that more was needed in Vietnam. Lip service was given to pacification or revolutionary development programs designed to bring safety and social justice to the countryside in order to "win the hearts and minds" of the rural population of South Vietnam and gain their active support for a government interested in their welfare and security and responsive to their needs. But comparatively meager resources were devoted to these programs and they were devoted too late. Often, such programs as were developed were largely planned, financed, and implemented by Americans and with little involvement or interest on the part of the government of South Vietnam. And again, there was no agency within the U.S. government solely responsible for such programs. In his book *Pacification*, Richard Hunt details American failure to understand and adjust to a counterinsurgency environment and strategy in which it was understood how military force should be applied to provide security to South Vietnam's rural population. And, as Robert Komer has pointed out, "In the last analysis, the U.S. effort in Vietnam . . . failed largely because it could not sufficiently revamp or adequately substitute for a South Vietnamese leadership, administration, and armed force inadequate to the task."[10]

Thus, fragmented and inefficient planning and execution marked the administration of American civil programs. These programs remained superficial and achieved few lasting results. Indeed, there was a general shallowness of knowledge and indifference to consideration of Vietnam as a society and a culture with its own structures and history. Even though a constitution was written and democratic elections were conducted at the national level, the basic structure of South Vietnamese society, government, and power relationships was not disturbed. And so the existence of South Vietnam as a nation continued to be sustained, as it had been at the outset of the American involvement, only by the commitment of American military power. Military operations were seldom coordinated with or directed toward progress in the pacification program. Military leaders on the ground failed to grasp the causes or the significance of the steady attrition of the authority of the government of South Vietnam in the countryside, a loss of political authority that was directly linked to the way the war was conducted. Indeed, the effects of military operations—the uprooting of the rural populace, its concentration in refugee camps or in the larger cities of South Vietnam, the creation of "free fire zones," the breakdown of government in the rural areas, and the demoralization of many aspects of traditional Vietnamese society—worked against the pacification program. As one observer noted,

> Instead of the weaknesses within South Vietnam being eliminated, they were being aggravated. . . . It was never understood that nation building was the offensive construction programme designed to strengthen the government's assets and eliminate its weaknesses, while the military operations were defensive and

destructive, designed to hold the ring for the constructive program, and in so doing, to weaken the enemy's military assets.[11]

It was also not understood by the United States that the South Vietnamese were seen by the North Vietnamese as mere puppets of the Americans. While we saw the war as aggression by the North against the South, they viewed Vietnam as one country, part of which they were trying to rescue from the puppets in order to unify the nation.[12] So the many and spectacular American military victories over Vietcong and North Vietnamese forces in most cases could not be translated into political gains for the South Vietnamese government. When American forces withdrew from an area, the enemy continued to find shelter, or at least passive acquiescence to his presence, from the rural population of South Vietnam. The two wars, political and military, were pursued as two relatively unrelated activities. But success in the military war could make no lasting difference without corresponding success in the political war. As John Prados characterizes it in his book *The Hidden History of Vietnam War*, "It was like sweeping water that flows back as soon as the brush passes. American firepower and tactics were devastating, and could hardly lose in battle, but they could hardly win 'the Nam.'"[13]

An American-sponsored Phoenix program designed to identify and eliminate Vietcong cadres in the rural areas met with some success and with much criticism. In his book *Stalking the Vietcong*, Stuart A. Herrington, an American Phoenix adviser, recounts how this American program was "a classic example of an attempt to graft an American-conceived plan onto a stubbornly resistant Vietnamese situation" and how it put the rural populace in an impossible position of accommodating to the Vietcong at night and to the South Vietnamese government forces in the day.[14]

The American failure in Vietnam was not a failure caused by the limitations placed on military action by civilian control, as many military commanders and other commentators continue to charge. Indeed, overwhelming American military power was brought to bear. The United States enjoyed complete control of the sea and air and had a striking superiority in materiel, weapons, and mobility on the ground. The American failure was caused by the lack of realization that military power could not solve what was a basically political problem. Overwhelming American military power was never directed toward solving that political problem. Military power was seldom used in ways that would contribute to the political stability and competence of the South Vietnamese government or to the safety of the people of South Vietnam.

To insist that the cost of not intervening to save South Vietnam would be greater than the cost that could be incurred in defending American interests in Southeast Asia was to place an unlimited commitment on American resources devoted to South Vietnam and was to have a stultifying effect on any serious examination of alternatives. Indeed, the strategy adopted assigned more rationality to the North Vietnamese decision-making process than it did to our own. By the gradual application of power, the United States would find the elusive point at which the war would become too costly to the old revolutionaries in North Vietnam, causing them to abandon their age-old nationalist goals in South Vietnam. But there would be no limit on the effort the United States would expend in driving them to that point. In their application of this rather naive strategy, the nation's leaders repeatedly misjudged the enemy's ability to frustrate America's aims and to match American escalation and reescalation at every stage. The North Vietnamese essentially adopted the same approach: fight until the enemy's losses become so great that he will be frustrated and quit. The difference was that North Vietnam was willing to endure far greater proportional losses than was the United States. Hanoi's total resolve and complete commitment to ultimately unifying the country regardless of the cost was never fully appreciated. Peace was less important to them than was the unity of Vietnam. The United States was fighting a limited war for limited purposes, while the North Vietnamese felt they were fighting an unlimited war to unify their country.

At some point it should have been clear—as it later became clear—that the costs, be they political, military, or economic, incurred by the United States in defending its hapless ally in South Vietnam could exceed the costs of disengagement or, conversely, that the costs we were willing to pay in a protracted war could not guarantee military victory. But to state this or to question seriously Vietnam's place in our national priorities was not encouraged in the Johnson or the Nixon administration and was seen, when it did occur, as indicating an unacceptable lack of resolve in meeting the worldwide communist challenge. Those few officials, such as Secretary of Defense McNamara and Secretary of Defense Laird, who foresaw the eventual cost or indicated at some point that they felt the cost had become too high were shuffled off the scene or ignored.

Only when the price of attaining U.S. objectives became so dear in lives, dollars, and public confidence and the benefits became so intangible, remote, and even implausible did our national leadership match the objectives that were being pursued with the resources and time needed to obtain them. Only when the cost had already become too high were the objectives that were being pursued and the strategy being followed to attain them matched to see if they were in accord. After the Tet offensive, this occurred for perhaps the first time. Objectives were matched to the resources required to achieve those objectives, and the strategy being followed was modified in some respects when it was seen that the costs—political, material, and human—of obtaining those results within a reasonable period of time would be more than the nation was willing to pay, if they could be achieved at all. The existing policy was shown not to be producing the results expected in a reasonable time or at an acceptable cost. The American public could not see an end to the war. In order to produce quicker or more decisive results, the commitment of resources would have to be increased vastly, and the whole nature of the war and its relationship to the United States would be changed. There were strong indications that large and growing elements of the American public had begun to believe that the cost had already reached unacceptable levels and that the objective was no longer worth the price. The forthcoming American election brought home to President Johnson finally that the policy being pursued in Vietnam, no matter how he had tried to limit it, would no longer be supported by the American public and that Vietnam and the conduct of the war there had become a divisive political issue. The political reality was that without necessarily renouncing the former policy, a new and less costly strategy had to be found. In his speech to the nation on March 31, 1968, President Johnson tried to remove that issue from the public debate. He spoke of peace in Vietnam, and he withdrew from the political battle for the presidency in order to remove that issue from political contention.

This is the situation that faced Richard Nixon as he assumed the presidency in 1969. He did not have an easy task, but his task was possibly less complicated than was that of President Johnson. It could not have taken him and his national security adviser, Henry Kissinger, long to realize that the war in Vietnam was not winnable militarily by the United States. His policy of negotiating with the North Vietnamese while trying to improve the competence, armament, and credibility of the South Vietnamese army did little to change the situation on the ground in a favorable way. Therefore, Nixon's policy of negotiation and "peace with honor" while reducing American casualties and involvement through Vietnamization soon became cynical. It was finally to leave South Vietnam to its own devices with empty promises to return in force if the armistice agreement were to be broached, as it most surely would be, by North Vietnam.

The role of the Joint Chiefs in this circumstance raises many pertinent questions concerning their influence, usefulness, and effectiveness in the national decision-making process. As chief military advisers to the president, they are bound to give him their best military advice unconstrained by political considerations. And they are bound to respect civilian control of the military instrument of power. The president is the commander in chief. So at some point it would seem essential that they salute, accept the political limitations imposed on them by civilian authority, and plan military operations to achieve national objectives within those political limitations. If these political considerations might preclude attaining the results desired, then the military chiefs have an obligation to inform political leadership of the limitations of military force within those policy restraints. But it is the president as commander in chief under the Constitution who decides how and for what purposes U.S. military force will be employed.

During the early years of the Vietnam War, however, the Joint Chiefs seemed incapable of accepting the president's political limitations and, indeed, seemed incapable of or unwilling to accept the necessity of conducting a limited war with limited resources in Vietnam, in which military actions were designed specifically to elicit a diplomatic and not a military outcome. Some have accused them of dusting off and attempting to implement old contingency plans, of doing what they were trained to do in a large-scale war, even though conditions in Vietnam were dramatically different. It appears that the Joint Chiefs made no independent analyses of what manpower levels would be needed to achieve White House objectives (denial of communist victory) within the restraints placed on the military operations in Vietnam by the president or of what military gains actually could be achieved within those constraints. Their advice on how to win was always predictable: do what General Westmoreland asks, lift the political and geographical restraints under which our forces operate, and increase the size of the strategic reserve through mobilization. These actions would then allow them to pursue the illusion of a military victory. But this was advice that President Johnson was never willing to accept. And based on Johnson's experience, it seems that President Nixon and his national security adviser, Henry Kissinger, seldom consulted the nation's military leaders other than the field commander in their search for military options for Vietnam.

On the other hand, it does not appear from the available documents that any of the senior military leaders threatened or even contemplated resigning to dramatize his opposition to the limitations on the conduct of the war insisted on by the president and his advisers. Far from seeking to present their views in public, each member of the Joint Chiefs, who (with the exception of the chairman) was also chief of his respective service, sought to protect the position of his service and his own status inside the administration while striving to change White House policy from within. The ventilation of disagreements with presidential policies did not become a high priority for the senior members of the military establishment during the entire period of U.S. involvement in Vietnam, nor was either president inclined to listen to their often parochial advice.

President Johnson was aware of the possible political repercussions of such a military defection, and he temporized over the years in order not to push his loyal military leaders to such a point. At a conference in Honolulu in 1966, he told Westmoreland, "General, I have a lot riding on you. . . . I hope you don't pull a MacArthur on me." Although President Johnson never approved the military strategy that the Joint Chiefs continued to recommend, he never explicitly ruled it out either. He allowed the military chiefs gradual increases in their combat forces in Vietnam and held out the possibility of greater operational leeway in the future. He pointed out the political and fiscal realities that he felt prevented his meeting all their requests while never rejecting completely all those requests. He slowly increased the resources and authority of General Westmoreland in a process of gradual and reluctant escalation.

Denied by civilian authority of a strategic concept and the military freedom that they felt was necessary to win the war, the military chiefs were pacified by gradual increases in force levels and in bombing targets and, eventually, by the replacement of a secretary of defense who had become anathema to them. But these increases in military authority and resources were always within the president's guidelines. President Johnson retained the political constraints on military action and, in effect, determined his own strategy. And so the military chiefs, while each sought a larger role for his own service, in effect became sophisticated yes-men for the president's policies, assuring the public, as did General Westmoreland, that every request from the field commander had been met and seldom raising in public their view of the eventual military consequences of the president's restrictions. The consequences of this failure to develop a precise, clear military strategy were certainly unintended by President Johnson. They included a costly bombing campaign against North Vietnam and the commitment of more than half a million American troops to a ground war in Asia without any fundamental agreement within our government as to how success was to be achieved or what really represented success.

Thus, the major American effort in Vietnam was always piecemeal, indecisive, contradictory, and misdirected. Each decision in Washington represented a compromise between a president determined to preserve his domestic programs while defending freedom in Southeast Asia with the least possible disruption in American life and the Joint Chiefs and the field commander who saw no alternative but an American takeover of the war and an all-out military effort against a dangerous and tenacious enemy while mobilizing to maintain American military capabilities to deal with contingencies in other parts of the world. In their book *The Irony of Vietnam: The System Worked*, Leslie Gelb and Richard Betts argue that the decision process functioned well in the Johnson administration, that alternatives were considered, and that each decision was a compromise between a president eager to limit the war and his military chiefs who wished to pursue it at an increased level.[15] But this was not a decision-making process that should be praised or emulated. By presenting a facade of unanimity concerning the conduct of the war and of the objectives being pursued, the president and the Joint Chiefs, in effect, inhibited rational national debate within the American body politic concerning U.S. objectives in Southeast Asia and the forces and resources to be devoted to the attainment of those objectives. When this debate did come, it was initiated by scattered groups of antiwar protesters and their congressional allies who often offered no workable policy alternatives.

President Johnson compromised in order to retain the continued support of his military leaders, which he felt was necessary to maintain support within the nation for American objectives and actions in Vietnam. He never changed his objectives while maintaining the pace of the action and the conduct of operations in the war within the political limits he felt to be necessary. But he never made clear his objectives, the resources to be allocated to the achievement of those objectives, and the political restraints that were to be maintained on military operations. He never insisted that his military advisers constrain their military advice within the political and resource constraints he had established. He never insisted that any of the chiefs who did not agree with his policy restrictions step down. And when it became clear that his military chiefs did not accept these political constraints and continued to recommend that national policy be changed so as to fight the war on their basis rather than on that of the president, he never removed them—as his predecessor, Harry Truman, had removed a field commander who had opposed his policies. President Johnson's greatest fault as a national leader was that he chose not to choose economically or militarily between the Great Society and the war in Vietnam. Instead, he sought a series of pragmatic solutions for avoiding what he believed would be a divisive national debate over that choice. There seemed to be little common understanding between the civil and the military leaders. Military goals were not developed to accomplish the objectives of a declared policy. The policy aims almost directly precluded the chances of success for the military strategy implemented by the military commanders. It was never the objective of the United States to "achieve military victory" in South Vietnam. It was made clear and specific at various times by various administration figures that the nation's goal was not to defeat North Vietnam without invading North Vietnam. The goal was to convince North Vietnam to cease its support of the war in South Vietnam, a goal difficult for the military to implement or ever to achieve.

From the beginning, President Johnson set out to fight a different kind of war in Vietnam, a limited war that allowed only limited force to achieve limited objectives within a limited geographic area, without declaring war, without "defeating" anyone, and without disturbing the normal everyday life of America. In particular, he did not want to risk the accomplishments of his

Great Society for that "bitch of a war" on the other side of the world by waging a total war. He refused to call up the reserves and maintained tight restrictions on military operations, such as not allowing the mining of Haiphong Harbor and the selective bombing of North Vietnam. Because of the limited use of force, the Rolling Thunder campaign in the eyes of the administration became a bargaining tool, a political and psychological weapon—a system of "sticks and carrots" to persuade the North Vietnamese to stop their support of the southern insurgency and to negotiate. It was not to be used, as the military commanders desired, as a means to destroy the enemy's industry, to break his will, and to win the war. Similarly, the ground war in the South would not be pursued outside the borders of South Vietnam. This commitment to a limited war with limited resources in a limited geographic region, along with a lack of modern facilities, led to a policy of gradual escalation to meet these limited objectives.

President Nixon and his administration faced the same problems. But his goal perhaps was somewhat simpler. On his being sworn in, President Nixon and his advisers, without consulting the Joint Chiefs, quickly concluded that American casualties had to be reduced or eliminated if the American people were to continue to support him and the American effort in Vietnam. He developed the program of Vietnamization to achieve that goal and had his national security adviser, Henry Kissinger, almost endlessly negotiate with the North Vietnamese to end the war. It seems clear that he seldom consulted the Joint Chiefs, the secretary of defense, or other members of his administration until a decision had been reached in the White House. When it became clear that the North Vietnamese would not agree to a "mutual withdrawal" of forces from the South (although the Americans were withdrawing in any case), the American objective became merely obtaining the release of our prisoners of war in the North while leaving the South with a "peace with honor," with large amounts of American equipment, and with a vague promise to take "swift and severe retaliatory action" in case the communists violated the armistice agreement. Significant numbers of North Vietnamese forces were left in the South, and both sides issued instructions to their forces to "take as much land as possible" during the negotiations. It was clear that each side did not consider that a peace agreement would end the war in Vietnam.

In the end, it is the president and Congress who must determine and enunciate national objectives and the role of force in achieving those objectives. But the military, in accepting and working within those national objectives, must realistically define the capability of force to achieve those policy objectives, to not overstate the capabilities of its forces, and to make it clear to civilian authority just what force can accomplish and cannot be expected to accomplish in a given situation and within specific policy and material guidelines. The question, then, remains as to how to make the advice of the Joint Chiefs pertinent to the needs of the president and his secretary of defense. Clearly, a primary requirement is clarity and consistency in the statement of national objectives that military force is designed to support or implement. It is important that the determination of national objectives be the result of prior, conscientious deliberation rather than of default, of wishful thinking, of unilateral goals or determinations, or of assumptions or impressions as occurred during the Vietnam conflict. Once established, these objectives should be frequently subject to scrutiny and debate within the administration to ensure that these goals remain consistent with external conditions and with national political realities and capabilities and that the costs do not exceed the importance of the objective to be achieved.

Other presidents have wrestled with the problem of developing military advice within the constraints of political limitations and realities. President John F. Kennedy early in his administration admonished the Joint Chiefs to "base their advice not on narrow military considerations alone but on broad gauged political and economic factors as well." But clearly, it is not the role of the Joint Chiefs to recommend political and economic policy, and there is no evidence that they followed President Kennedy's directive. Looking at the war in Southeast Asia during the 1960s, one can conclude that there seemed to be little common understanding between the civil and military leaders as to what was to be achieved. Military goals were not developed to accomplish the objectives of a declared political policy. The policy aims almost directly precluded the chances of success of the military strategy implemented. The dangerous illusion of a military victory became the military mission even though it was not the national objective. The senior military leaders opposed the president's policy continuously and vociferously. This is not a decision-making process that can be tolerated under our system of government.

By the time Nixon assumed the presidency, a limit on the number of additional American forces to be committed to South Vietnam had been imposed by the previous administration, and he was prepared to accept it. But he had to find a way to disengage American forces from this unfortunate land and thus to reduce American casualties. He tried almost all the things that the Joint Chiefs had recommended and that President Johnson had refused to do. He invaded Cambodia and Laos, bombed Hanoi, and mined Haiphong Harbor. None of these military actions seemed to have any effect on the determined North Vietnamese. They continued to pursue their strategy of unity with the South by a "people's war" that the Americans had not undertaken and thus could not win.

Epilogue

And so what have we now learned from a careful analysis of the American decision-making process, the thoughts of the senior participants and observers in that decision-making process, and the new insights and points of view provided us by North Vietnamese officials? Clearly, the pursuit of military victory by U.S. forces in Vietnam was a dangerous illusion at least from the time of the death of Ngo Dinh Diem in 1964. From that time forward, there did not exist a legitimate and "independent noncommunist South Vietnam" that had the capability or interest in providing services and security to the rural population of South Vietnam and thereby winning their loyalty. American efforts to substitute for that government and army through the force of our arms was doomed to failure. Both presidents Kennedy and Johnson at some point in the decision-making process stated that they would not send American boys to do what South Vietnamese boys should be doing. But for various reasons and on the advice of their senior counselors, they did. And this nation found out tragically that 549,000 American soldiers, however courageous, well trained, equipped, supported, and supplied, were not the answer to South Vietnam's political problems. From 1964 to 1973, the so-called Republic of Vietnam existed only because of the willingness of the United States to send its soldiers to fight in its behalf. When that support was removed, the inevitable results could have been predicted, whether it was in 1964 or in 1973.

Another illusion created by American leaders was that the conflict in Vietnam represented the aggression of one sovereign state against another. What the United States called North Vietnamese "aggression" was seen from the point of view of the North Vietnamese and many of its southern sympathizers as nothing more than an attempt to complete the process of unifying

Vietnam free from foreign rule and under a revolutionary government, a process that had begun years before, that had been won from France on the battlefield in the first Vietnam War, and that had been promised in the armistice of the Geneva agreements. The war in Vietnam could have been seen as similar to the Chinese struggle between two elements both seeking the control and unity of their country after World War II. China, of course, was more important, but the United States refrained from sending troops to try to save its hapless ally there. Why this nation decided to intervene militarily in the similar indigenous struggle in Vietnam remains an American tragedy.

Because of the nature of the war, it might have been predicted that the chimera of military victory for South Vietnam and for the United States was always an illusion. American forces could win every battle but, as the French had discovered years before, could not overcome the ardor for unity and independence that burned in the hearts of the old nationalists of both North and South Vietnam. The "mind-set" of the North Vietnamese was that their nation was one and that no sacrifice was too great to achieve that unity denied to them by outside powers for hundreds, perhaps thousands, of years. The method chosen was a people's war to involve the rural populace in its own victory. The United States felt that it could win a conventional war against a fairly primitive conventional army. The method chosen by the United States was a war of fire and maneuver among a supposedly friendly foreign population and with little regard for the political consequences of its military actions.

Eisenhower's domino principle, accepted uncritically by a succession of American leaders, was a simplistic formula and had little or no validity in Southeast Asia. Nationalist and communist Vietnam was never a threat to the other nations of Southeast Asia and was never an agent of the Soviet Union or of communist China. As former Vietnamese diplomat Luu Doan Huynh stated, "If I may say so, you were not only wrong, but you had, so to speak, lost your minds. Vietnam a part of the Chinese expansionist game in Asia? For anyone who knows the history of Indochina, this is incomprehensible."[1]

Vietnam's invasion and occupation of Cambodia sometime later stopped genocide in that nation that in some ways was directed toward Vietnamese. Indeed, the North Vietnamese with whom we talked were somewhat upset by the fact that the international community viewed its occupation of Cambodia as an "invasion" when they rather saw it as a humanitarian operation to stop the genocide that the Khmer Rouge were undertaking there.

The United States at any time after 1964 could have attained a "peace with honor" by negotiating a settlement with North Vietnam or with the National Liberation Front for a coalition government in South Vietnam that eventually would have sought unity with the North. This could have been done with less harm to American international prestige and less harm to our national security than was occasioned by a fruitless, costly, and eventually humiliating military debacle. The Central Intelligence Agency reported this fact to President Johnson in 1967, but it was not widely circulated in the American government. But presidents Kennedy, Johnson, and Nixon all were not ready to accept a coalition government in the South that would include communists. The United States was committed emphatically and publicly to preventing a communist takeover of the South. In the interminable negotiations with President Nixon and his national security adviser, Henry Kissinger, the North Vietnamese insisted on a coalition government in the South that would not include President Thieu or any members of his government. The United States just as adamantly refused to dump Thieu. Only when the North Vietnamese dropped this demand was an agreement possible.

One fact emerges clearly from a study of the American decision-making process during this nation's involvement in Vietnam. That fact is that American strategic intelligence concerning North Vietnam was consistently accurate. Another fact that also is clear is that the senior decision makers in the U.S. government seldom if ever believed it or acted on it. Those two facts, in part, helped create the dangerous illusion of U.S. military victory in Vietnam.[2]

Subsequent to the end of the war, the American military continued to react in a conventional, unimaginative fashion. In the future, American military commanders insisted, American military forces would be used only in conventional wars where our advantages in firepower and mobility could be directed with overwhelming force against a massed enemy and "victory" could be ensured. There would be no more gradualism, no more political limitations, no more sanctuaries, no more fighting without winning, and no "substitute for victory." The Nixon Doctrine, propounded by the president in Guam in mid-1969 just as the "Vietnamization" program got under way, attempted to put this American approach into a broader context. At that time, President Nixon indicated that the United States "should avoid that kind of policy that will make countries in Asia so dependent upon us that we are dragged into conflicts. . . . The United States is going to encourage, and has the right to expect, that this problem [internal security] will increasingly be handled by . . . the Asian nations themselves."[3]

This led, in the minds of many American decision makers, military and nonmilitary, to the "Vietnam syndrome," the idea that military force had limited utility as well as little public support in the conduct of American foreign policy, that diplomacy should be allowed to work, and that the United States did not have important interests in many parts of the world. "No more Vietnams" became the watchword for both the military and those opposed to military intervention by the United States. Henceforth, American military officers insisted, the United States should not employ military force unless it had a clear idea as to why it was fighting, had public support, and was prepared to devote the resources and time required to see the war through to a victorious conclusion.

On November 28, 1984, during the large American military buildup, Secretary of Defense Casper Weinberger enunciated six criteria to be applied for the use of American military forces in the future. These criteria, which, in effect, codified the "Vietnam syndrome," seemed to be essential rules for avoiding another Vietnam. These guidelines, of course, declared what not to do with military force rather than when to take bold and imaginative military action. The Weinberger tests were thus designed to echo criticisms of the conduct of the Vietnam War from the American military. They ruled out the use of force except for vital national interests. They also demanded assurance of domestic support in advance of committing troops and called for clear political and military objectives. Another demand was the reasonable intention of achieving military victory when once engaged.[4] These criteria constituted a hurdle to the use of force so high that Secretary of State George Shultz later called them "a counsel of inaction bordering on paralysis."

The evolving world situation soon called into question the usefulness of Secretary Weinberger's criteria as a guide to action. After two major military operations, President George H. W. Bush reflected on the use of force in his valedictory address at the U.S. Military Academy at West Point. The outgoing president argued against fixed rules or rigid criteria. Instead of relegating the use of force by the United States to a last resort in extreme circumstances, as Weinberger had seemed to do, Bush endorsed military action for important but less vital national purposes. The Bush criteria were put into action in choices concerning U.S. military actions in Bosnia and Somalia. Through this evolution, a new and more flexible criterion became elaborated in military doctrine. *Joint Publication 3-0, Doctrine for Joint Operations*, published in 1995, goes far beyond earlier criteria by making significant distinctions among types of conflicts and alternative political goals. In war, the doctrine states, "the goal is to win as quickly and with as few casualties as possible, achieving national objectives and concluding hostilities on terms favorable to the United States." In "military operations other than war involving the use of force," however, the general goals are "to support national objectives, deter war, and return to a state of peace."

The document emphasizes that strategic direction for the employment of military forces comes from the National Command Authority (NCA) through the Chairman of the Joint Chiefs of Staff and the necessity for military activities "to be synchronized with other instruments of national power and focused on common national aims." The doctrine also places on the NCA, through the Chairman of the Joint Chiefs, the responsibility to ensure that "military objectives are defined, understood, and achievable."[5]

Thus, the leaders of the American military after Vietnam, as they have moved into positions of leadership and responsibility in their respective services, seem to have learned some of the lessons of Vietnam. They have transformed the American military from an inflexible focus on "defeating the enemy" at all costs (which it can still do) to a more flexible military able and willing to undertake many and varied missions to achieve various national objectives that they undoubtedly will encounter in the future. This has occurred in Haiti, Bosnia, and Kosovo. It has also occurred in Iraq by necessity as religious rebellion took place throughout the country after American troops deposed a despotic leader. In Iraq, it was the very premise of the American commander's successful plan for the so-called surge of American forces.[6] It appears to be planned in Afghanistan.

Already young soldiers have had to master the fundamentals of nation building, which was anathema to the American army of Vietnam days. The Bush administration also was initially reluctant to use the military to support nation-building efforts when it came into office. Now that the Soviet Union and nuclear war are no longer the major threats to America and now that the U.S. Army no longer looks to fighting on the plains of central Europe, it has become necessary for U.S. forces to be able to work with other people and nations to achieve its security objectives. At the Pentagon, Defense Secretary Robert M. Gates has cautioned the army not to assume that the counterinsurgency campaigns in Iraq and Afghanistan are anomalies. In October 2008, Gates stated that "unconventional wars" were "the ones most likely to be fought in the years ahead." A 2005 Pentagon directive advised the military to treat "stability operations" as a core mission.[7]

On February 27, 2008, the army published a revised field manual, *FM 3-0 Operations*, which incorporates army doctrine and adds the mission of stabilization of war-torn nations, making that mission equally important in doctrine to defeating enemies on the battlefield.[8] This was described as a major development that draws on the hard-learned lessons of Iraq and Afghanistan. In both countries, initial military successes by the U.S. Army gave way to long, grueling struggles among religious groups to establish control. The manual describes the United States as facing an era of "persistent conflict" in which the military will often operate among civilians in countries where local institutions are fragile and efforts to win over a wary population are crucial. Thus, American doctrine from Vietnam to the present day has changed from "no substitute for victory" to a spectrum of conflict extending from stable peace to general war to include "stability operations." Almost as a reminder of the failures of Vietnam, the manual states,

"Army doctrine now equally weights tasks dealing with the population—stability or civil support—with those related to offensive or defensive operations. Winning battles and engagements is important but alone is not sufficient. Shaping the civil situation is just as important to success."[9]

The army of the twenty-first century has elevated the mission of stabilizing war-torn nations, making it equally important in the proper circumstances as defeating the enemy on the battlefield. It remains to be seen whether training and organizational changes will follow suit.

Notes

PREFACE

1. McNamara et al., *Argument without End*, preface.
2. Blight and Welch, *On the Brink*; Blight, Allyn, and Welch, *Cuba on the Brink*, 250–62; Blight and Lang, "Burden of Nuclear Responsibility."
3. Schandler, "The Pentagon and Peace Negotiations after March 31, 1968."
4. "Missed Opportunities? II," transcript, corrected version, 39.

CHAPTER 1

1. Walton, *The Myth of Inevitable U.S. Defeat in Vietnam*, 5.
2. Braestrup, *Big Story*.
3. Mueller, "Reflections on the Vietnam Anti-War Movement and on the Curious Calm at the War's End," 151.
4. Palmer, *The 25-Year War*, 46.
5. Summers, "A Strategic Perception of the Vietnam War," 35.
6. Summers, *On Strategy*, 1.
7. Kinnard, *The War Managers*.
8. *Foreign Relations of the United States, 1949*, vol. VII, pt. 2, 1215–20.
9. U.S. Congress, *United States–Vietnam Relations, 1945–1967*, vol. 2, sec. IV.B.3, 39. See also vol. 3, sec. IV.C.1, 46–55.
10. *Public Papers of the Presidents: Lyndon B. Johnson, 1965, Vol. I*, 395.

CHAPTER 2

1. MacMillan, *Paris, 1919*, 54.
2. Duiker, *Ho Chi Minh*, 361.

3. Eisenhower, *The White House Years*, 400–402.
4. "Missed Opportunities? II," transcript, corrected version, 35.
5. Eisenhower, *The White House Years*, 349–56.
6. Duiker, *Ho Chi Minh*, 348.
7. "Missed Opportunities?," 354–55; see also U.S. Congress, *United States–Vietnam Relations*, vol. 1, secs. II.B.1, B11–B13, B22–B31, and Buzzanco, *Masters of War*, 41–45.
8. Eisenhower, *The White House Years*, 369–72.
9. *Public Papers of the Presidents: Dwight D. Eisenhower, Vol. II, 1954*, 2397.
10. Eisenhower, *The White House Years*, 371.

CHAPTER 3

1. *Public Papers of the Presidents: Dwight D. Eisenhower, Vol. II, 1954.*
2. Embassy, Paris to State Department, December 19, 1954, quoted in *United States–Vietnam Relations*, vol. 1, sec. IV.A.3, 22.
3. U.S. Congress, *United States–Vietnam Relations, 1945–1967*, vol. 2, sec. IV.A.2, 25; Hoopes, *The Devil and John Foster Dulles*, 242–44.
4. Record, *The Wrong War*, 4.
5. Eisenhower, *The White House Years*, 374.
6. Joint Chiefs of Staff, *The History of the Joint Chiefs of Staff.*
7. BDM Corporation, *A Study of Strategic Lessons Learned in Vietnam*, 3-1-3-2.
8. Cochran, "American Planning for Ground Combat in Vietnam, 1952–1965," 65.
9. Spector, "The First Vitalization," 109–15; see also U.S. Congress, *United States–Vietnam Relations*, vol. 2, sec. IV.A.4, 22–31.
10. Cable, *Conflict of Myths*, 177–78.
11. Prados, *The Hidden History of the Vietnam War.*
12. McNamara et al., *Argument without End*, 78–86.
13. "Missed Opportunities? II," transcript, corrected version, 38–39, 48.
14. Jacobs, *Cold War Mandarin*, 42–43.
15. "Missed Opportunities? II," transcript, corrected version, 49.

CHAPTER 4

1. Duiker, *Ho Chi Minh*, 463–64.
2. "Missed Opportunities? II," transcript, corrected version, 38–39.
3. Duiker, *Ho Chi Minh*, 493–94.
4. "Missed Opportunities? II," transcript, corrected version, 40–41.
5. "Missed Opportunities? II," transcript, corrected version, June 20–23, 1997, 49.
6. "Missed Opportunities? II," transcript, corrected version, February 23–26, 1998, 6, 33.

7. "Missed Opportunities? II," transcript, corrected version, February 23–26, 1998, 6, 33.

8. "Missed Opportunities? II," transcript, corrected version, February 23–26, 1998, 50–52, 56, 58–59.

9. McNamara, *In Retrospect*, 113–17; Johnson, *The Vantage Point*, 62–66; Taylor, *Swords and Plowshares*, 308–11; U.S. Congress, *United States–Vietnam Relations*, vol. 3, sec. IV.C.1, 40–55.

10. Duiker, *Ho Chi Minh*, 513–15, 525–26; U.S. Congress, *United States–Vietnam Relations, 1945–1967*, vol. 3, sec. IV.A.5. 31, 64–65.

11. "Missed Opportunities? II," transcript, corrected version, 15–16.

12. *Foreign Relations of the United States, Vietnam, 1964–1968, Volume I: Vietnam, 1964*, 165.

13. Curry, *Edward Lansdale*, 222–24.

14. Curry, *Edward Lansdale*, 226–29.

15. Duiker, *The Communist Road to Power in Vietnam*, 245.

16. U.S. Congress, *United States–Vietnam Relations*, vol. 3, sec. IV.B.5, 41–42; Taylor, *Swords and Plowshares*, 311; Herring, *America's Longest War*, 137.

17. U.S. Congress, *United States–Vietnam Relations, 1945–1967*, vol. 3, sec. IV.B.3, 37–60.

18. U.S. Congress, *United States–Vietnam Relations, 1945–1967*, vol. 2, sec. IV.B.1, 125–33.

19. U.S. Congress, *United States–Vietnam Relations, 1945–1967*, vol. 3, sec. IV.B.3, 26–29.

20. U.S. Congress, *United States–Vietnam Relations, 1945–1967*, vol. 3, sec. IV.B.2, i–iv, 1–35.

21. "Missed Opportunities? II," transcript, corrected version, June 20–23, 1997, 121–24.

22. "Missed Opportunities? II," transcript, corrected version, February 23–26, 1998, 102.

23. U.S. Congress, *United States–Vietnam Relations, 1945–1967*, vol. 3, sec. IV.C.2.(a), i–ii.

24. Prochnau, *Once upon a Distant War*.

25. "Missed Opportunities? II," transcript, corrected version, 48.

26. Duiker, *Ho Chi Minh*, 625–27.

27. U.S. Congress, *United States–Vietnam Relations, 1945–1967*, vol. 3, sec. IV.B.2, 19–20.

28. U.S. Congress, *United States–Vietnam Relations*, vol. 3, sec. IV.B.5, i–viii.

29. "Missed Opportunities? II," transcript, corrected version, June 20–23, 1997, 65.

30. Hunt, *Pacification*.

31. "Missed Opportunities? II," transcript, corrected version, 51–52.

32. "Missed Opportunities? II," transcript, corrected version, 32.

33. "Missed Opportunities? II," transcript, corrected version, 53.

34. Duiker, *Ho Chi Minh*, 534.

35. Duiker, *Ho Chi Minh*, 535.

36. Westmoreland, *Report on the War in Vietnam*, 71.
37. Johnson, *The Vantage Point*, 143–44.

CHAPTER 5

1. Windchy, *Tonkin Gulf*, 317; Goulden, *Truth Is the First Casualty*, 37, 48–79; U.S. Congress, Committee on Foreign Relations, *The Gulf of Tonkin*.
2. *Public Papers of the Presidents: Lyndon B. Johnson*, 927–28; Johnson, *The Vantage Point*, 119–20; Taylor, *Swords and Plowshares*, 321; U.S. Congress, *United States–Vietnam Relations*, vol. 4, sec. IV.C.2.B, 19–27.
3. Robert S. McNamara et al., *Argument without End*, 167.
4. *Public Papers of the Presidents, Lyndon B. Johnson*, 930–32; 93; Johnson, *The Vantage Point*, 118–19.
5. U.S. Congress, Committee on Foreign Relations, U.S. Senate, 100th Congress, 2nd Session, *The U.S. Government and the Vietnam War*, vol. 2, 349–50.
6. U.S. Congress, *United States–Vietnam Relations*, vol. 6, sec. IV.C.6.A, 23–24.
7. Johnson, *The Vantage Point*, 118–19.
8. Johnson, *The Vantage Point*, 120.
9. Westmoreland, *Report on the War in Vietnam*, 95; Westmoreland, *A Soldier Reports*, 62–65, 71–74, 77–81, 90–98.
10. U.S. Congress, *United States–Vietnam Relations*, vol. 6, sec. IV.C.7.B, 124–25.
11. Johnson, *The Vantage Point*, 120.
12. Johnson, *The Vantage Point*, 121.
13. Clodfelter, *The Limits of Airpower*, 35–37, 100–102; Drew, *Rolling Thunder 1965*, 26–29.
14. U.S. Congress, *United States–Vietnam Relations*, vol. 6, sec. IV.C.7.A, 54–57. For accounts of the political turmoil in South Vietnam during this period, see Duncanson, *Government and Revolution in Vietnam*, 342–51, and Shaplen, *The Lost Revolution*, 266–322.
15. U.S. Congress, *United States–Vietnam Relations*, vol. 6, sec. V.C.7.B, 125.
16. Taylor, *Swords and Plowshares*, 337–38.
17. "Missed Opportunities? II," transcript, corrected version, 61.
18. Johnson, *The Vantage Point*, 126–27.

CHAPTER 6

1. U.S. Congress, *United States–Vietnam Relations, 1945–1967*, vol. 6, sec. IV.C.7(a), 1; Clodfelter, *The Limits of Airpower*, 62.
2. U.S. Congress, *United States–Vietnam Relations, 1945–1967*, vol. 6, sec. IV.C.7(a), 3; Clodfelter, *The Limits of Airpower*, 66.

3. U.S. Congress, *United States–Vietnam Relations, 1945–1967*, vol. 6, sec. IV.C.7(a), 9–10.

4. National Security Council, NSSM 1, "Summary of Responses to NSSM 1— The Situation in Vietnam," *Congressional Record* 118, no. 176 (May 10, 1972), E4981; U.S. Congress, Committee on Foreign Relations, U.S. Senate, *Bombing as a Policy Tool in Vietnam*, 12.

5. U.S. Congress, *United States–Vietnam Relations 1945–1967*, vol. 6, sec. IV.C.7(a), 16; Clodfelter, *The Limits of Airpower*, 77–78.

6. Prados, *The Hidden History of the Vietnam War*, 187.

7. U.S. Congress, *United States–Vietnam Relations, 1945–1967*, vol. 6, sec. IV.C.7(a), 20–28.

8. U.S. Congress, *United States–Vietnam Relations, 1945–1967*, vol. 6, sec. IV.C.7(a), 31–32.

9. U.S. Congress, *United States–Vietnam Relations, 1945–1967*, vol. 6, sec. IV.C.7(a), 33–34.

10. U.S. Congress, *United States–Vietnam Relations, 1945–1967*, vol. 6, sec. IV.C.7(a), 60–65.

11. Clodfelter, *The Limits of Airpower*, 90–91; see also U.S. Congress, *United States–Vietnam Relations, 1945–1967*, vol. 6, sec. 4.C.7(a), 179–80.

12. U.S. Congress, Committee on Armed Services, U.S. Senate, *Air War against North Vietnam*; see also U.S. Congress, *United States–Vietnam Relations, 1945–1967*, vol. 6, sec. 4.C.7(b), 99.

13. U.S. Congress, Committee on Armed Services, U.S. Senate, *Air War against North Vietnam*; see also U.S. Congress, *United States–Vietnam Relations, 1945–1967*, vol. 6, sec. 4.C.7(b), 93–97.

14. U.S. Congress, *United States–Vietnam Relations, 1945–1967*, vol. 6, sec. IV.C.(b), 122.

15. U.S. Congress, *United States–Vietnam Relations, 1945–1967*, vol. 6, sec. IV.C.(b), 127.

16. U.S. Congress, *United States–Vietnam Relations, 1945–1967*, vol. 6, sec. IV.C.(b), 124–25.

17. Clodfelter, *The Limits of Airpower*, 35–36.

18. U.S. Congress, *United States–Vietnam Relations, 1945–1967*, vol. 6, sec. IV.C.(a), 178.

19. U.S. Congress, *United States–Vietnam Relations, 1945–1967*, vol. 6, sec. IV.C.(a), 179.

20. U.S. Congress, *United States–Vietnam Relations, 1945–1967*, vol. 6, sec. IV.C.(a), 175–76.

21. U.S. Congress, *United States–Vietnam Relations, 1945–1967*, vol. 6, sec. IV.C.(a), 177.

22. "Missed Opportunities II: Military Conversations," 25.

23. U.S. Congress, *United States–Vietnam Relations, 1945–1967*, vol. 6, sec. IV.C.(b), 3.

24. "Missed Opportunities II: Military Conversations," 25.

25. U.S. Congress, *United States–Vietnam Relations, 1945–1967*, vol. 6, sec. IV.C.7(b), 31.

26. U.S. Congress, *United States–Vietnam Relations, 1945–1967*, vol. 6, sec. IV.C.7(b), 33.

27. "Missed Opportunities II: Military Conversations," 25.

28. Clodfelter, *The Limits of Airpower*, 128–29.

29. U.S. Congress, *United States–Vietnam Relations, 1945–1967*, vol. 6, sec. IV.C.7(b), 35–36; Clodfelter, *The Limits of Airpower*, 140–42.

30. Clodfelter, *The Limits of Airpower*, 142.

31. Vu Can, *North Vietnam*, 24–25.

32. Duiker, *Sacred War*, 200.

33. "Missed Opportunities II: Military Conversations," 25.

34. Salisbury, *Behind the Lines*, 114.

35. Vietnam News Agency, June 5, 1971.

36. "Missed Opportunities II: Military Conversations," 25.

37. Sharp, *Report on the War in Vietnam*, 38–39.

38. U.S. Congress, *United States–Vietnam Relations, 1945–1967*, vol. 6, sec. IV.C.7.(b), 123–24.

39. U.S. Congress, *United States–Vietnam Relations, 1945–1967*, vol. 6, sec. IV.C.7(b), 170.

40. Schandler, "The Pentagon and Peace Negotiations after March 31, 1968."

41. Tilford, *Setup*.

42. Littauer and Uphoff, *The Air War in Indochina*, 281.

43. Tilford, *Setup*.

CHAPTER 7

1. U.S. Congress, *United States–Vietnam Relations, 1945–1967*, vol. 4, sec. IV.C.4.1, 1.

2. U.S. Congress, *United States–Vietnam Relations 1945–1967*, vol. 4, sec. IV.C.4.1, 2–6; see also Westmoreland, *A Soldier Reports*, 123.

3. U.S. Congress, *United States–Vietnam Relations, 1945–1967*, vol. 5, sec. IV.C.4, 56–59.

4. Johnson, *The Vantage Point*, 139–41; U.S. Congress, *United States–Vietnam Relations, 1945–1967*, vol. 4, sec. IV.C.5, 55–60.

5. U.S. Congress, *United States–Vietnam Relations, 1945–1967*, vol. 4, sec. IV.C.5, 68–69, 124–26; Johnson, *The Vantage Point*, 140–41.

6. U.S. Congress, *United States–Vietnam Relations, 1945–1967*, vol. 4, sec. IV.C.5, 126.

7. U.S. Congress, *United States–Vietnam Relations, 1945–1967*, vol. 4, sec. IV.C.5, 81.

8. "Ground War in Asia," *New York Times*, June 9, 1965, 46, col. 1.

9. U.S. Department of State, *Department of State Bulletin*, vol. 52, 1041; U.S. Congress, *United States–Vietnam Relations, 1945–1967*, vol. 4, sec. IV.C.5, 344–35; Westmoreland, *A Soldier Reports*, 135–36, 138–39.

10. Taylor, *Swords and Plowshares*, 341–42; U.S. Congress, *United States–Vietnam Relations, 1945–1967*, vol. 5, sec. IV.C.6(a), 8–9; Westmoreland, *A Soldier Reports*.

11. U.S. Congress, *United States–Vietnam Relations, 1945–1967*, vol. 4, sec. IV.C.3, 101, and sec. IV.C.5, 77–79; Taylor, *Swords and Plowshares*, 342–43.

12. Westmoreland, *A Soldier Reports*, 129–30; U.S. Congress, *United States–Vietnam Relations, 1945–1967*, vol. 4, sec. IV.C.5, 57–58, 9–10.

13. Westmoreland, *Report on the War in Vietnam*, 129.

14. U.S. Congress, *United States–Vietnam Relations, 1945–1967*, vol. 5, sec. IV.C.6(a), 8–9.

15. U.S. Congress, *United States–Vietnam Relations, 1945–1967*, vol. 4, sec. IV.C.5, 7–8; Westmoreland, *A Soldier Reports*, 95.

16. Westmoreland, *A Soldier Reports*, 142.

17. U.S. Congress, *United States–Vietnam Relations, 1945–1967*, vol. 4, sec. IV.C.5, 104–105.

18. U.S. Congress, *United States–Vietnam Relations, 1945–1967*, vol. 4, sec. IV.C.5, 105; Johnson, *The Vantage Point*, 147.

19. McNamara, *In Retrospect*, 203.

20. Taylor, *Swords and Plowshares*, 349; U.S. Congress, *United States–Vietnam Relations, 1945–1967*, vol. 4, sec. IV.C.5, 104–105.

21. U.S. Congress, *United States–Vietnam Relations, 1945–1967*, vol. 4, sec. IV.C.5, 105, and vol. 6, sec. IV.C.7(a), 6–8.

22. U.S. Congress, *United States–Vietnam Relations, 1945–1967*, vol. 6, sec. IV.C.7(a), 8.

23. Valenti, *A Very Human President*, 354–55; Johnson, *The Vantage Point*, 151.

24. Johnson, *The Vantage Point*, 148, 151–52. The discussions and opinions involved in this decision-making process have been detailed in Berman, *Planning a Tragedy*; VandeMark, *Into the Quagmire*; and, more recently, McMaster, *Dereliction of Duty*.

25. *Public Papers of the Presidents: Lyndon B. Johnson, 1965*, vol. II, 794–99.

26. Johnson, *The Vantage Point*, 153.

27. Tuchman, *Practicing History*, 257.

28. Transcript of a conversation between Herbert Schandler and Colonel Quach Hai Luong, June 20–23, 1997, 2.

29. "Missed Opportunities?," 61.

30. "Missed Opportunities?," 145–46.

31. "Missed Opportunities?," 154.

32. JCSM 625-65, August 27, 1965, Subject: Concept for Vietnam, quoted in U.S. Congress, *United States–Vietnam Relations, 1945-1967*, vol. 5, sec. IV.C.6(a), 15.

33. Transcript, 88–90.

34. U.S. Congress, *United States–Vietnam Relations, 1945–1967*, vol. 5, sec. IV.C.6(a), 14.

35. U.S. Congress, *United States–Vietnam Relations, 1945–1967*, vol. 5, sec. IV.C.6(a), 15.

36. U.S. Congress, *United States–Vietnam Relations, 1945–1967*, vol. 5, sec. IV.C.6(a), 22.

37. "Missed Opportunities?," 146.

38. U.S. Congress, *United States–Vietnam Relations, 1945–1967*, vol. 5, sec. IV.C.6(a), 4–25.

39. U.S. Congress, *United States–Vietnam Relations, 1945–1967*, vol. 5, sec. IV.C.6(a), 20–23.

40. U.S. Congress, *United States–Vietnam Relations, 1945–1967*, vol. 5, sec. IV.C.6(a), 30.

41. Westmoreland, *A Soldier Reports*, 160.

42. For details of the American logistical buildup, see Heiser, *Vietnam Studies*, 8–34.

43. U.S. Congress, *United States–Vietnam Relations, 1945–1967*, vol. 5, sec. IV.C.6(b), 34–41.

44. U.S. Congress, *United States–Vietnam Relations, 1945–1967*, vol. 5, sec. IV.C.6(b), 53–54.

45. U.S. Congress, *United States–Vietnam Relations, 1945–1967*, vol. 5, sec. IV.C.6(b), 80–81.

46. U.S. Congress, *United States–Vietnam Relations, 1945–1967*, vol. 5, sec. IV.C.6(b), 83–93.

47. U.S. Congress, *United States–Vietnam Relations, 1945–1967*, vol. 5, sec. IV.C.6(b), 93–100.

48. U.S. Congress, *United States–Vietnam Relations, 1945–1967*, vol. 5, sec. IV.C.6(b), 108–10.

49. U.S. Congress, *United States–Vietnam Relations, 1945–1967*, vol. 5, sec. IV.C.6(b), 61–67.

50. U.S. Congress, *United States–Vietnam Relations, 1945–1967*, vol. 5, sec. IV.C.6(b), 73–75.

51. U.S. Congress, *United States–Vietnam Relations, 1945–1967*, vol. 5, sec. IV.C.6(b), 82–85.

52. Taylor, *Swords and Plowshares*, 375–76. For accounts of allied participation in the war, see Larsen and Collins, *Vietnam Studies*. See also Thompson, *Unequal Partners*, 73–112.

53. U.S. Congress, *United States–Vietnam Relations, 1945–1967*, vol. 5, sec. IV.C.6(b), 214–15, 93–100.

54. Trewhitt, *McNamara*, 227–45; Johnson, *The Vantage Point*, 372.

55. U.S. Congress, *United States–Vietnam Relations, 1945–1967*, vol. 5, sec. IV.C.6(b), 222–24.

56. U.S. Congress, *United States–Vietnam Relations, 1945–1967*, vol. 5, sec. IV.C.6(b), 223.

57. Johnson, *The Vantage Point*, 20.

58. Address by General William C. Westmoreland to the National Press Club, November 21, 1967, 7, 11.

CHAPTER 8

1. U.S. Congress, *United States–Vietnam Relations*, vol. 5, section IV.C.C, 2.
2. "Missed Opportunities? II," transcript, corrected version, 74.
3. "Missed Opportunities? II," 68–69.
4. Westmoreland, *Report on the War in Vietnam*, 163.
5. Ford, *CIA and the Vietnam Policymakers*, 104–13.
6. Duncanson, *Government and Revolution in Vietnam*, 53.
7. Son, *The Vietcong Tet Offensive, 1968*, 25–26.
8. Westmoreland, *Report on the War in Vietnam*, 157.
9. MACV 01614, 0409 February 1968, General Westmoreland to General Wheeler.
10. U.S. Congress, *United States–Vietnam Relations*, vol. 5, sec. IV.C.6.C, 12–16.
11. Braestrup, *Big Story*.
12. McCarthy, *Eugene 3*, 265–67.
13. Schandler, *The Unmaking of a President*, 920; U.S. Congress, *United States–Vietnam Relations*, vol. 5, sec. IV.C.6.C, 80–88.
14. "Missed Opportunities? II," 74–75.

CHAPTER 9

1. U.S. Bureau of the Budget, *Budget of the United States Government for the Fiscal Year Ending June 7, 1996*; see also U.S. Congress, Joint Economic Committee, *Economic Effect of Vietnam Spending, Hearings*, 205.
2. A major portion of this discussion is condensed from Helsing, *Johnson's War/Johnson's Great Society*.
3. King, "The Casualties of the War in Vietnam."
4. Johnson, *The Vantage Point*, 318.
5. U.S. Board of Governors of the Federal Reserve System, *Fifty-Fifth Annual Report of the Board of Governors of the Federal Reserve System, 1958*, 331–32; Bach, *Making Monetary and Fiscal Policy*, 137.
6. Johnson, *The Vantage Point*, 406–407.
7. Karnow, *Vietnam*, 596.

CHAPTER 10

1. Nixon, *RN*, 349.
2. Kimball, *Nixon's Vietnam War*, 188–89.
3. Berman, *No Peace, No Honor*, 52.
4. Kissinger, *White House Years*, 436.
5. Kimball, *Nixon's Vietnam War*, 181–82.

6. Transcript of a conversation between Colonel Herb Schandler and Colonel Quach Hai Luong, Institute for International Relations, Hanoi, Vietnam, February 23–26, 1998, 32.

7. Kissinger, *White House Years*, 35.

8. Berman, *No Peace, No Honor*, 52–53.

9. Nixon, *RN*, 380–82; see also Shawcross, *Sideshow*.

10. Nixon, *No More Vietnams*, 108.

11. Nixon, *RN*, 446–51. For additional details of the Cambodian operation and the American public's reaction, see Shawcross, *Sideshow*. For a refutation of Shawcross's explanation, see Kissinger, *Ending the Vietnam War*, appendix, 567–81.

12. Nixon, *RN*, 449–51, 455–57; Heineman, *Campus Wars*, 246–50.

13. DeBenedetti, *An American Ordeal*, 253, 286.

14. Kissinger, *White House Years*, 979.

15. There remains some controversy as to whether General Abrams recommended this attack or whether the attack was forced on him by Washington. Kissinger, *The White House Years*, 991, indicated that the dry-season offensive was recommended by Bunker, Abrams, and Thieu. They were in favor of a bold Laotian operation to cut the Ho Chi Minh Trail in Laos near the Demilitarized Zone. Kissinger then goes on to describe President Nixon's strategy in gaining approval for this move from the members of his administration (994–1000). In his biography of General Abrams, *Thunderbolt*, Lewis Sorley states only that "an all-South Vietnamese invasion of Laos was planned and conducted" (305). In his later book *A Better War*, Sorley quotes Al Haig as stating, concerning the origin of the operation, "I would say that the pressure came from here, from the White House" (263).

16. Kimball, *Nixon's Vietnam War*, 248.

17. Kissinger, *White House Years*, 1010.

18. Kissinger, *Ending the Vietnam War*, 233.

19. For a description of the use of airpower in this campaign, see Lavalle, *Airpower and the 1972 Spring Invasion*. A more brief version is contained in Givens, *Turning the Vertical Flank*, 49–64.

20. Nixon, *RN*, 603–606.

21. Berman, *No Peace, No Honor*, 81.

22. Nixon, *RN*, 349.

23. Berman, *No Peace, No Honor*, 41–43.

24. Berman, *No Peace, No Honor*, 52–53, 66.

25. Berman, *No Peace, No Honor*, 43–44.

26. Kissinger, *Ending the Vietnam War*, 182; Berman, *No Peace, No Honor*, 77–78.

27. Berman, *No Peace, No Honor*, 155–56; Zhai, *China and the Vietnam Wars, 1950–1975*, 204–205.

28. Kissinger, *White House Years*; Berman, *No Peace, No Honor*, 80–81.

29. Kissinger, *Ending the Vietnam War*, 210, 337.

30. Kissinger, *Ending the Vietnam War*, 385; Kissinger, *White House Years*, 1412.

31. Kissinger, *Ending the Vietnam War*, 374–76; Nixon, *RN*, 705–706.

32. Kissinger, *Ending the Vietnam War*, 387–408; Kissinger, *White House Years*, 1415–46.

33. The Christmas bombing is examined in detail in Michel, *The 11 Days of Christmas*. A shorter version is in Ambrose, *Americans at War*, 162–76.

34. Berman, *No Peace, No Honor*, 215.

35. Michel, *The 11 Days of Christmas*, 236.

CHAPTER 11

1. Summers, *On Strategy*, 95–105.

2. Conference, Institute for International Relations, Hanoi, Vietnam, February 23–26, 1998, Transcript, 23.

3. Transcript, conversation between Colonel Herb Schandler and Colonel Quach Hai Luong, 5.

4. Transcript, conversation between Colonel Herb Schandler and Colonel Quach Hai Luong, February 23–26, 1998, 20.

5. Transcript, conversation between Colonel Herb Schandler and Colonel Quach Hai Luong, February 23–26, 1998, 22.

6. Transcript, conversation between Colonel Herb Schandler and Colonel Quach Hai Luong, February 23–26, 1998, 22.

7. McNamara et al., *Argument without End*, 42; see also McNamara, *In Retrospect*, 29.

8. Johnson, *The Vantage Point*, 152.

9. McMaster, *Dereliction of Duty*, 65.

10. Komer, *Bureaucracy Does Its Thing*, 18; Hunt, *Pacification*; see also *United States–Vietnam Relations*, vol. 6, sec. IV.C.8.

11. Thompson, *No Exit from Vietnam*, 146, 149.

12. McNamara et al., *Argument without End*, 192–93.

13. Prados, *The Hidden History of the Vietnam War*, 120.

14. Herrington, *Stalking the Vietcong*.

15. Gelb and Betts, *The Irony of Vietnam*.

EPILOGUE

1. McNamara et al., *Argument without End*, 81.

2. Ford, "Why CIA Analysts Were So Doubtful about Vietnam"; Ford, "Thoughts Engendered by Robert McNamara's *In Retrospect*"; Ford, *CIA and the Vietnam Policymakers*.

3. *Public Papers of the Presidents: Richard Nixon, 1969*, 548–49.

4. Office of the Assistant Secretary of Defense, Public Affairs, *The Uses of Military Power*.

5. Joint Chiefs of Staff, *Joint Publication 3-0*, viii, I-2–I-4.

6. Ricks, "A Military Tactician's Political Strategy," A7.

7. Gordon, "After Hard-Won Lessons, Army Doctrine Revised," 1–3.

8. *FM 3-0, Operations*, Headquarters, Department of the Army, Washington, DC, February 27, 2008.

9. Carter, "Army Manual Stresses Nation Building," 1–3.

Bibliography

Allen, George. *None So Blind: A Personal Account of the Intelligence Failure in Vietnam*. Chicago: Ivan R. Dee, 2001.

Ambrose, Stephen E. *Americans at War*. Jackson: University Press of Mississippi, 1997.

Andradé, Dale. *Trial by Fire: The 1972 Easter Offensive: America's Last Vietnam Battle*. New York: Hippocrene, 1995.

Bach, George L. *Making Monetary and Fiscal Policy*. Washington, DC: Brookings Institution Press, 1971.

Barrett, David M. *Uncertain Warriors: Lyndon Johnson and His Vietnam Advisers*. Lawrence: University Press of Kansas, 1993.

BDM Corporation. *A Study of Strategic Lessons Learned in Vietnam: Volume 5, Planning the War*. McLean, VA: BDM Corporation, 1980.

Berger, Carl, ed. *The United States Air Force in Southeast Asia, 1961–1973: An Illustrated Account*. Rev. ed. Washington, DC: Office of Air Force History, United States Air Force, 1984.

Berman, Larry. *No Peace, No Honor: Nixon, Kissinger, and Betrayal in Vietnam*. New York: Free Press, 2001.

———. *Planning a Tragedy: The Americanization of the War in Vietnam*. New York: Norton, 1982.

Bernstein, Irving. *Guns or Butter: The Presidency of Lyndon Johnson*. New York: Oxford University Press, 1996.

Blaufarb, Douglas. *The Counterinsurgency Era*. New York: Free Press, 1977.

Blight, James G., Bruce J. Allyn, and David A. Welch. *Cuba on the Brink: Castro, the Missile Crisis and the Soviet Collapse*. Exp. and rev. paperback ed. Lanham, MD: Rowman & Littlefield, 2002.

Blight, James G., and janet M. Lang. "Burden of Nuclear Responsibility: Reflections on the Critical Oral History of the Cuban Missile Crisis." *Peace and Conflict: Journal of Peace Psychology* 1, no. 3 (1995): 225–64.

Blight, James G., and David A. Welch. *On the Brink: Americans and Soviets Reexamine the Cuban Missile Crisis*. Rev. paperback ed. New York: Hill & Wang, 1990.

Braestrup, Peter. *Big Story: How the American Press and Television Reported and Interpreted the Crisis of Tet 1968 in Viet Nam and Washington*. 2 vols. Boulder, CO: Westview, 1976.

———, ed. *Vietnam as History: Ten Years after the Paris Peace Accords*. Washington, DC: University Press of America, 1984.

Buzzanco, Robert. *Masters of War: Military Dissent and Politics in the Vietnam Era*. Cambridge: Cambridge University Press, 1996.

Cable, Larry E. *Conflict of Myths: The Development of American Counterinsurgency Doctrine and the Vietnam War*. New York: New York University Press, 1986.

Carter, Sara. "Army Manual Stresses Nation Building." *Washington Times*, March 3, 2008, 1–3.

Catton, Philip E. *Diem's Final Failure: Prelude to America's War in Vietnam*. Lawrence: University Press of Kansas, 2004.

Chapuis, Oscar. *The Last Emperors of Vietnam: From Tu Doc to Bao Dai*. Westport, CT: Greenwood, 2000.

Clifford, Clark, with Richard Holbrooke. *Counsel to the President: A Memoir*. New York: Random House, 1991.

Clodfelter, Mark. *The Limits of Airpower: The American Bombing of North Vietnam*. New York: Free Press, 1989.

Cochran, Alexander S., Jr. "American Planning for Ground Combat in Vietnam, 1952–1965." *Parameters: Journal of the U.S. Army War College* 14, no. 2 (Summer 1984): 63–69.

Cohen, Eliot A. *Supreme Command: Soldiers, Statesmen, and Leadership in Wartime*. New York: Free Press, 2002.

Cooper, Chester. *The Lost Crusade: America in Vietnam*. New York: Dodd Mead, 1970.

Curry, Cecil B. *Edward Lansdale: The Unquiet American*. Washington, DC: Brassey's, 1998.

DeBenedetti, Charles. *An American Ordeal: The Antiwar Movement of the Vietnam Era*. Syracuse, NY: Syracuse University Press, 1990.

Dixon, Joe C., ed. *The American Military and the Far East, Proceedings of the Ninth Military History Symposium, U.S. Air Force Academy, 1980*. Washington, DC: Office of Air Force History, 1980.

Drew, S. Nelson. *Rolling Thunder 1965: Anatomy of a Failure*. Maxwell Air Force Base, AL: Air University Press, 1986.

———, ed. *NSC-68: Forging the Strategy of Containment*. Washington, DC: National Defense University Press, 1994.

Duiker, William J. *China and Vietnam: The Roots of Conflict*. Berkeley: University of California Press, 1986.

———. *The Communist Road to Power in Vietnam*. Boulder, CO: Westview, 1981.

———. *Ho Chi Minh: A Life*. New York: Hyperion, 2000.

———. *Sacred War: Nationalism and Revolution in a Divided Vietnam*. New York: McGraw-Hill, 1995.

———. *Vietnam: Nation in Revolution.* Boulder, CO: Westview, 1983.

Duncanson, Dennis J. *Government and Revolution in Vietnam.* New York: Oxford University Press, 1968.

Dyson, F. J., R. Gomer, S. Weinberg, S. C. Wright, et al. *Nuclear Weapons in Southeast Asia, Study S-266.* Jason Division, Institute of Defense Analysis, Contract DAHC15 67 C 0011, published March 1967, declassified December 2003.

Eisenhower, Dwight D. *The White House Years: Mandate for Change, a Personal Memoir, 1953–1956.* Garden City, NY: Doubleday, 1963.

Ford, Harold P. *CIA and the Vietnam Policymakers: Three Episodes, 1962–1968.* Washington, DC: Central Intelligence Agency, 1998.

———. "Thoughts Engendered by Robert McNamara's *In Retrospect.*" *Studies in Intelligence* 35, no. 5 (1996): 95–109.

———. "Why CIA Analysts Were So Doubtful about Vietnam." *Studies in Intelligence*, no. 1 (1997): 85–95.

Foreign Relations of the United States, 1949. Vol. VII. Washington, DC: U.S. Government Printing Office, 1976.

Foreign Relations of the United States, Vietnam, 1961–1963. Washington, DC: U.S. Government Printing Office, 1991.

Foreign Relations of the United States, Vietnam, 1964–1968. Vol. I. Washington, DC: U.S. Government Printing Office, 1992.

Gardner, Lloyd C. *Pay Any Price: Lyndon Johnson and the Wars for Vietnam.* Chicago: Ivan R. Dee, 1995.

Gardner, Lloyd C., and Ted Gittinger, eds. *The Search for Peace in Vietnam, 1964–1968.* College Station: Texas A&M University Press, 2004.

Gelb, Leslie H., and Richard K. Betts. *The Irony of Vietnam: The System Worked.* Washington, DC: Brookings Institution Press, 1979.

Geyelin, Phillip L. *Lyndon Johnson and the World.* New York: Praeger, 1966.

Givens, Robert P. *Turning the Vertical Flank: Airpower as a Maneuver Force in the Theatre Campaign.* USAF Cadre Paper No. 13.

Gordon, Michael R. "After Hard-Won Lessons, Army Doctrine Revised." *New York Times,* February 8, 2008, 1–3.

Goulden, Joseph C. *Truth Is the First Casualty—The Gulf of Tonkin Affair: Illusion and Reality.* Chicago: Rand McNally, 1969.

Haig, Alexander M., Jr., with Charles McCarry. *Inner Circles: How America Changed the World: A Memoir.* New York: Warner, 1992.

Halberstam, David. *The Best and the Brightest.* New York: Random House, 1969.

———. *The Making of a Quagmire.* New York: Random House, 1965.

Heineman, Kenneth J. *Campus Wars: The Peace Movement at American State Universities in the Vietnam Era.* New York: New York University Press, 1993.

Heiser, Joseph. M., Jr. *Vietnam Studies: Logistical Support.* Washington, DC: Department of the Army, 1974.

Helms, Richard, and William Hood. *A Look over My Shoulder: A Life in the Central Intelligence Agency.* New York: Random House, 2003.

Helsing, Jeffrey W. *Johnson's War/Johnson's Great Society: The Guns and Butter Trap.* Westport, CT: Praeger, 2000.

Herring, George C. *America's Longest War: The United States and Vietnam, 1950–1975*. 2nd ed. New York: Knopf, 1979.

Herrington, Stuart A. *Stalking the Vietcong: Inside Operation Phoenix: A Personal Account*. Novato, CA: Presidio Press, 1997.

Hoopes, Townsend. *The Devil and John Foster Dulles*. Boston: Little, Brown, 1973.

Hunt, Richard. *Pacification: The American Struggle for Vietnam's Hearts and Minds*. Boulder, CO: Westview, 1995.

Jacobs, Seth. *Cold War Mandarin: Ngo Dinh Diem and the Origins of America's War in Vietnam, 1950–1963*. Lanham, MD: Rowman & Littlefield, 2006.

Johnson, Lyndon Baines. *The Vantage Point: Perspectives of the Presidency, 1963–1969*. New York: Holt, Rinehart and Winston, 1971.

Joint Chiefs of Staff. *Joint Publication 3-0: Doctrine for Joint Operations*. Washington, DC: Joint Chiefs of Staff, February 1, 1995.

Joint Chiefs of Staff, Historical Division, Joint Secretariat. *The History of the Joint Chiefs of Staff. The Joint Chiefs of Staff and the War in Vietnam: History of the Indochina Incident, 1940–1954, Vol. 1*. Washington, DC: Joint Chiefs of Staff, 2004.

Jones, Howard. *Death of a Generation: How the Assassinations of Diem and JFK Prolonged the Vietnam War*. New York: Oxford University Press, 2003.

Karnow, Stanley. *Vietnam: A History*. New York: Penguin, 1983.

Kimball, Jeffrey. *Nixon's Vietnam War*. Lawrence: University Press of Kansas, 2004.

———. *The Vietnam War Files: Uncovering the Secret History of Nixon-Era Strategy*. Lawrence: University Press of Kansas, 2004.

King, Martin Luther, Jr. "The Casualties of the War in Vietnam." In *Beyond Vietnam and Casualties of War in Vietnam*. Los Angeles: Clergy and Layman Concerned About Vietnam, The Nation Institute, 1986.

Kinnard, Douglas J. *The War Managers*. New York: DaCapo, 1991.

Kissinger, Henry. *Ending the Vietnam War: A History of America's Involvement in and Extrication from the Vietnam War*. New York: Simon & Schuster, 2003.

———. *White House Years*. Boston: Little, Brown, 1979.

Komer, Robert W. *Bureaucracy at War: U.S. Performance in the Vietnam Conflict*. Boulder, CO: Westview, 1986.

———. *Bureaucracy Does Its Thing: Institutional Constraints on U.S.-G.V.N. Performance in Vietnam*. Santa Monica, CA: RAND Corporation, 1998.

Kraslow, David, and Stuart H. Loory. *The Secret Search for Peace in Vietnam*. New York: Random House, 1968.

Krepinovich, Andrew F., Jr. *The Army and Vietnam*. Baltimore: Johns Hopkins University Press, 1986.

Ky, Nguyen Cao, with Marvin J. Wolf. *Buddha's Child: My Fight to Save Vietnam*. New York: St. Martin's, 2002.

Larsen, Stanley R., and James L. Collins, Jr. *Vietnam Studies: Allied Participation in Vietnam*. Washington, DC: Department of the Army, 1975.

Lavalle, A. J. C. *Airpower and the 1972 Spring Invasion*. USAF Southeast Asia Monograph Series, Vol. 2, Monograph 3.

Littauer, Raphael, and Norman Uphoff, eds. *The Air War in Indochina*. Rev. ed. Boston: Beacon, 1971.

Logevall, Fredrik. *Choosing War: The Lost Chance for Peace and the Escalation of the War in Vietnam*. Berkeley: University of California Press, 1999.

MacGarrigle, George L. *The United States Army in Vietnam: Combat Operations: Taking the Offensive: October 1966 to October 1967*. Washington, DC: Center of Military History, United States Army, 1998.

MacMillan, Mary. *Paris, 1919: Six Months That Changed the World*. New York: Random House, 2003.

McCarthy, Eugene. *Eugene 3: The Year of the People*. Garden City, NY: Doubleday, 1969.

McMahon, Robert J., ed. *Major Problems in the History of the Vietnam War*. Lexington, MA: D.C. Heath, 1990.

McMaster, H. R. *Dereliction of Duty: Lyndon Johnson, Robert McNamara, the Joint Chiefs of Staff, and the Lies That Led to Vietnam*. New York: Harper, 1997.

McNamara, Robert S. *In Retrospect: The Tragedy and Lessons of Vietnam*. New York: Times Books, 1995.

McNamara, Robert S., et al. *Argument without End: In Search of Answers to the Vietnam Tragedy*. New York: Public Affairs, 1999.

Michel, Marshall L., III. *The 11 Days of Christmas: America's Last Vietnam Battle*. San Francisco: Encounter Books, 2002.

Miller, Robert Hopkins. *The United States and Vietnam 1787–1941*. Washington, DC: National Defense University Press, 1990.

Military History Institute of Vietnam. *Victory in Vietnam: The Official History of the People's Army of Vietnam, 1954–1975*. Translated by Merle L. Pribbenow. Lawrence: University Press of Kansas, 2002.

"Missed Opportunities? Revisiting the Decisions of the Vietnam War, 1945–1968." Transcript of the Proceedings of a Conference Held 20–23 June 1997 at the Institute for International Relations, Hanoi, Vietnam. Providence, RI: Brown University, Wilson Institute for International Studies, 1998.

"Missed Opportunities? II: Revisiting the Decisions of the Vietnam War, 1945–1968." Transcript of the Proceedings of a Conference Held 23–26 February 1998 at the Institute for International Relations, Hanoi, Vietnam. Providence, RI: Brown University, Wilson Institute for International Studies, 1998.

"Missed Opportunities II: Military Conversations." Transcript of the Proceedings of a Conversation between Colonel Herb Schandler, Colonel Quach Hai Luong, Kathy Le, and Le Hong Truong, Held 23–26 February 1998 in Hanoi, Vietnam. Providence, RI: Brown University, Wilson Institute for International Studies, 1998.

Momyer, William W. *Airpower in Three Wars: WWII, Korea, Vietnam*. Reprint ed. Maxwell Air Force Base, AL: Air University Press, 2003.

Mueller, John. "Reflections on the Vietnam Anti-War Movement and on the Curious Calm at the War's End." In *Vietnam as History: Ten Years after the Paris Peace Accords*, ed. Peter Braestrup. Washington, DC: University Press of America, 1984.

Neese, Harvey, and John O'Donnell. *Prelude to Strategy: Vietnam, 1960–1965*. Annapolis, MD: Naval Institute Press, 2001.

Neu, Charles E., ed. *After Vietnam: Legacies of a Lost War*. Baltimore: Johns Hopkins University Press, 2000.

Nixon, Richard. *No More Vietnams*. New York: Arbor House, 1985.

———. *RN: The Memoirs of Richard Nixon*. New York: Touchstone, 1978.

Office of the Assistant Secretary of Defense, Public Affairs. *The Uses of Military Power: Remarks Delivered by Secretary of Defense Casper Weinberger at the National Press Club*. News Release No. 609-84, November 28, 1984.

Osborne, Milton E. *Strategic Hamlets in South Vietnam: A Survey and Comparison*. Southeast Asia Program, Department of Asian Studies, Data Paper No. 55, Ithaca, NY, April 1965.

Palmer, General Bruce, Jr. *The 25-Year War: America's Military Role in Vietnam*. Lexington: University Press of Kentucky, 1984.

Porter, Gareth. *Perils of Dominance: Imbalance of Power and the Road to War in Vietnam*. Berkeley: University of California Press, 2005.

Prados, John. *The Blood Road: The Ho Chi Minh Trail and the Vietnam War*. New York: Wiley, 1999.

———. *The Hidden History of the Vietnam War*. Chicago: Ivan R. Dee, 1995.

———. *Lost Crusader: The Secret Wars of CIA Director William Colby*. New York: Oxford University Press, 2003.

Prochnau, William. *Once upon a Distant War: Young War Correspondents and the Early Vietnam Battles*. New York: Times Books, 1995.

Public Papers of the Presidents: Dwight D. Eisenhower, Volume II, 1954. Washington, DC: U.S. Government Printing Office, 1954.

Public Papers of the Presidents: Lyndon B. Johnson, 1965, Volume I. Washington, DC: U.S. Government Printing Office, January 1966.

Public Papers of the Presidents: Lyndon B. Johnson, 1965, Volume II. Washington, DC: U.S. Government Printing Office, January 1966.

Public Papers of the Presidents: Richard Nixon, 1969. Washington, DC: U.S. Government Printing Office, January 1971.

Record, Jeffrey. *Making War, Thinking History: Munich, Vietnam, and Presidential Use of Force from Korea to Kosovo*. Annapolis, MD: Naval Institute Press, 2002.

———. *The Wrong War: Why We Lost in Vietnam*. Annapolis, MD: Naval Institute Press, 1998.

Ricks, Thomas E. "A Military Tactician's Political Strategy." *Washington Post*, February 9, 2009, A7.

Salisbury, Harrison. *Behind the Lines: Hanoi, December 23, 1966–January 7, 1967*. London: Secker & Warburg, 1967.

Schandler, Herbert Y. "The Pentagon and Peace Negotiations after March 31, 1968." In *The Search for Peace in Vietnam, 1964–1968*, ed. Lloyd C. Gardner and Ted Gittinger. College Station: Texas A&M University Press, 2004.

———. *The Unmaking of a President: Lyndon Johnson and Vietnam*. Princeton, NJ: Princeton University Press, 1977.

Shaplen, Robert M. *The Lost Revolution*. New York: Harper & Row, 1965.

Sharp, U. S. Grant. *Report on the War in Vietnam (as of 30 June 1968)*. Washington, DC: U.S. Government Printing Office, 1968.

———. *Strategy for Defeat: Vietnam in Retrospect*. San Rafael, CA: Presidio Press, 1978.

Shawcross, William. *Sideshow: Kissinger, Nixon and the Destruction of Cambodia.* New York: Simon & Schuster, 1979.

Shepherd, Jack, and Christopher Wren. *Quotations from Chairman LBJ.* New York: Simon & Schuster, 1968.

Sorley, Lewis. *A Better War: The Unexamined Victories and Final Tragedy of America's Last Years in Vietnam.* New York: Harcourt Brace, 1999.

———. *Honorable Warrior: General Harold K. Johnson and the Ethics of Command.* Lawrence: University of Kansas Press, 1998.

———. *Thunderbolt: General Creighton Abrams and the Army of His Times.* New York: Simon & Schuster, 1992.

Smith, John T. *Rolling Thunder: The American Strategic Bombing Campaign against North Vietnam, 1964–1968.* Surrey: Air Research Publications, 1994.

Son, Pham Van. *The Vietcong Tet Offensive, 1968.* Saigon: Printing & Publications Center, RVNAF, 1968.

Spector, Ronald. "The First Vitalization: U.S. Advisors in Vietnam, 1956–1960." In *The American Military and the Far East: Proceedings of the Ninth Military Symposium, U.S. Air Force Academy, 1980*, ed. Joe C. Dixon. Washington, DC: Office of Air Force History, 1980.

Summers, Harry G., Jr. "A Strategic Perception of the Vietnam War." In *Assessing the Vietnam War*, ed. Lloyd J. Mathews and Dale E. Brown. McLean, VA: Pergamon-Brassey's, 1967.

———. *On Strategy: A Critical Analysis of the Vietnam War.* Novato, CA: Presidio Press, 1982.

———. *Vietnam War Almanac.* New York: Facts on File, 1985.

Tang, Truong Nhu. *A Viet Cong Memoir: An Inside Account of the Vietnam War and Its Aftermath.* New York: Vintage, 1985.

Taylor, General Maxwell. *Swords and Plowshares.* New York: Norton, 1972.

Thayer, Thomas. *War without Fronts: The American Experience in Vietnam.* Boulder, CO: Westview, 1985.

Tho, Tran Dinh. *The Cambodian Incursion, Indochina Monographs.* Washington, DC: U.S. Army Center of Military History, 1979.

Thompson, Sir Robert G. K. *Defeating Communist Insurgency.* Westport, CT: Praeger, 1966.

———. *No Exit from Vietnam.* London: Chatto & Windus, 1969.

Thompson, W. Scott. *Unequal Partners: Philippine and Thai Relations with the United States, 1966–75.* Lexington, MA: D.C. Heath, 1975.

Tilford, Earl H., Jr. *Setup: What the Air Force Did in Vietnam and Why.* Maxwell Air Force Base, AL: Air University Press, 1991.

Transcript of the Proceedings of a Conversation between Col. Herb Schandler, Col. Quach Hai Luong, Kathy Le and Le Hong Truong, February 23–26, 1998, Hanoi, Vietnam, unpublished.

Trewhitt, Henry L. *McNamara: His Ordeal in the Pentagon.* New York: Harper & Row, 1971.

Trullinger, James Walker, Jr. *Village at War: An Account of Revolution in Vietnam.* New York: Longman, 1980.

Tuchman, Barbara W. *Practicing History: Selected Essays*. New York: Ballantine, 1981.

Turley, G. H. *The Easter Offensive: Vietnam, 1972*. Novato, CA: Presidio Press, 1985.

U.S. Congress, Committee on Armed Services, U.S. Senate, 90th Congress, 1st Session. *Air War against Vietnam, Hearings before the Preparedness Investigating Subcommittee*. Washington, DC: U.S. Government Printing Office, 1967.

U.S. Congress, Committee on Foreign Relations, U.S. Senate, 90th Congress, 2nd Session. *The Gulf of Tonkin, the 1964 Incidents*. Washington, DC: U.S. Government Printing Office, 1968.

U.S. Congress, Committee on Foreign Relations, U.S. Senate, 92nd Congress, 2nd Session, October 12, 1972. *Bombing as a Policy Tool in Vietnam: Effectiveness*. Washington, DC: U.S. Government Printing Office, 1972.

U.S. Congress, Committee on Foreign Relations, U.S. Senate, 99th Congress, 2nd Session. *The U.S. Government and the Vietnam War: Executive and Legislative Roles and Relationships, Part I, 1945–1961*. Washington, DC: U.S. Government Printing Office, 1984.

U.S. Congress, Committee on Foreign Relations, U.S. Senate, 100th Congress, 2nd Session. *The U.S. Government and the Vietnam War: Executive and Legislative Roles and Relationships, Part II, 1961–1964*. Washington, DC: U.S. Government Printing Office, 1985.

U.S. Congress, Committee on Foreign Relations, U.S. Senate, 100th Congress, 2nd Session. *The U.S. Government and the Vietnam War: Executive and Legislative Roles and Relationships, Part III, January–July 1965*. Washington, DC: U.S. Government Printing Office, 1988.

U.S. Congress, Committee on Foreign Relations, U.S. Senate, 103rd Congress, 2nd Session. *The U.S. Government and the Vietnam War: Executive and Legislative Roles and Relationships, Part IV, July 1965–January 1968*. Washington, DC: U.S. Government Printing Office, 1994.

U.S. Congress. *United States–Vietnam Relations, 1945–1967*. 12 volumes. Prepared by the Department of Defense and Printed by the U.S. Congress, House Committee on Armed Services. Washington, DC: U.S. Government Printing Office, 1971.

U.S. Department of State. *Department of State Bulletin*. Vol. 52. Washington, DC: U.S. Department of State, 1965.

U.S. Marines in Vietnam. *The Landing and the Buildup: 1965*. Washington, DC: History and Museums Division, Headquarters, U.S. Marine Corps, 1978.

Valenti, Jack. *A Very Human President*. New York: Norton, 1975.

VandeMark, Brian. *Into the Quagmire: Lyndon Johnson and the Escalation of the Vietnam War*. New York: Oxford University Press, 1991.

Vu Can. *North Vietnam: A Daily Resistance*. Hanoi: Foreign Language Publishing House, 1975.

Walt, Lewis W. *Strange War, Strange Strategy: A General's Report on Vietnam*. New York: Funk & Wagnalls, 1979.

Walton, C. Dale. *The Myth of Inevitable U.S. Defeat in Vietnam*. Portland, OR: Frank Cass, 2002.

Westmoreland, William C. *Report on the War in Vietnam*. Washington, DC: U.S. Government Printing Office, 1968.

——. *A Soldier Reports*. Garden City, NY: Doubleday, 1976.

White, Theodore H. *The Making of a President, 1964*. New York: New American Library, 1965.

Windchy, Eugene C. *Tonkin Gulf*. Garden City, NY: Doubleday, 1971.

Zhai, Quang. *China and the Vietnam Wars, 1950–1975*. Chapel Hill: University of North Carolina Press, 2000.

Index

air strikes, 63–64, 70
American advisors, 3
American failure in Vietnam, 1, 164; as seen by political scientists, 1; influence of Vietnam War on American policy, 1; views of military leaders, 1; breakdown in strategy, 1; caused by constraints on use of force, 2; lost by unsympathetic press, 2; was a civil war, 2–3
American view: of Ho Chi Minh, 13; of unity of Communist threat, 13; of South Vietnam, 17
analysis of bombing campaign, 72–89
Annam, 10
Army of the Republic of Vietnam (ARVN), 30, 39
ARVN. *See* Army of the Republic of Vietnam
Associated Press, 115

Ba Gia, 96
Ball, George C., 99, 100
Bien Hoa, 54–55
Binh, Madame Nguyen Thi, 145
bombing of north, 52–53
bombing pause, 66, 67, 107–108
books about Vietnam, 1
Braestrup, Peter, 129

Brinks Hotel, 55
British, 11
Buddhist-Catholic quarrel, 46
Buddhist demonstrations, 39, 152–153
budget process, 133–136
Bundy, McGeorge, 53, 60–61, 93
Bundy, William, 99
Bush, President George H. W., 176

Cambodia, 14, 101, 139–140, 141, 174
Central Intelligence Agency (CIA): analysts downplayed effects of bombing, 56; detected change in communist strength, 46–47; paramilitary operations transferred to MACV, 36; reports, 36; saw antigovernment cadre in south as indigenous, 152
Chinese: Empire, 9; nationalists, 11; recognizes DRV, 12; risk of intervention, 52, 104–105; United States wants to avoid direct confrontation, 157
Church, Frank, 143–144
CIA. *See* Central Intelligence Agency
civilian officials, 61, 112–113, 116
Clifford, Clark: new secretary of defense, 72; sent to Far East by

About the Author

Dr. Herbert Y. Schandler, colonel, Infantry, U.S. Army (Retired), is particularly qualified to write this book. His experience with the Vietnam War at many levels is unique. Schandler graduated from the U.S. Military Academy (West Point) in 1952. After assignments in Korea and Europe and at Harvard University and West Point, Schandler was assigned as executive officer, Second Battalion, Second Infantry, Fort Devens, Massachusetts. The battalion was soon transferred on paper to the First Infantry Division and began its deployment to Vietnam. In Vietnam, the battalion was assigned to Lai Khe, just north of the city of Ben Cat. In November and December, the battalion successfully defended itself in two major operations against the Vietcong north of Lai Khe.

After seven months, Schandler was transferred to the Plans and Operations Division (J-3), MACV. He served in J-33, the Revolutionary Development Division of J-3, and was actually located in the Vietnamese Ministry of Revolutionary Development in Saigon. He was charged, along with two other majors, with developing an organization that integrated the military/civilian effort in Vietnam. The plan was implemented as Civil Operations and Revolutionary Development Support (CORDS).

Schandler left Vietnam in November and was assigned to the Vietnam Desk, Strategic Plans and Policy Division, Office of the Deputy Chief of Staff for Operations, Department of the Army, at the Pentagon in Washington, D.C. Here he was in a perfect position to interpret for the Chief of Staff, U.S. Army, the organizational changes that were occurring in MACV as the CORDS organization was implemented.

Schandler was promoted to lieutenant colonel and later was transferred to the Office of the Assistant Secretary of Defense for International Security Affairs, where he was made assistant for Southeast Asian affairs on the Policy Planning Staff. He participated in the group that undertook a comprehensive reassessment of U.S. strategy for the new secretary of defense, Clark Clifford, after the Tet offensive and the request for major reinforcement to Vietnam by General Westmoreland. Unexpectedly, the North Vietnamese agreed to negotiations, and Schandler represented the assistant secretary of defense on an interagency group that developed negotiating positions for the U.S. delegation to the Paris peace talks. In addition, Schandler was assigned to write the last chapters concerning the Tet offensive of what later came to be known as the Pentagon Papers.

In July 1969, he was ordered back to Vietnam to command an infantry battalion. He served for several months as the inspector general of the 101st Airborne Division while waiting for a battalion to become free through normal rotation. In January 1970, he took command of the Third Battalion, 187th Infantry, 101st Airborne Division (Airmobile). The tasks of his battalion were to weaken the Vietcong in the area, clear and remove the mines left by previous combatants, build or improve roads leading to the former hamlets, train the local defenders, and move civilians from the refugee camps to newly built and government-controlled hamlets along the Thua Thien River, the area known to the French as "la rue sans joie" (the street without joy). The 3/187th Infantry Battalion accomplished all these missions.

After a year of study at the Air War College, Schandler was assigned to the Office of the Chief of Staff, U.S. Army, General William Westmoreland. He was subsequently promoted to colonel. During this period, the so-called Pentagon Papers were published by the *New York Times*. Using these papers and interviews with many of the participants, Schandler completed his dissertation and was awarded a PhD degree by Harvard University in 1974. He retired from the army in 1975. His study was published as *The Unmaking of a President: Lyndon Johnson and Vietnam* (1979).

In February 1998, while serving as a professor at National Defense University (NDU) in Washington, D.C., Schandler volunteered to accompany a group of historians to Hanoi to participate in talks with former North Vietnamese leaders concerning the various perspectives of the two sides during the war. Brown University had set up interviews at the Vietnamese Institute of International Relations in Hanoi with former secretary of defense Robert S. McNamara, who had made several trips to Hanoi to speak with these Vietnamese leaders. The group was to continue that dialogue without Secretary McNamara, who would not return to Vietnam. Schandler visited Hanoi in

1989 and 1990 as a member of this group. These interviews resulted in the book *Argument without End: In Search of Answers to the Vietnam Tragedy* (1999) by Robert McNamara and others. Dr. Schandler contributed a chapter titled "U.S. Military Victory in Vietnam: A Dangerous Illusion?"

Schandler retired in 2004 from the Strategy Department, Industrial College of the Armed Forces, NDU, as George C. Marshall Professor of Grand Strategy.